THERE ARE ALTERNATIVES!

There are Alternatives!

Four Roads to Peace and Security

Johan Galtung

International Peace Research Institute, Oslo
Geneva International Peace Research Institute
Peace Research Institute, Alicante
Berghofstiftung, Berlin

United States distributor
DUFOUR EDITIONS, INC.
Booksellers and Publishers
Chester Springs, PA 19425
215-458-5005

SPOKESMAN

First published in 1984 by:
Spokesman
Bertrand Russell House
Gamble Street
Nottingham
England
Tel. 0602 708318
Copyright © Johan Galtung, 1984

British Library Cataloguing in Publication Data

Galtung, Johan
    There are alternatives!: four roads to peace and security.
    1. Disarmament
    I. Title
    327.1'74   JX1974

ISBN 0-85124-393-2
ISBN 0-85124-394-OPbk-0

Distributed in the United States by:
Dufour Editions Inc.
Chester Springs
Pennsylvania 19425
Tel. (215) 458-5005

Printed by the Russell Press Ltd., Nottingham

Contents

Preface

This book is dedicated to the peace movement. By that I mean all those people, millions and millions, in East and West who know a nuclear war simply must not happen, who know that arms races cannot go on indefinitely without leading to a war, who know that disarmament conferences will not stop the arms race, who are saying this clearly, who act accordingly, and who are desperately looking for a way out. The book is an effort to explore such alternatives, and an invitation to the reader to criticise and develop them further in the same or different directions. It is based on more than 200 talks on this topic between June 1981 and October 1983, in 20 countries East and West, North and South, and is very much inspired by what I have learnt from the discussions with audiences of politicians, military people, people in general, peace movement or not. For these people, still in search of alternatives, are the true believers in the best aspects of Western civilisation, not those with locked-in minds that always produce the same answer: more armament. Should we manage to get out into the daylight again it will be because the pressure from the peace movement is strong enough, and in the right direction.

In these meetings I have felt the despair of people. They hardly believe a word of what governments tell them. Not only do they feel they have been lied to too often. They also doubt that official experts, even when they are alone and do not have to defend their policies against the attacks from an increasingly big and increasingly sceptical part of the population, have the slightest idea of how to stop this drift towards a major war. It looks as if it has all got out of hand and that today's policies are ritualistic repetitions of yesterday's policies, at ever higher and more suicidal levels of insecurity. But people are also critical of the peace movement, and peace researchers, for offering only endless criticism of the present arms race in general, and the Euro-missiles in particular. It is simply not true, as many people contend, that there is no interest in alternatives, only in simple slogans like "No to nuclear weapons". The problem is rather that the inability of the governments to come up with anything but continued qualitative and quantitative armament is reflected in the paucity of constructive thought in the peace movement, lest explorations of alternatives will "split the movement". But such alternatives exist. They are completely realistic, practised by several countries in Europe already — they are there for everybody to see. There is no iron law condemning us to live in an age of ever increasing insecurity. The trends can be reversed. But for that to happen the peace movement has to become much stronger in the arena of very concrete politics. I think it will.

The book is also inspired by Fredrik Galtung, 12 years old, and Irene Galtung, 6 years old. Some time ago Fredrik said the following: "There is so much about nuclear war on TV. You say you are a peace researcher, and we move a lot. Where would it be safest to live in Europe, if we have a choice?" The book is, in a sense, an effort to answer that question, not as a guide to security in present-day Europe only, but as an exploration of what insecure countries could do to become more secure.

Irene said, a short while ago: "Papi, in kindergarten they say there is a terrible, very strong bomb. Will that bomb kill us all? They also say that you are against it. But are you strong enough?" Hardly. I am not even sure I feel flattered by the comparison. Will the bomb kill us? I doubt there is anybody reasonably informed and honest who can answer *no*. And what right do these people have to make my little daughter, a little miracle of joy and energy, feel that something horrible is coming and can come any day? That we live on borrowed time? These people who themselves will be hiding in their little holes somewhere, who are without the courage to have a popular vote on the issue, and even try to avoid votes in the parliaments, those bastions of the democracy they praise so highly — what right do they have? None. They should start listening to the millions who reject their policies, including children, instead of trying to fight them, or even deceive them.

I would like to express my particular gratitude to the many who have discussed the manuscript, and particularly to Reneo Lukić, to Sverre Lodgaard, to Arthur Westing who read the first draft and to Dietrich Fischer with whom I have had a continuous and very productive co-operation these two years. Angelika Kuhn and Ingrid Rudolph of the Wissenschaftskolleg, Berlin have done an excellent job typing the manuscript. The many discussions with colleagues, particularly in the *Goals, Processes and Indicators of Development Project*, have been most useful. I would also like to thank the Freie Universität, Fachbereich 15 Politische Wissenschaft, for inviting me to give the contents of the book as a lecture course during the summer semester 1983 and to the many and excellent students for good questions and comments. That the responsibility for the text nevertheless rests with the author goes without saying.

The book is written in a slightly circular way, presenting the argument in a simple manner in Chapter 1, then going into detail in the next chapters, and particularly in Section 5.2* to 5.5 where the alternatives are concerned. Some readers may find the formulas in Chapter 3 frightening, in that case drop 3.1 and 3.4. Sections 3.2 and 3.3 will give the gist of the argument. And for those who want more, the references at the back of the book should be useful.

Think. Discuss. Act. *There are alternatives!*

Johan Galtung
Berlin, October 1983

---

*Cross-references like this in the text refer to the main sections and their subsidiary parts. In this case the reference is to Section 5, on "Alternative Security Policies", part 2, on "Transarmament".

1

There are exits

1. How: A strategy for security

"I could see where you could have the exchange of tactical weapons against troops in the field without it bringing either one of the major powers to pushing the button."
US President Ronald Reagan (*International Herald Tribune* 21 October 1981)

Can there be much doubt about what has been going on over the last few years? Is it not common sense that it is in the interest of both superpowers that major wars, if they take place, are fought mainly on the territory of third parties and — if possible — by these third parties themselves? Europeans arc often so ethnocentric that they think the Cold War is limited to Europe. We easily forget that the Cold War confrontation of ideologies and material/security interests is equally clearly articulated in East Asia. And that the superpowers have already fought on third party territory twice: Korea 1950-1953, Vietnam 1955-1975 (although with only the US directly involved). In neither case did it come to strategic exchange of ultimate weapons between the superpowers, but nuclear threats were used by the US side against the proxy on the other side. After all, the US had already committed a totally unnecessary nuclear genocide on Asian soil, at 8.45 am on 6 August 1945 — Hiroshima — possibly in revenge for Pearl Harbour. It came out of the blue sky, with no warning (instead of on an unpopulated island). They had few qualms about doing such things on Asian territory, with Asians bleeding to death for reasons only partly of their own making. Of course, nobody in his or her good senses will deny that it is in the interest of any country to manoeuvre in such a way that the likelihood of nuclear war on their own territory is minimised. But when close allies are involved, of the same race and culture on either side, the arguments have to become more complicated, more subtle.

Thus, I think it is fair to say that Europeans on both sides felt considerably better when the basic strategy was MAD, mutual assured destruction, Big Brother destroying his Soviet counterpart Bolshoj Brat and vice versa. The flight of the missiles from one superpower to the other, not to mention the human loss, would be greatly lamented. But there is a difference between the bomb that hits oneself and the bomb that hits the superpower heartland, an ocean, or those vast Eastern European plains far away. Is it really strange if the two superpowers also found this MAD? Correspondingly, in the almost inconceivable circumstances of a war against Norway and Finland, would not battle on Swedish territory have certain advantages, particularly if Sweden through non-proliferation treaties had pledged herself not to develop the kind of arms reserved for only the Big?

What I am hinting at differs from the current concern with intermediate nuclear missiles (SS20, Cruise/Pershing II) in two ways.

First, the focus on land-based IRBM (intermediate range ballistic missiles) and GLCM (ground-launched cruise missiles) is only a mid-way station. Siting land-based IRBMs in continental Western Europe is certainly a way of "sharing costs and risks" within the NATO alliance (Weinberger, Rogers); with the sea-based ones only costs would be shared. They can even serve to attract some of the Soviet intercontinental ballistic missiles (ICBMs) which, it should be remembered, can also be used for the middle range simply by changing the launching angle (although the converse is not true) away from US targets. Knowing this, the Western European allies might more easily agree to a first strike, both to hit Soviet missiles before they are launched, and to get these awesome targets away from their own soil.

But there is a serious flaw: *the formula is asymmetric*. The Soviet Union might decide both to hit where the bomb comes from and where the ultimate command comes from, from the US heartland. Only if the bombs do not hit the Soviet heartland, or the Soviet Union itself, could the war possibly be kept limited in the sense of keeping the area and the targets limited — to us, to the 500 million non-superpower Europeans, East and West. The corresponding formula worked in Korea and Vietnam. This is where the build-up of the short range tactical nuclear capacity enters the picture, with arms stationed with the allies on both sides, the small brethren. This formula would be more symmetric and must be what Reagan was thinking of in his famous, and honestly outspoken, formulation quoted above. But then the Soviet Union has promised all-out nuclear response to any Western nuclear first-use — for instance within the framework of the very aggressive, offensive strategy known as Airland Battle (2000) — but presumably first against Western Europe, which with the new missiles appears as most threatening.

During summer 1983 the situation with regard to "intermediate nuclear forces", INF, in Europe seemed to be about as follows, with the proviso that the picture is from Soviet sources because they give a more complete image, and that all such figures should be taken with more than a pinch of salt.

The Soviet Union had 455 land-based missiles, divided among the old SS-4s and SS-5s (with 1Mt loads and ranges of 2,000 and 4,100kms) and the "modernised" SS-20 (with a range of 5,000 kms, and three warheads, each carrying 150Kt). The Western side had "only" 18 land-based missiles, the French S-3 (with a range of above 3,000 km, load 1Mt). The Soviet Union then, had 18 sea-based missiles stationed on six diesel submarines in the East Sea; as against 80 French M-20s on five submarines with about the same range and load as the French missiles, stationed in Southern France, and 64 British Polaris missiles on four submarines with a range of 4,500 kms and three warheads each with a load of 200Kt. Thus, counting both land-based and sea-based missiles there were 473 on the Soviet side against the well-known figure of 162 on the Western side; a ratio of 3:1. To this should then be added 465 Soviet aeroplanes carrying nuclear weapons (TU-22, TU-16) and 695 on the Western side, divided between 651 US planes (FB-111A, F-111, F-4, A-6 and A-7; forward-based systems) and the 44 French Mirage IV. All together this gives 938 carriers (missiles and planes) for the Soviet Union and 857 for the Western side — a slight superiority for the Soviet Union. In terms of warheads it gives 2,155 for the Soviet Union as against 3,056 for the Western side, or 1.4 more for the West. If 108 Pershing II and 464 Cruise missiles (range 2,500kms, load 200Kt) are added, then the Western side would be very superior, up to 3.628 warheads (the French "modernisation" programme with seven warheads and the British with 10 warheads for Trident missiles would increase the British-French contribution from 290 to 1,326 warheads). The basic, overriding, difference, however, is that US systems in Europe can reach the Soviet Union, and with Pershing II, even Moscow, in 12 minutes, whereas the Soviet Union has nothing corresponding that can reach the United States.

Second, I assume the motivation for preferring a European battlefield to be relatively symmetrically distributed between the superpowers. No one knows better than they the damage the bombs will do. No one knows better than they how disinclined they are to stop the arms race as they would either want some edge over the other side (to "prevail"), or that the other side has no such edge ("parity"). But leaving the different goals aside, they are even incapable of agreeing on what "rough parity" would mean, given the tremendous asymmetries and role of non-quantifiable variables in the whole process. Both sides try to present their own armament as "modernisation", and as a legitimate reaction to efforts by the other side to arrive at a first strike capability. Both are prisoners of their own logic. What could be more natural than a tacit superpower agreement to the effect of displacing the theatre of war, even if it is a puppet theatre with the superpowers both pulling the strings and being spectators? Of course they will vehemently deny this. They will overbid each other in saying that no area-limited war is possible in trying to assure their allies that the coupling of allies-to-superpower, also on the enemy side, is as firm as ever. Reagan's remark was a major *gaffe*: it would have been interesting to have attended the meeting he had with his advisors afterwards. And yet the Soviet Union will probably follow suit, stationing similar missiles (SS22s) on Eastern European territory (East Germany, Czechoslovakia, Bulgaria — less probably in Romania and Poland).

Will this transfer of the nuclear battlefield work? Only insofar as the Europeans permit it. No doubt the US (and the USSR) have a strong argument: the Europeans were egoistic in preferring a deterrence based on the mutual assured destruction of the superpowers, with the Europeans living, even prospering, under this (dubious) nuclear umbrella. The Europeans are equally right that the opposite position, a transfer to tactical nuclear exchange in the European (meaning also non-USSR) theatre, would be utter superpower egoism, of the type demonstrated in East Asia. Had the US strategic missiles been stationed in US areas as densely populated, with as well educated, politically conscious people as is the case for the missiles now to be emplaced in Western Europe, the US would have had a peace movement at least of the quantitative magnitude and the qualitative depth as the European one.

The dreaded but likely outcome is certainly that the transition towards a limited European theatre continues and that the NATO IRBM capacity is built up, wholly or partly according to the plans. This would, of course, increase the pressure on the Russians to have something *similar*, meaning missiles as powerful, precise, and invulnerable (because of speed and/or trajectory) *and* missiles stationed in corresponding places. It is quite clear what that would mean: land-based missiles in East Germany (for weapons corresponding to Pershing II), and the Soviet cruise missiles, SS-CX4, sea-based, on ships in international waters off the US coasts. There are few things the US would be so sensitive to, among other reasons because the US is so vulnerable, due to her imperialistic policies; she is probably as little supported by the local Latin populations as the Soviet Union in Eastern Europe. Hence the Caribbean based Rapid Deployment Force. Possibly the Soviet Union might give up such designs. In that case they would continue their deployment of ICBMs and IRBMs, to be launched in all possible ways against all possible targets, including the US — making a mockery of any US attempt to limit a nuclear war. That they should come to the conclusion, after Cruise/Pershing II have been emplaced, that they should submit and reduce the SS20s with no substitution, is a clearly metaphysical speculation. I am unaware of any empirical case of this kind. And the theory is also suspect, as can be seen from one simple counter-question. If the USSR is now too strong, why doesn't the United States back down? And why do they expect the USSR to do what they do not, if for no other reason because of national pride? Do they have any good reason to believe the USSR to be more submissive than they are themselves? Why should the USSR not "catch up" when that is what the US say that *they* do? Why should the USSR disarm under pressure when the US would never do so?

So the arms race continues without delay, as a tactical nuclear, and conventional, Europe-limited arms race, with Norway and Denmark included through the US prepositioning schemes, or as a strategic ICBM/IRBM race, as before. Or both. And non-stationed IRBMs may also be emplaced in Israel, Pakistan and Korea, or withdrawn to Siberian soil — only then it is the East Asian theatre, the USSR-China-Korea-Japan conflict formation. So it continues till there is that incident, that military confrontation that triggers off the war that simply must not take place, whether by accident, escalation, design, or what not.

So, what is there to be done? Is there somewhere a strategy of security as opposed to these formulas so eminently suited to increased insecurity? Much can be said about this, some of it in the rest of this book. But let me indicate four answers right away, derived from asking a very simple question: which countries are today the "most secure", meaning the "least insecure", and what might be the basis of their security? Using the 29 countries of Europe as a sample (not counting the Soviet Union and the five mini-states), my own tentative answer would be in terms of four classes of countries:

1. *Most secure:* Switzerland, Yugoslavia, Albania (3 countries).
2. *Second:* Finland, Austria, Sweden, Malta (4 countries).
3. *Third:* France, Greece, Romania, Iceland, Ireland, Spain, Cyprus (7 countries).
4. *Most insecure:* the client states in the NATO and WTO systems (15 countries).

This is not the place to go into any details (see Chapter 5 below). But some of the logic of the argument, the dimensions of reasoning, can be made explicit. There are four dimensions underlying the classification.

First, *the extent to which the country has a credible non-provocative defence*, and not an offensive military capacity. There are three types here: *conventional military defence* with short range but high fire power, mobile and autonomous units that are dispersed in order to be as invulnerable and as unworthy of a nuclear attack as possible; *paramilitary defence* (guerilla) and *nonmilitary defence* (social defence). These three are certainly combinable, with the first being more important as a territorial defence, the other two as occupation defence. Switzerland and Yugoslavia both have come very far in this direction: the client states not at all, dependent, as they are, on superpower strategies.

Second, non-alignment, *the degree of decoupling from the superpowers*. In a war what matters is the extent to which the country is a part of a superpower design, and can be used by them as a launching platform for attacks on the other side. Membership or non-membership of blocs in times of peace does matter. No country in the world today feels threatened by Switzerland or the other countries in class 1 above, nor by the countries in class 2 — hence they are not likely to be exposed to any major threat or attack out of fear either. But attack can also come for other reasons — so this source of security has to be coupled to the other points.

Third, *the extent to which the country itself has inner strength*, by being reasonably self-reliant in essentials (food, energy, health, defence); not being too centralized; having some reservoir of intermediate technology to fall back upon; not being too easily fragmented by class, ethnic and other conflicts; above all by being autonomous. Again, Switzerland is a good case, systematically working (see its 1973 defence plan) along such lines. So is Yugoslavia. The client states may have plans in this direction but little action, hence they are bad providers of security for their own citizens, and should be exposed as such. For security certainly has this inner dimension. But it also has another, non-military outer dimension, and that is the last point.

Fourth, *the extent to which the country is useful to others* if left in peace, so that belligerents prefer to leave it intact. Switzerland obtains this through its banking services, the Red Cross, the many conference sites (all of Switzerland, not only the UN, is a site of that kind) and sometimes through its good offices as a go-between. Most countries in Europe have something to offer in that direction, something useful they can do better than others, but it is often overshadowed by the aggressive defence policy these countries have been engaging in.

The basic thesis of this book is that although no policy today is without some risk, it would be considerably less risky for a country to follow these four leads than to be a party to superpower strategy, with the ever increasing probability of becoming the theatre of war. For this to happen the country does not even have to leave NATO: it could do like France (and Greece and Iceland, in some periods) and leave the military integration — Romania is very similar to this on the other side — but continue in the political alliance. It could also try to change the military strategy, through no-first-use strategies, withdrawing nuclear arms intended for fighting rather than deterring wars. It could develop defensive defence, building down the offensive components — a look at the defence budgets of Switzerland, Yugoslavia, Finland, Austria and Sweden will show that the average expenses per capita are quite low relative to comparable NATO countries. It could become less vulnerable economically, physically and structurally — something it probably should do anyhow, given the current structural crises in East and West, showing up as political and economic crises. And it could engage more actively in peace policies; both by being more useful and by being a better go-between.

Needless to say, all of this has to be reasoned at least relatively carefully, and it has to be spelt out, at least in some detail. The global context has to be brought in, the entire range of the East-West conflict, not only the European "theatre". And that is what this book is about. But first some words about why this whole issue is so urgent. Not that the next section is news for anybody who is in the peace movement, but it somehow has to be said. And be read, perhaps particularly by those who say "Believe me, I am every bit as much against these *horrible* weapons as you are, only I think we have to show determination and willingness to build up our strength even further in order to get rid of them". Somehow such people are very able to restrain their urge to express in more detail how horrible these weapons are. So the next section is dedicated to them.

2. Why: The new weapons

Much has been written about the new post-Second World War weapons in general and the weapons of mass destruction in particular: the atomic, biological, chemical, radiological and ecological weapons. In addition there are all the new generations of conventional weapons, but the focus here will be on the non-conventional ones, particularly on nuclear (atomic) arms. The literature about their effects is enormous. The task here is to try to summarize it and put it in the proper perspective.

Let us divide the world into six parts in order to understand better the effects of the new weapons. Clearly there is the old distinction between the human part and the non-human part, and the division of the former into human beings proper and the human made environment, here referred to as "human settlements". In the old days warfare was about human beings, killing them or maiming them, and then about human settlements, destroying and burning them. Agriculture is a part of human settlements and many conflicts were over cattle or destructive of cattle and crops; later on, over industrial resources or destructive of them. But the non-human-made environment was left reasonably untouched by warfare, until recently.

To capture this more clearly let us divide the world in the following way; subdividing the environment into five parts:

$$\begin{array}{ccccccccc}
& & & & & atmosphere & & & \\
The\ world & = & homosphere & + & biosphere & + & hydrosphere & + & cosmosphere \\
& & \swarrow \quad \seararrow & & \downarrow & & lithosphere & & \\
& & human \quad\ human & & animals; & & & & \\
& & beings \quad\ settle\text{-} & & plants; & & & & \\
& & \qquad\quad ments & & micro\text{-} & & & & \\
& & & & organisms & & & &
\end{array}$$

(Needless to say much finer distinctions can be made in all the categories.) The old weapons were focused on the homosphere, not on the rest. Characteristic of the weapons of mass destruction is that they go much further. *In their ultimate consequence they are omnicidal weapons*, so that one could use the following formula:

$$\begin{array}{ccccc}
Omnicide & = & genocide & +\ sociocide & +\ ecocide \\
& & \swarrow \quad\ \searrow & & \downarrow \\
& & struc\text{-} \quad\ cul\text{-} & & bio\text{-},\ atmo\text{-},\ hydro\text{-},\ litho\text{-}, \\
& & ture \qquad ture & & cosmocide
\end{array}$$

This will now have to be spelt out.

That the weapons are genocidal hardly needs exploration. Present scenarios for nuclear wars operate with figures in the order of 10^8 or 10^9, the hundreds or thousands of millions of deaths; for single weapons, even for one single warhead, one may realistically assume millions and tens of millions of deaths. Whether the present stock is sufficient to wipe out all of human-kind is perhaps still debatable; with moderate assumptions about the rate of growth of the destructive power of that stock it will certainly no longer be debatable within a short span of time.

What goes for human beings also goes for human settlements given their generally high level of vulnerability. But the term "sociocide" used here is intended to refer to more than the mere destruction of the material aspects of human settlements. It includes social structure and human culture. This does not mean that the survivors, if there are any, will not have a social structure and a culture; human beings wherever they are and under whatever conditions, even those of a concentration camp, develop structure and culture. The sociocidal aspect refers to the type of structure and culture. It is then assumed that the new social structure will be a combination of a small group of decision-makers, cowardly surviving in bunkers, highly authoritarian either by self-selection to that kind of job or by dint of a position of power in highly vertical structures, and in addition by dint of the cataclysmic events of a nuclear war — and then, on the other hand, small groups of humans, scattered around, probably also with highly authoritarian structures, trying to cope with the problems of post-holocaust existence. The totality of this would be the new social structure, a grotesque caricature of human society, with the "leaders" trying to reach out to the rest no doubt in efforts to relieve the pain, but equally undoubtedly in efforts to retain control. The non-leaders will fight among themselves for the crumbs of relief, probably accepting the spoils while at the same time rejecting the "leaders" who will be seen by very many as responsible for the calamity, and not very different from the "leaders" on the other side. It should also be remembered that war plans include nuclear bombing of one's own side, in addition to the obvious fact that it may be difficult during the war to establish whose bomb one is actually suffering from.

The culture will probably undergo a similar polarisation. On top of it all will be written two words: NEVER AGAIN, the same words that were so frequently seen after the First and Second World Wars. They would be honestly intended, but the exact conclusions will be different, depending on who draws them. Some people will draw the conclusion "no more atomic weapons", others will draw the conclusion "more atomic weapons" — it went wrong only because we did not have enough! If the debate between those who see war as a lesser evil and those who see war as the highest evil was more emotional after the Second World War than after the First, then it stands to reason that it will be even more emotional after a nuclear holocaust. It should be noted that as usual both sides will be able to quote the Christian Bible since this particular document contains formulations that can be picked up by either — there is both real legitimation of desertification ("Verwüstung" in the Lutheran Bible) when carried out by legitimate authority (God) *and* the turn to compassion, understanding the enemy, even turning the other cheek. Needless to say, this polarisation of culture goes very well with the polarisation of structure mentioned above.

It has sometimes been said that a nuclear war would bring humanity back to conditions of the Middle Ages; some even say the Stone Age. I would not use any such description. I find them too insulting to the Middle Ages and the Stone Age, to the many people who decently laboured under those conditions of material hardship relative to the comforts enjoyed by one tenth, maybe even one fifth of human-kind today, and find it much better to conclude that we are dealing with a phenomenon of a totally new kind. Suffice it only to mention the enhanced radiation weapons (ERW), also known as the neutron bombs, capable of killing human beings through the radiation effect, yet being less destructive of material components because a lesser portion of the total energy is released as blast and heat. Or, let us mention the opposite bomb, the reduced redundant radioactivity bomb (RRR) which has exactly the opposite characteristic: much less of the total energy is released as radiation, much more as blast and heat. With that kind of bomb, which actually would come closer to the notion of a "clean" bomb, one would have the weapon that could be associated economically with capitalism, killing capital in all forms, retaining more human beings who can be used as producers, not to mention as consumers when the wheels start turning again. The neutron bomb has also been referred to as "capitalist", probably by somebody who does not understand capitalism. Did people really sit in the Stone Age, and in the Middle Ages, calculating mathematically these types of effects? Were they that cold blooded, or did they not at least have the excuse of some passion behind the wars? Or has an incredible moral degradation set in? Were the leaders of those days so cowardly that they were hiding in bunkers instead of assuming personal risks?

However this may be, the White Death of nuclear war can better be compared to the Black Death if some reference to something usually associated with the Middle Ages has to be found; in other words to what was then seen as a natural catastrophe. It seems to have wiped out 40 per cent of the European population at that time; we would be lucky if we escape from a nuclear war with losses as low as that. And that would only mean counting the initial losses. In addition there are the losses through the multiplier effects in space and time: the radioactive fallout carried by wind and water through space, and through time as cancer showing up much later in human bodies and dysgenic effects that might be visited upon us in untold numbers of generations — we simply do not know. The Black Death spread in space, but not in time, through these types of mechanisms.

However, it is when we go to the third component of the equation about omnicide that the real differences show up: *ecocide*. The general formula is very simple: the higher the level of evolution of a biological organism, the more vulnerable to radiation. Animals will go before plants do, and most resistant will be the micro-organisms; higher animals (vertebrates) before lower animals (invertebrates); higher plants (flowering) before lower plants (non-flowering). But this means that the basis for all life, the miracle of photo-synthesis, will be removed because there will be no green plants capable of performing it. And where the primary producers have been killed, and there is little migration into the area because the radiation is too hostile, the micro-organisms known as reducers will do the rest of the job, ending with mineralisation and nitrification. The atmosphere composition will be tilted in favour of nitrogen and CO_2, away from oxygen. The hydrosphere may be less affected, except that it can no longer be a habitat for biota unable to find enough nutrients and to withstand the contamination. The lithosphere will lose its soil (humus) and desertification will set in. From that point on recovery seems to be extremely difficult even when aided by human inputs because of the hostile context (sandstorms, for instance). Under such circumstances energy from the sun can no longer be captured and packaged in a way humans can make use of. Recovery rates for some ecosystems are, of course, more favourable: decades for grassland (prairie), centuries for forests. For agriculture it may be less if the human inputs are available — the question is whether they are. Being generally very simple, monocultural systems, they are already immature and low on natural healing power, with no redundancy that can help towards restoration of maturity.

So far the weapons do not touch the cosmosphere, but with satellite and anti-satellite war going on in outer space this will no longer be true. There will be radioactive debris all over, and quite possibly other effects unthought of so far. Whatever these effects may be the cosmosphere will certainly come through to us in a different way because of possible "holes" in the ionosphere, electromagnetic pulses (EMP) of which we know relatively little today, and so on.

I may summarise it: it is Neville Shute's *On the Beach* and George Orwell's *1984*, both wrapped into one. This is true not so much because of the direct, immediate effects of nuclear weapons as because of the way in which nature, including the human made part of it, is based on chains and cycles; these are systems where effects are transmitted from one corner to the other and back again, sometimes reduced, sometimes amplified. Sometimes effects may cancel out each other. But evil effects tend not to do so, they rather reinforce each other as when radiation gets more of a bite on some organism that already has been exposed to excessive heat, or when excessive heat assails a human being trapped in a building that has been kicked down by a blast. In addition, the whole system changes, many components may still be there but in totally different proportions, making old mechanisms work in a way different from before. And the recovery systems themselves may be knocked out: in the short run the disaster relief organisation, including primary, secondary and tertiary health services; then human reproduction simply because of partial or complete sterilisation of men and women due to radiation; then the same for animals and plants in addition to possible damage to the photo-synthetic mechanism itself. In short, the destruction is not only at the component, but also at the system level.

I let this suffice as a way of arriving at the major point: nuclear holocaust is not only a crime against humanity as it has often been said; it is also a crime against human society and culture, and a crime against the environment, making it a universal crime, *a crime of cosmic dimensions*. These are big words, and they should be underpinned again by putting them in a proper perspective.

A nuclear holocaust is the very opposite of develpment, it is *anti-development*, not in the sense of putting us back historically because we were never exposed to nuclear holocaust, but in the sense of rejecting almost everything humankind has been struggling for, some of which it has obtained, over the last millennia. But in addition to that the nuclear holocaust is *anti-evolution*, it is Darwin in reverse, a decapitation of the evolutionary chart precisely because the "highest" organisms are also the most vulnerable ones. Whether the micro-organisms and the cockroaches left behind, given some millions of years, will be able to bring forth human beings again, we do not know — probably not. They might also come to the conclusion that it would not be worthwhile, if given the opportunity to reflect on the matter!

What this means is nothing less than the following: not humans in general but certain very particular human beings have arrogated to themselves the right to attack the very work of creation, of the Creator — as seen by the monotheistic religions. In terms of the occidental religions, based on the Old Testament, it suffices to read the very opening of the Bible, *Genesis*, to see what this desertification means: it means cancelling most of the work that God did on the *second* day of creation (the plants), the *fifth* day of creation (the fishes and the birds), the *sixth* day of creation (animals and human beings). It would leave us with an inanimate earth, except for the micro-organisms. However, God did not imagine a world filled with radioactive dust and ashes because he had, according to Genesis, a more forward looking perspective for his act of creation. These latter day anti-creators not only push the act of creation back, but also try to make their action irreversible, sealing it with radioactivity.

It is at this point that one might ask a question, using a mild understatement: *who gave them the right to do this?* who gave them the right to engage in the enactment and preparation of such crimes, such extreme blasphemy against the Yahveh of the Jews, the God of the Christians and the Allah of the Muslims? Who gave them the right to cancel the whole setting within which the complex cycles of transmigration and rebirth, believed in by Hindus and Buddhists, go on? Who gave them the right to tamper with and destroy the very essence of that dialectic of nature that Daoism is about? Who gave them the right not only to plan genocide, but also to destroy the whole social setting with its structure and culture, however imperfect, that constitute the very essence of humanist faith? In short, who gave them the right to plan for such cosmic crimes, to set themselves up as anti-gods?

Answer: *Nobody did.* They came into this not so much because they drifted into it, prisoners of the paradigms of pre-nuclear thinking, not quite seeing where they were heading. And yet if there were any justice in the world the whole universe should somehow rally against them, showing very clearly that on the one side there are the nuclear planning groups, West and East, plus some cockroaches and micro-organisms; and on the other side all the rest of us. All the rest of us, human beings with all our imperfections, of all genders and ages, classes, nations and races; of all religions and a-religions and anti-religions. It should make all of us rise together with animals and plants, with air and water, minerals and the sun and the moon and the stars against those who threaten our universe. More particularly, it should make all religions and religious officials stand up as one body against this supreme act of blasphemy, monotheistic, polytheistic, pan-theistic, anti-theistic and a-theistic creeds alike, plainly stating the truth that this is totally, utterly unacceptable. And they should be joined in this by everybody else, if for no other reason just for the one I feel every morning into the eyes of my own beloved children, both with peace in their names (Fredrik and Irene): will they be permitted to live their lives or will it be taken away from them by this coldly calculated madness?

But this must be done retaining that basic Catholic insight found in so many faiths: the distinction between the *peccato* and the *peccatore*. It does not help excommunicating the nuclear planners; what helps is to show them ways out of their thought prison, and indeed to show them that it is a prison. Many of the high officers and officials have already come to this insight and more will do so. Let us only hope that time does not run out on us all.

3. Who: The peace forces

An idea without an actor is as empty as an actor without an idea. Peace ideas call for peace forces, of which there are many. Let us start with the peace movement. Whether one agrees or disagrees with the peace movement in Europe and North America, there is agreement about one point: it has become a political factor of major importance. Although the

"zero option" is very far from what the peace movement stands for, there
is hardly any doubt that European governments adopted this position in
autumn 1981 due to the pressure of the peace movement, and that the
position of the European governments in turn influenced the official US
stand before the "disarmament negotiations" started on 30 November
1981. One simple reason for this is that it would be very difficult today for
any government of the left, meaning social democrat, in Western Europe
to get into a position of power if it is in opposition — or to keep power if it is
in that position — in the longer run against the will of the peace movement.
It has to come to terms with it, one way or the other. And this probably also
works the other way: a political party or combination of parties that takes
up a position close to the peace movement will get its reward — if not
necessarily the majority, like *die Grünen*.

How come it is so strong? Participants may say it is because of the
urgency of the matter, not only the catastrophic nature of nuclear war but
also the seemingly increasing probability that nuclear war may take place,
and in Europe. They will also point to the necessity of an alert and
mobilised public opinion in a situation where the establishment seems to be
unable to cope with the matter, as evidenced by the many years of by and
large fruitless "disarmament negotiations", in spite of, or because of,
countless plans in that direction. Worse than that, the explicitly callous and
provocative attitude of the Reagan administration has probably
contributed more than anything else to the growth of the peace movement,
which might make him an honorary member had the situation not been that
serious. This has certainly also activated some organisational patterns left
dormant after the end of the Vietnam war. There was an unused
organisation capacity.

However, a deeper analysis would bring in general social changes that in
and by themselves may be less related to the immediate concern with peace
and war. To see this more clearly, let us try a brief summary of the
difference between the peace movement of the 1980s and that of earlier
periods. With the exception of the tremendous campaign against nuclear
testing in the early 1960s, the peace movement of earlier decades was
mainly the movement of two groups, both small, and rather different. On
the one hand there was a pacifist and often sectarian Christian, or religious
in general, movement with a relatively absolutist, strong moral stand. On
the other hand there were people in the West who for one reason or
another saw the superpowers in a highly asymmetric perspective, with the
Soviet Union being not only "better" but in itself a peace force, and for that
reason worthy of support in the West, making up for the lack of an
independent movement in the East. Needless to say, co-operation between
more or less pacifist, and more or less communist, groups was and is
always problematic, with the latter trying to make use of the former, and
the former becoming increasingly sophisticated in their way of handling
that problem as time went by. Thus, the normal peace movement pattern
was one of small but very active groups organising signature campaigns
and demonstrations, and being capable of mobilising bigger groups only
when the issues crystallised more clearly politically, and the danger of the
arms race and arms use in various parts of the world (particularly Vietnam)

became clear to larger groups of the population.

Recently, however, and that is the mark of the 1980s, at least 10 more groups have come into the picture and very prominently so. Each of them has brought into the peace movement not only vast numbers of people, but also new perspectives, new ways of dealing with the whole matter, and new channels into the harder nucleus of the European countries, with their various degrees of militarisation, bordering on *de facto* coup d'état and occupation of the country by the military complex.

First of all: *women*. Clearly this has to do with the emancipation of women in general, with the advent of 50 per cent of human-kind as potential subjects, not only actual objects of political processes. What women have brought into the movement can hardly be overestimated. There is a perspective of holism whenever women enter, a refusal to reduce the peace/war issue to a question of disarmament negotiation tactics, of counting of rockets the way men love to do. Many more factors are taken into account, problems are seen in a broader context, thus also forcing men to see them likewise. And in addition to that, women have shown a unique capacity for new languages, new ways of acting and talking about war and peace; suffice it only to mention the marches to Paris in 1981, Minsk 1982 and Washington 1983, going even in the Soviet Union! Clearly women relate more directly to the reproductive process, bringing the family level closer to the level of international politics. But the utter futility of the whole effort to try to secure peace by means of a deterrence that never can become stable is brought up more clearly by women than by men. There is a healthy disrespect for the whole pattern of thinking found within the field of "security studies", and that in itself is a rather major contribution — as so clearly expressed by the women around the Greenham Common base.

Second, *youth*. One may argue that they have always been there, but that is not necessarily the case — now it is more youth in general. A major point here is no doubt the education revolution of our societies, putting at the disposal of even very young people, and perhaps particularly them, a vast amount of knowledge that people two or three times older in earlier periods — also to a large extent today — might envy them. It is not rare to find young people able to debate technicalities with officials "very high up" in a way that only ten or five years ago could only be heard in small, closed circles of "experts". The availability of information, concepts and analyses in an inexpensive form (pocket book) is certainly very important in this connection, as is the widespread knowledge of languages. In earlier ages such things were monopolies held by certain groups in certain classes; today this is much less so. And in addition, of course, comes the whole host of other issues that have mobilised youth recently, as indicated below.

Third, *the green movement*, standing for a bundle of issues, and for that reason often characterised as a colourful movement rather than merely a green one. The interesting thing is to see the convergence that is taking place now in the early 1980s between the ecologically inspired green movement of the 1970s and the new peace movement. Sooner or later the new peace movement will have to come to grips with the problem of *alternative* security policies, not only with how to obtain a Europe free from nuclear weapons. One presupposes the other. And that thinking is likely to lead to conclusions in terms of security based on societies that have a greater inner strength, are less dependent on foreign trade for essentials (food, energy) and less dependent on technocratic centres for administration and satisfaction of basic needs. Also, defence thinking is likely to lead to conclusions in terms of more autonomous, local defence based on small, mobile and dispersed units (military, paramilitary and/or non-military). But these two types of conclusions go exactly in the direction of what the green movement has been arguing for ecological and generally democratic reasons: more local self-reliance, decentralisation, a less technocratic society.

And the green movement, on the other hand, will have to ask questions about how the type of society the movement wants to build, more human in its goals and processes, will have to relate to the problems of defence and security in general. Of course that thinking will go in the direction of trying to hook security onto the new social patterns that the movement is arguing anyway. This already gives a basis for a major convergence. Whether one starts from one end or from the other, the type of society one arrives at, and the type of security policy, would be very different from the "blue", capitalist movement with its emphasis on centralism, trade and offensive weapons systems. It should only be added to this that the "pink" movement, the social democrats/socialists, until recently have not been able to contribute much thinking of their own to this debate. Their contribution has mainly been in terms of a slightly softer, more controlled version of the type of security politics the "blue" people tend to promote, with the key exceptions of Alva Myrdal, and West Germans like Erhard Eppler and, perhaps, Egon Bahr and Willy Brandt.

Fourth, *the local level.* Something new is happening in the world when city councils, particularly in Britain, but now in very many countries pass resolutions declaring their own territory nuclear-free zones. Operationally it is relatively clear what this means on paper: no nuclear energy, no passage for nuclear material including waste material, and of course no production or deployment of nuclear weapons. In practice it may be less clear what will happen as the central government in all countries claims a monopoly of defence policy, and also seems to have the ultimate power when it comes to energy policy. These matters have been defined by the centre as being "in the interest of the nation", regardless of the local level. However, the enormous risks of having such installations on one's own territory have also become increasingly clear to the population, and city councillors who pass resolutions of the type mentioned can be said to a large extent to act as an expression of popular sentiment, even if this is not necessarily reflected in party platforms that have been defined at the national level.

This *localisation of security politics,* because of the awesome consequences, is a new factor. And it brings out very clearly a major policy dilemma: if the national government wants to install nuclear weapons systems it will probably prefer more conservative, "blue" municipalities with less trouble and stay away from "pink/green" municipalities where the population could be mobilised to highly embarrassing confrontations. As such confrontations within the "blue" type of thinking also will be seen as decreasing the credibility of the national defence stance, it is quite possible that the national government would prefer to avoid them. But the consequence of that, in turn, is of course that if a war should come there would be higher mortality for conservative than for more radical voters, simply because the former have permitted nuclear weapon targets to be installed on their territory, and the latter have not. In other words, defence politics has become much more real to people! And in Britain more than half the population live in such nuclear-free-zone municipalities. A new perspective on multiparty politics, indeed — a new perspective on parliamentary democracy.

Fifth, *the trade unions.* Here again an interesting new phenomenon is emerging. Whereas before, issues of peace and war tended to come at the end of the agenda of major trade union meetings, they are now in the very forefront, and politicians make use of trade union meetings for major policy declarations in this field. It is not strange that this should happen. The gains of the trade union movement in recent decades have been tremendous, increasing the material standard of living of workers to a point unthought of before. Needless to say, this has had to do with economic growth, and the ability of the ruling classes in western societies to share at least some of that growth with the workers mainly responsible for the production of the growth. Clearly these workers would not like to see their gains disappear in a nuclear explosion — "what have we worked for all these years if it is all going to disappear in a nuclear war?" An argument of that kind certainly also applies to the economic crisis which also will be at the top of the agenda of the meetings mentioned. But then economic matters always were; there is nothing new in that since trade unions by their nature have been not only economy oriented but also to some extent economistic in their approach to politics. What is new is the focus on peace/war issues — a focus which brings major new groups of the population into the peace movement.

Sixth, *social democrats.* This point is closely linked to the preceding one. But there is also another dimension to it which seems to be new. It has been indicated above that social democrats, with very few exceptions, have not been in the forefront when it comes to original thinking about peace/war matters, although it can be argued that they have been in the forefront when it comes to practice: *no social democratic government in Europe ever went to war as an aggressor.* My own experience, however, has been that it is easier to find alternative thinking about security matters among conservatives than among social democrats, and when the latter turn to security problems it tends to be limited to thinking about arms control. Maybe there is a parallel here to their approach to capitalist society: it is not so much a question of introducing an alternative economy ("socialist") as how to control the capitalist economy through negotiations and agreements. But rank-and-file social democrats themselves, today, do not seem to be content with that state of affairs. There is movement and a search for something different, and this search is bound to bring results when the vast masses of people who adhere to this major current in European politics really get moving. It may also be that social democrats would, as they have in the past, be more able to take up contacts with the

Eastern European countries as some of the thinking about economic affairs is shared. Clearly this is also a political bread and butter necessity: the social democrats have the peace movement in their own house, partly from the traditional hard left with more communist leanings, and mainly, today, from the new softer left, the green movements within the social democratic parties. In short, they have to move and will move, once they liberate themselves from the myth that nuclear defence is less expensive and hence useful in building a social welfare state.

Seventh, *the churches*. What is new here is that the peace movement has reached churches in general, not only the more sectarian and more fundamentalist. It is the common churchgoer, the congregation found on Sundays that now seems to be on the move, up to bishops' conferences. Whether they express their feelings in theological terms, that "nuclear war is blasphemy against God" or not, does not matter so much. There is a general feeling of deep moral uneasiness with the whole situation expressed in their positions. Maybe this uneasiness also is deeper than what has been indicated so far, maybe it is also a discontent with a Christianity much too clearly tied to the interests of those groups that also are central in state formation, the establishment itself. Maybe it has also become a question of freedom of expression within the Christian churches. Topics bordering on state interests — traditionally taboo as subjects for theological research and Christian expression — are no longer off limits. To the extent that this is the case there may be an alliance here between alternative security thinking and new currents in theology, relatively similar to the type of alliance mentioned above in connection with the green movement. Again, things are coalescing in a way they did not before, with a tremendous chance for Christianity to become a moral force.

Eighth, *professions*. The interesting thing in this connection is that one group after the other seems to come out looking at the whole matter of nuclear war and security not in general terms, but from their professional point of view. Nuclear scientists have always done so, not only because of their particular competence, but also to some extent to atone for the sins of that particular profession in releasing such forces. But today physicians of all kinds come out with very clear descriptions of what nuclear war would mean, denouncing it as a disaster for which there is no cure as the whole system itself might break down. Only preventive medicine can help. Lawyers are very explicit about the illegality. Priests speak out. And it can safely be predicted that one profession after the other will do the same, increasingly bringing new perspectives into the debate and the political struggle. What is interesting in this connection is not that these people participate in the peace movement; to some extent they always have as individuals. They have more impact when they participate from their professional perspective, bringing into the movement new types of professional competence, thereby broadening the argumentation against the use of weapons of mass destruction and also, hopefully, broadening the search for alternatives.

Ninth, *generals/admirals for peace:* an impressive group of very high ranking officers retired or resigned from service in NATO countries who here throw in their considerable expertise and status in favour of the peace movement. Only the shared anxiety in facing the prospects of a nuclear holocaust can explain the ease with which this group has been accepted by, and accepts, other groups in the peace movement. And behind them are many, many officers of lower ranks doing or contemplating the same, not to mention the thousands who remain in the armies but move in thought, speech and action towards nuclear pacifism.

Altogether this is rather impressive. And it is perhaps not too presumptuous to mention that there is also a tenth group — very small, but quite articulate — that has played some role in the peace movement, particularly in the European countries north of the Alps: the *peace researchers*. Since that group came into being at the end of the 1950s and early 1960s it has spread relatively quickly and now provides movements of this kind with an alternative source of information and insight, breaking the monopoly that "security research" in its more militaristic vein has had on these affairs until recently. Needless to say, the peace research movement will only remain valuable insofar as it retains its independence of the peace movement and does not become to the peace movement the non-questioning servant that security research has tended to become to Ministries of Foreign and Defence Affairs; an informal redundancy with highly predictable stands on most issues.

Does this mean that all one now has to do is to wait a little, and then the movement will collect the fruits of its endeavours: countries will simply become good models of what the peace movement stands for, observing many of its ideas, as they once did to a movement in many ways quite similar, the labour movement? Certainly not.

To answer that question, the example of the fate of the peace movement of the early 1960s is instructive, and should serve as a stern warning: a movement against nuclear testing focused on the dangers of fallout in the atmosphere and hydrosphere, and hence in food products, particularly the health hazards. The response to that narrowly defined movement was clear: continue with the testing, but do it in such a way so that there will be little or no fallout — in other words underground. The result of this was the Partial Test Ban Treaty of August 1963, providing the nuclear powers with a less illegitimate basis for doing what they wanted to do. They continued the testing in such a way that even more devilish weapons could be developed — the weapons we are concerned with today. As a result of this Pyrrhic victory the peace movement of those years dwindled to its more usual low level, the hard core remaining with the two groups mentioned, and nuclear testing actually increased rather than decreased, protected from the inquisitive glances of the public eye.

It is easily perceived that something similar could happen today. There is always the temptation to get high numbers in a movement by rallying around specific causes about which there is consensus, such as the abolition of land-based intermediate range missiles. And the obvious danger is that the other side will take such narrow slogans very literally, responding to the "No Pershing/Cruise; no SS20" with the "zero option", and even by withdrawing and not deploying intermediate range nuclear missiles, relying on inter-continental ballistic missiles that can also serve shorter ranges, and on offensive conventional arms and the short distance nuclear weaponry, the tactical nuclear arms in Europe. There is a corresponding danger in the much better slogan of "nuclear-free Europe from Poland to Portugal": it might become nuclear-free and be filled with chemical weapons instead. In short, a key danger for the peace movement is also to become too modest in its demands, that it does not live up to its historical obligation to take the debate about *alternative* security policies seriously, knowing well that some of the ranks will split at least temporarily over such issues. But if the peace movement cannot take this decisive step from the quantity of millions, rallying in non-violent demonstrations against collective suicide, to the quality of deeper, more considered perspectives, then who else can do it? Those trapped in thought prisons derived from pre-nuclear thinking? Hardly. But then all the signs are that the peace movement is now doing exactly this and becoming even stronger in the total struggle for a more peaceful world. There is a quantity-quality process going on, with not only higher numbers of participants, but also deeper reflection.

Obviously, this type of movement does not have the same strength in all countries. Generally speaking one may perhaps say that the protest movement is strongest in democratic "client countries", meaning countries whose governments are subservient to the superpower where nuclear policy is concerned, yet have a democratic political structure and culture. Thus, one finds particularly strong movements in countries like the Federal Republic of Germany, the Netherlands, Belgium, Denmark, Norway and Britain. That these are not the only conditions is clearly seen by the fact that the movement is weak in Italy where the information level is low, and only very recently has become strong in Greece, but impeded by the Greece/Turkey issue in a way which is difficult to detach from the more general peace issue. However much the Greek movement may insist that the conflict with Turkey is an artificial one, clearly security problems have to be a public concern, not monopolised entirely, as in Spain, by a small "club de caballeros". The Falklands/Malvinas war was also a shock to the movement in Britain — nationalism is deeper than many believe, although there was also an age factor here.

In "protest countries" — the non-aligned countries and the semi non-aligned such as France — the movement tends to be weak, to a large extent because the population thinks the government has already done something about the issue. Obviously, the populations in Switzerland and Yugoslavia, Austria and Finland, and to some extent also Sweden and Malta feel a type of security that the populations of neighbouring NATO countries do not feel — or at least they do not feel the same ever present, gnawing insecurity. For that reason it may also be predicted that if the protest movement is successful, and turns the country into a protest country, the result may be that the movement dwindles away, or becomes a client movement to its own country's government. But there is certainly some distance to go before that will happen.

This leads to the obvious question: are there similar movements in Eastern Europe? Yes and no. We know full well that the systems are different, not only economically but also in terms of the possibility of democratic expression. To search for such *mass movements* is a little like squaring the circle; to search for something not (yet) existing, within the current terms of reference. There will be individuals, courageous and strong, there will be some groups, there may be sporadic protest actions. But in general the alignment between government and the open expression of popular sentiment will be ensured through acts of repression, and the consciousness will be low for lack of debate. On the other hand, the value of even small non-authorised peace movements in Eastern Europe should not be underestimated — 10 organised persons against military action may be as much of a shock to governments in the East as 100,000 in the West — 50 as much or more than half a million. Where everybody speaks few tend to listen; where everybody listens few dare speak — but *when* they speak they are heard. The marginal utility is higher, precisely because the Eastern governments cling so desperately to an opinion monopoly on peace and security affairs, not only an action monopoly. They would themselves gain so much from democracy in these matters!

However, the partner in the East for the peace movement in the West is also the official peace movement, and some of the governments in Eastern Europe, although it may be difficult to have contacts with both at the same time, and particularly at the same place. Also, Eastern Europeans governments differ. Thus, Romania under the leadership of Nicolae Ceausescu is an important part of the general peace movement in Europe, with even-handed attempts to calm down the superpowers, retaining a high level of decoupling, and (it seems) not open to Soviet offensive arms; also working for the Balkans as a nuclear-free zone. The demonstrations in Bucharest in the autumn of 1981 brought together at least 300,000 participants, and they shouted slogans of peace, not what they could also have said, "Give us bread!" In short, the government took a risk in sponsoring and organising this demonstration, testifying to its genuine nature.

But the point is not only whether the governments are able to or want to mobilise popular sentiment on their side; the key point is what the attitudes of the Eastern European governments are in this matter. It is clearly in the interest of the Soviet Union not to have on its border unfriendly regimes. In fact, the regimes should serve as a guarantee to the Soviet Union that the border countries cannot be used for offensive activities against the Soviet Union. The 1948 treaty of friendship and co-operation with Finland guarantees this. This is entirely compatible with the type of politics that Romania engages in, and may even be to the advantage of the Soviet Union. To show the world that the Warsaw Treaty Organisation is capable of harbouring a protest country as much as the North Atlantic Treaty Organisation is already something even if this, of course, is denigrated in the West. To have such protest countries (although at the moment there is only one, Romania) play a possible role in a second détente process, if it is ever to come about, would be another point. As matters stand right now, a second détente seems to be more in the interest of the Soviet Union than of the United States, hence it is possible that protest countries in the eastern camp could have more latitude than corresponding countries in the western camp.

This, then, leads to the interesting situation that the protest movement in

the West may find some resonance in protest governments (and others) in
the East, whereas protest movements in the East (such as Solidarity in
Poland) find resonance all over the West. With their own governments the
protest movements are never popular; there is not that much difference
between early phases of the Solidarity movement (say, till 1981), and the
present (autumn 1983) phase of the peace movement in the West. They are
both autonomous popular movements; neither of them a tool of
governmental forces on the other side. The Soviet government has
financed some peace organisations through the World Peace Council — but
that is the communist part of the old peace movement, not the new peace
movement which is seen as "splitting the peace forces" by Moscow. But it
may very well be that the Western peace movement idea of a nuclear
weapon-free zone in Europe might find its best starting point in an area
where there is an Eastern European government willing to move in this
direction — and that is not in north-eastern Europe but in south-eastern
Europe (for instance a zone comprising Greece, Yugoslavia, Bulgaria and
Romania, possibly even including Albania). In short, good peace movement
politics here would be to keep all options for alliance open — with Eastern
European governments, and with authorised and non-authorised peace
movements. Nuclear arms are also means of controlling allies East and
West; any government wanting more autonomy will therefore appreciate a
strong peace movement.

It should be remembered in this connection that Eastern European
countries are relatively collectivist where foreign policy is concerned.
Public opinion studies indicate that, whereas the population in these
countries may be at odds with their governments in domestic matters, they
share many official assumptions about world politics in general, and the
Cold War in particular. This means that official statements relatively
similar to what comes out of the peace movement in the West may be quite
representative of Eastern European public opinion — except for a hard
right-wing dissident core very much cherished by conservative Western
governments. But it also means that there is not that individual dedication
and willingness to fight found in the West; the costs are too high. It all
becomes more official and institutional. But even in the West the peace
movement is strongest in democratic and client countries, particularly in
north-western Europe. It is of course weaker in autocratic countries
(Turkey) and also in protest countries because the population may feel less
motivated when official statements are already peace-oriented — as
mentioned above. East and West are not that different.

In conclusion, it might be said that there is no doubt that a new peace
actor has come into existence: the Western peace movement. But it is not
so much a third, invisible, party at the negotiation table in Geneva; it may
rather be referred to as a second party, both in Geneva *and* inside the
West. It represents popular and populist interests and sentiments. But the
superpowers represent the opposite and have considerable shared
interests; that of remaining superpowers. To remain superpowers they
have to have super-weapons, and monopoly over them. Even when the
weapons are deployed far away from superpower heartland the
superpowers remain firmly in control — even if the control is that of the

local commander, it is a superpower local commander — in general with no double-key formula (meaning veto power). The superpowers have a shared interest in keeping the peace movement at bay, in seeing to it both that public opinion does not become too restless and that it does not have too much success. The superpowers have to appear as if they are trying to do something about the situation, yet they want to remain superpowers, not giving in to unpredictable popular forces directed at both of them, saying "a plague on both your houses".

And then there is the peace movement as the opposition to Western governmental military policies, usually heavily under-represented in the national parliaments, relative to its strength in the population. With the relationship between governments East and West blocked and the opposition in the East muted — to say the least — this is the only *open* conflict over the peace issue, and it has to carry much of the dialogue of the whole East-West system. With the ritualistic locked-in position of most Western governments this means that the peace movement carries considerable historical responsibility. Is the peace movement, highly unco-ordinated as it is, able to discharge that responsibility?

As mentioned earlier, the peace movement of today is more mature than the movement of yesterday. It is not easily deceived by naive or deceitful "through-armament-to-disarmament" formulas, and is highly sceptical of "disarmament negotiations". If the movement is able to keep up the pressure it may also continue to have success, but beyond the sense of "bringing-the-parties-to-the-negotiation-table". To the extent that the peace movement has been instrumental here it is also a Pyrrhic victory since negotiations around that table seem to stimulate armament rather than disarmament (because the parties are comparing their arsenals of weapons item by item, they become more conscious of each deficit and of course draw the conclusion that they have to catch up; see Chapter 4).

The point is rather that the peace movement has revealed a gap between popular sentiment and what governments pursue militarily in alliance meetings which is so great that one may reasonably ask whether these alliances really exist, except as governmental clubs. It is not only governmental expertise that is challenged, but the whole basis of their security policy. It is not only Poles that represent a problem to WTO; it is also the populations of the emerging protest countries in Western Europe that seem to have no faith in "security" as pursued by their governments. They see the danger in terms of nuclear armament, not in terms of a possible Soviet attack. Will Poles really fight for the Soviet Union? Will they accept that only the other side can be blamed for a war? Will the millions in the West European peace movement fight for the United States, or cast the Soviet Union in the role of the sole aggressor? In case of a war they may not openly revolt against their increasingly militarist regimes, but they may certainly fail to co-operate, and may engage in passive resistance. The alliances may still look formidable from the outside, but increasingly they have become like empty shells. Only those shells, unfortunately, are filled with more explosives of mass destruction than ever before, and increasingly so.

Hence, the peace forces are many: the peace movements in the West; the

There are alternatives!

authorised and non-authorised movements in the East; the neutral and non-aligned and protest governments West and East; the non-aligned movement, the UN. It ought to be enough — but on the other side are the military complexes and their supporters. A small minority, but very, very strong.

In conclusion, some words about public opinion in the Western countries. The *International Herald Tribune* and the Atlantic Institute conducted a public opinion poll in nine countries, all of them United States "allies", prior to the summit meeting in Williamsburg of the Western leaders in May 1983. Among the questions asked was a general one: "Which of the following are your greatest concerns for yourself and your country today?" Below, however, the focus is only on the questions and answers directly relating to the subject of the present book — the greater concern actually being "unemployment". There are a number of interesting conclusions to draw from this table.

Table 1.1

Greatest concern for yourself and your country (%)

	Great Britain	France	Italy	Japan	Netherlands	Norway	Spain	United States	W. Germany
1. Inadequate defence	8	6	6	10	7	4	5	12	4
2. Threat of war	26	34	44	36	33	31	48	25	16
3. Nuclear weapons	32	19	33	28	47	42	29	20	42
4. (3)-(2)	+6	−15	−11	−8	+14	+11	−19	−5	+26

Reduce defence spending and use some of the money for social services, health and education

	Great Britain	France	Italy	Japan	Netherlands	Norway	Spain	United States	W. Germany
1. Support	58	81	68	58	54	54	82	69	67
2. Oppose	32	5	13	11	27	41	2	27	15
3. (1)-(2)	26	76	55	47	27	13	80	42	52

Increase trade with the Soviet Union and the other East European countries

	Great Britain	France	Italy	Japan	Netherlands	Norway	Spain	United States	W. Germany
1. Support	39	57	41	41	36	56	74	46	54
2. Oppose	46	28	28	15	36	35	10	49	23
3. (1)-(2)	−13	+29	+13	+26	0	+21	+64	−3	+31

First, just looking at the top line of figures: clearly only very small minorities in the nine countries concerned are of the opinion that "inadequate defence" is the greatest concern. On the other hand their leaders talk as if that is the greatest concern, in many of these countries ranking much above unemployment, inflation and so on when expressed in terms of budgetary priorities. The figures are actually so small that any armament policy in these nine countries definitely is not merely a minority policy but actually the policy of a very small minority. Although it makes almost no sense to compare these small figures it should only be noted, in passing, that the countries with the highest percentages are the United States and what still pass as the two most faithful allies, Japan and Great Britain.

Second, what people are worried about is evidently the "Threat of war" and "Nuclear weapons". Of course, it is difficult to say exactly what people have been thinking of when they give such responses. But it is not unreasonable to assume that "Threat of war" relates to the East-West conflict as such, and since these are Western countries, possibly an expression of the fear of a Soviet attack. "Nuclear weapons" may relate more to the arms race as such and be an expression of the fear of drifting into a nuclear war because of arms race dynamics. Obviously these two answers and interpretations do not exclude each other, and judging by the figures both concerns are deeply embedded in the populations. But when compared to the first set of figures it does not look as if the population is of the opinion that the response should be to make defence more "adequate". In fact, the combination of these first three lines of the table is open to exactly the interpretation that is the underlying psycho-political basis for the peace movement: there is threat of war, even nuclear war, not because we have too little defence but because we have too much.

In this connection it is interesting to distinguish between the countries that emphasise "nuclear weapons" more and those that emphasise "threat of war" more; line No.4 in the table. The four countries that emphasise "nuclear weapons" more are exactly the four countries with the strongest peace movements among the nine: Great Britain, Netherlands, Norway and the Federal Republic of Germany. Conversely, the three countries with the lowest relative concern for nuclear weapons are the three Latin European countries, France, Italy and Spain, with relatively small peace movements.

Third, something of the same appears when we look at how people relate military expenditure to social expenditure, in other words the reactions to the proposal of transfers from the military budget to social services of various kinds. The support for such a transfer is overwhelming, a clear majority policy in all countries. The only country where there is a sizeable proportion of the population opposing this kind of transfer is Norway, and one interpretation might be that in that particular country the social services, health and education are still functioning quite well — which they certainly are not in Spain, hence Spain and Norway as the two extremes in the distribution. It will be noted that the three Latin European countries are the highest in choosing 'support' over 'oppose' as their answers, followed by the Federal Republic of Germany and Japan. Of course, it is difficult to draw firm conclusions on this basis but it might indicate that there are two types of motivations for opposing military expansion: one in Northern Europe deriving from the threat of nuclear war, and another in Latin Europe, deriving from the threat of decreasing social welfare. It

looks as if the Federal Republic of Germany has a peace movement riding
on both waves, both the internationally and nationally motivated opposition
to military expansionism.

Fourth, what are the attitidues to increased trade with the Soviet Union
and Eastern Europe? Most interesting in this table is the circumstance that
only two countries have more people opposing such a proposal than
supporting it: the United States, and — even more so — Great Britain.
Again this shows what a limited support any NATO policy of restriction
against trade with Eastern Europe enjoys. As is well-known this has
already led to considerable cleavages within the alliance.

Of course, public opinion is subject to fluctuations: there are moods
depending on circumstances, both influenced by longer trends and by
sharp, decisive events. Nevertheless it does not seem too audacious to draw
the conclusion from this study that any policy of less threatening postures,
withdrawal of nuclear weapons and increased trade between East and
West could count on substantial public support, whereas a policy of
armament, making the defence more "adequate", can count on solid
opposition. And that opposition is precisely what is known as the peace
movement.

4. What: Four roads to peace and security

It seems to me that there are four approaches in this field, four roads that
governments and movements can try to travel in order to arrive at peace,
at least in the narrow sense of war avoidance. They are: *conflict resolution,
balance of power, disarmament* and *alternative security policies.* Later on,
road No.4, the one most believed in here but certainly not to the exclusion
of the other three, will also be seen as four roads, or parallel paths — that
hopefully one day could become highway lanes.

Peace politics usually starts with conflict resolution. If we limit the
perspective to conflicts between countries and groups of countries
(territorial, governmental), then there is somewhere in a conflict usually —
not always — an *issue* or a bundle of issues, and *parties* are being formed.
There is a conflict when parties are in pursuit of incompatible goals, the
incompatibility being the issue. Thus, they may both want their own
ideology and political system to prevail or both want control over a certain
territory. Very soon this becomes extremely complicated. Issues get
interwoven with each other, parties and party lines become blurred and
overlapping. If anything ever was clear it gets lost. The reason for this is
that conflicts are never stable, they are always in some process: patterns of
attitudes and patterns of behaviour on either side (or all sides, there are not
necessarily only two) start building up, new issues emerge as a consequence
of hostile attitudes and behaviour and mesh with the old ones; new parties
emerge and mesh with the old ones, and so on.

The effort to cut through it all with some process of *conflict resolution*
often becomes like cutting the famous Gordian knot: there is no knot any
longer, for sure, only a vastly complex tangle, and the rope may get
destroyed in the cutting process. Hence, as most people will know from

personal relations, very many conflicts are perhaps never really solved but recede into the background, are forgotton. One way in which they are forgotten is because another conflict comes up that requires more attention. The East-West conflict is also an example of that: The "North-South conflict" received more attention because of the détente, *and vice versa,* from the end of the 1960s and receded into the background again with the intensification of the Cold War from the end of the 1970s.

However, some conflicts are resilient. Neither dissolved, nor forgotton, attitudes of hatred and destructive behaviour start accumulating. The other party is increasingly seen as standing in one's way. Professionals are called in: the ideologists and propagandists for the production of hatred, and the military for the production of means of destruction, ultimately for the production of destruction itself. The former is intended to hit the mind, the latter to hit the body — and in addition to the body all the things made by human beings, the human-made environment and recently also the rest of the environment. Let us focus on the means of material destruction of the other side and call them offensive arms. If one side acquires them the other also tends to feel provoked into doing so and the result is an offensive arms race which may not necessarily cause a war, but may end with a war, meaning with a bang rather than with a whimper.

One idea as to how wars can be avoided is now to try to make the arms race end with a whimper by finding a point, a so-called stable *balance of power,* where both sides can agree that enough is enough, and simply stop increasing the arsenal of means of destruction. Another idea would be that the point does not have to be a point; it does not have to be a static equilibrium either, but could be a dynamic equilibrium where both parties continue increasing their armament, but in a balanced way. This is the most optimistic interpretation of the arms race of recent decades.

Experience seems to show that sooner or later more bang than whimper comes out of any arms race. Hence, there is the third approach, the idea of *disarmament:* of coming to a point where instead of building up destructive power one tries to build it down. The question is how to do that, and one position has been that it can only be done if the balance of power referred to above is retained, if it is done in a mutually agreed fashion, and if the process is controlled, possibly even through on-site inspection. A negative rather than positive arms race, under the headings of *balanced, mutual* and *controlled* is called for.

This road to peace, however, also seems problematic and for that reason many people have come to the conclusion that there might be something wrong with the entire approach. Even if one sticks to the custom of referring to the whole destruction machinery as "defence" (there are not many countries left now that have not renamed their former Ministries of War, Ministries of Defence), there seems to be something about this machinery that makes it extremely difficult to identify that stable point or region of balance, and even more difficult to disarm from that point on. And that leads to the forth problématique, of *alternative security policies,* including other forms of defence that do not lead to the type of arms races that seem to accompany the quest for the balance of power. Moreover, what would constitute an answer to the problem of security in a disarmed world? Fundamental in this connection are defensive or non-aggressive and non-provocatory, conventional military defence, paramilitary defence (guerrilla) and non-military defence; as opposed to offensive military "defence", be that conventional or nuclear (or with other weapons of mass destruction).

In what follows there will be one chapter devoted to each of these four approaches, analysing their weak and strong sides. Here the focus will be on something else: *the indivisibility of the problématique.* Underlying this is one simple proposition: *The four approaches to peace have all to be pursued in a meaningful way at the same time. If one pursues only one of them, not even that one will be achieved.*

That there is some validity to this idea is easily seen. Thus, imagine only conflict resolution is pursued. There is an effort to find out what the real issue is, the innermost issue, and to try to develop some imaginative formula, accepted by both parties, supported by viable institutions and "structures" so that the conflict might eventually disappear, wither away. But what then about the military machinery, the "defence" machinery? It would still be there, and it seems to have a healthy life of its own. In fact, it may well be that it was exactly something like this that happened at the end of the détente period (roughly speaking mid-'60s to mid-'70s) in Europe. Imaginative formulas for conflict resolution had been found, codified in the Final Act of Helsinki. But very little had actually happened to the military machineries, except some agreed-upon formula for institutionalised growth — SALT I. What happened afterwards gives very little reason to believe that it is enough to arrive at conflict resolution. In fact, right now there is probably more conflict than ever before, among other reasons because of the propensity of military machineries to generate issues of their own and re-open the old ones. At least it is clear that it is not sufficient to try to solve the issues as long as the parties, in this case the alliances, remain. They are part of the conflict formation, as important as the issues, and tend to generate their own justification.

But does that mean that the pursuit of balance of power can at least keep the conflict within bounds? No. First of all, not unlike conflict resolution, it is very difficult to achieve, one simple reason being that both parties are likely to interpret the word "balance" like shopkeepers do, not as it is done in mechanics. It is not really assumed to mean parity, even "rough parity" — as defined by a very crude scale. Both parties, or at least one of them, might prefer to have a "positive balance", like any shopkeeper — an edge over the adversary. Only if at least one of them misperceives the situation will this be possible, and that particular combination would certainly not be stable. How important this is, however, is to a large extent dependent on the amount of conflict raw material there is floating around between the parties, material that can be processed into the type of attitude and behaviour out of which, if not hot wars, at least war-like interaction is made i.e. Cold War. And the net consequence is the negation of what one set out to achieve: balance of power. Instead there would be an arms race, brought about by the very search for balance, in a context of conflict. If no conflict, then it is all the more easy. With conflict, a war is the likely result of an arms race, even a war nobody really wanted.

Imagine, then, that one crosses the borderline from the "realist' (concerned with the politics of conflict resolution and the technicalities of balance of power) to the "idealist", concerned with the struggle to reduce the level of armament, of destructive power, and/or to make arms less lethal. Imagine there is success with the effort to disarm, but that the conflict is left unresolved and/or the disarmament takes place in a highly unbalanced way. The consequences are fairly obvious. There is always the danger that a conflict left unattended will generate the kind of situation where at least one of the parties, if not planning a war, might start fearing that the other side is planning one. The result, in all likelihood, will be rearmament — and the experience seems to show that in such cases there will be an overshoot relative to the level of armament existing before the reduction took place. One of the reasons for this is simple: it is always easier to rearm than simply to arm, for the same reason as it is easier to walk or drive along a road already travelled once. One knows what to do, difficulties can better be foreseen, the speed is higher, and is fuelled by the moral rage stemming from frustrated hopes. And then there is the other possibility: there was no balance, the militarily stronger party makes a threatening move, and the result is either the rearmament just mentioned or simply an invasion, an occupation, loss of freedom. The customary military phrase of *horror vacui,* the horror of the (militarily) empty space, is certainly not true under all circumstances but it is not untrue under all circumstances either. It might obtain precisely when there is a conflict left unresolved and there is a gross imbalance. So, again, he who aims at too little does not even get that: he gets rearmament, over-armament.

And the same applies to the fourth corner in the quadrangle: the least tested hypothesis, that of alternative security policies. As a part of such a policy a country neither disarms nor rearms. It *transarms,* meaning building a defence on the triple combination mentioned of conventional military, paramilitary and non-military defence. But the conflict is left unattended. There is no balance in a sense to be explored later (in 3.4): a realisation of the fact that one's own security has as a condition that the other party also is secure, that security has to be shared, common. There is no general disarmament. And the transarmed country looks as if it is permanently waiting for the worst to happen; it does not breathe peace. And that is the point: a high level defensive defence preparation has much to say in its favour, it may even deter so effectively that no attack takes place. But it also freezes conflicts rather than solving them by creating a sense of invulnerability, even of lofty isolation, of being immune not only to attack but also to criticism, and hence not having to pay any attention to it. Switzerland is perhaps a case here, having solved a problem for itself, but not as a part of a process together with others. It could lead to mutually non-provocative societies, even with all societies transarmed, decoupled from superpowers, with more inner strength and outer usefulness. But will it not become like the heavy arm of a medieval knight, proud of the fact that he has no lance to wield, but nevertheless suffocating inside his armour? And does a conflict not somehow have to be resolved to permit history to move on?

We know little of this latter case, so one speculation may be as good as the other. But the first two cases are very well known from post-Second World War history. In fact, one may even write that history in the terms suggested above. There was a phase filled with efforts to regulate if not also to dissolve the conflicts that started piling up (again) between the victors after they had defeated the Nazi scourge. Maybe it was not whole-hearted, but an effort it was. It did not succeed, and balance of power policies have been pursued ever since. The idea has been to buy security through ever-increasing military budgets. But the illusive benefit "security" has not only failed to appear; there has been diminishing, even negative returns for the dollars and roubles spent in the pursuit, even to the point that many people seem to feel that what is produced is insecurity rather than security. To achieve balanced, mutual and controlled disarmament under such conditions has always been even more difficult than to try to get security through balance of power. We are again in that phase now, in ways to be explored later, but with the shallow one-sidedness characteristic of all these efforts, failure seems highly predictable. Next in line, then, is the demand for alternative security policies, not only from the grassroots, from peace movements in general, but pursued at the governmental level. If this is also to be pursued with the same shallow one-sidedness, there will be a fourth failure in this linear train of one-sidedness, to be added to the two already well consummated, and the third that has not yet been officially declared as a failure. Four single-minded wrongs spread out in time certainly do not make one right; at best we would then be back again to square one. At worst we would have the war.

My conclusion is that peace politics must be seen as having at least four components that have to be approached synchronically, at the same time, not diachronically, one after the other. It makes no sense to run from one corner to the other in the diagram below:

Figure 1.2   The components of peace politics

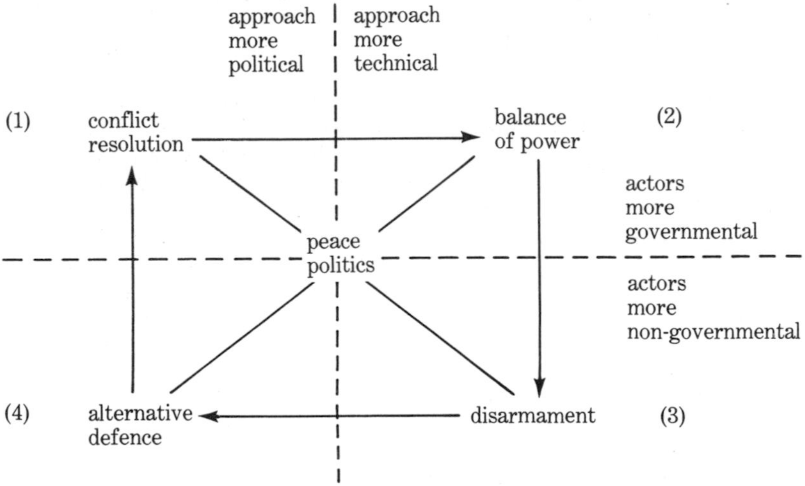

What should make sense would be to have an integrated policy that walks not only on two legs as the Chinese used to say, but on all four. Is our poor world capable of that, even assuming good will?

It is easily seen that one major difficulty in this connection is the division of labour traditionally existing between these four components. For one thing, the top two have been seen as the task of governments, the bottom two as something popular movements have been talking about — governments may have paid some attention and performed some ritual exercises, but little more. Good peace politics would make all four both governmental and non-governmental, and both political and technical.

Conflict resolution has been the task of the policy makers, expressed at the international level by the Foreign Offices. The balance of power has been the task of the Ministries of Defence in whose interest it has been to make it a very technical and secret matter indeed. Disarmament has fallen between two stools: between the peace movement to whom it is a moral necessity, and the government technicians who have been the professionals of the armament process, suddenly to find themselves called upon to reverse and undo their own creation. A very difficult task for any person indeed. And alternative security policy is the domain of nobody.

At the international level this division of labour is even more pronounced: conflict resolution is the task of the United Nations, partcularly the General Assembly and the Security Council. To pursue the balance of power is outside the tasks of the United Nations except insofar as the disarmament conferences, to some extent under the aegis of the United Nations, serve as a forum in which the degrees of balance can be evaluated under the guise of performing disarmament negotiations. And alternative security policies are, at most, the concern of some international, non-governmental peace organisations. At no point do all these components come together.

All of this is a very unfortunate situation indeed. To take a parallel from the field of health: it is as if such important health tasks as hygiene and sanitation; improvement of the nutrition level and the general standard of living of the population; immunisation; quarantine; and cure and care for the diseased were carried out by totally unrelated institutions in society. In most countries there are today Ministries of Health (or sections dealing with health within Ministries of Social Affairs etc.), concerned with the co-ordination of different aspects of the health process. One may object that it was not always like this, which is true. But then there was not that much health either — and if there are still considerable health deficits relative to what could be obtained in many countries, at least one of the reasons is the failure to develop co-ordinated health policies.

Of course, such co-ordinated policies may also make more grandiose mistakes, and the more so the higher the level of co-ordination. But this holds only up to a certain point: the dangers of too much co-ordination should not serve as an argument in favour of total lack of co-ordination. For what we are doing in the field of peace policies translated into health policies is a little bit like first trying to get at health through sanitation/hygiene alone; then, when there are still problems of health unsolved, giving it up, switching to nutrition instead, then switching to immunisation, and when that doesn't work either, going in entirely for curative medicine. As in the field of peace and war, single-minded approaches may help a little. But what one is trying to do in the field of health is to obtain some additional positive effect, often called "synergy", by not only enacting all policies but also having these different policies play together.

It is easily seen, at least in principle, that this is possible. A disarmament process has to some extent to be balanced, that is one consequence of this type of philosophy. Another consequence is that it has to take place in an atmospere of conflict resolution. And still another consequence is that as one disarms there also has to be some kind of armament. Some kind of alternative defence has to be built up, unless one assumes that the world has become safe enough for a total lack of any kind of defence against aggression — because there will be none. But this build-up has to be done in such a way that it does not add new conflict material, and that is tricky, a theme to be explored later.

At this point I only want to arrive at one conclusion: *peace politics is complicated,* to put it mildly. The level of complexity is also at the intellectual level: it is a question of keeping quite a lot of ideas in one's mind at the same time, and trying to let them interact with each other, shunning most of the simplifying single-factor theories, so dear both to bureaucracies of external affairs and of defence, of armament and of disarmament; as they are dear to many of the peace movements, solidly built around one single idea, be that conciliation, peace through strength, no to weapons in general or atomic weapons in particular, yes to alternative forms of defence. It is also complicated at the governmental level, and might lead to the conclusion that far better than an inter-departmental committee at the governmental level would be a special department, or *Ministry of Peace;* in all countries. There is nothing more inane in this idea than there once was in having a Ministry of Environment — yet that was accepted all of a sudden in the early 1970s in so many countries, probably because it was seen as essential in removing some obstacles (pollution, depletion) in the way of continued economic growth. There is certainly a limit to what ministries can do, but at least they have the advantage of having an overview of the issues, permitting an integrated view and sometimes even integrated action that would be impossible when the issues are fragmented from each other into separate ministries. Another concrete consequence is that environmental concerns, and in this case peace concerns, can be pleaded more effectively at the cabinet level when represented by a ministry. In principle.

But having said that one could also turn the argument to the level below and the level above: why not also a municipal board for peace (as there is one for environment in many municipalities in many countries) with professional peace workers. And why not a United Nations Peace Programme, (a UNPP, like the UNEP, United Nations Environment Programme) combining functions that today are divided between the secretariats of the political organisations (the General Assembly and the Security Council), the peace-keeping operations, the disarmament organisations, and so on? In short, a plea for the emergence of peace politics at all levels, and not only in the minds of men and women, but also as even boring, day-to-day administrative routines. At any rate, it is the hope that the next chapters will show that there is more than enough work to do.

2

Conflict Resolution

1. The global reach: superpower values and interests

Peace politics has no beginning and no end because everything has to be done synchronically, but nobody has so far been able to write, or at least to print, a book that way. There is something linear about a book, and this one is no exception so I have to start somewhere. And it does make good sense to start with the prospects for conflict resolution — which presupposes some exploration of the conflict itself. After all, this belongs to the heart of the matter.

What is the so-called East-West conflict about? We know more or less who the parties are, but what are, basically, the issues? Unfortunately, they are deep, far-reaching and genuine and cannot be wished away. They are inextricably linked to two particular countries, the United States and the Soviet Union, remarkably similar in their dissimilarities. And they are also inextricably linked to two particular ideologies, liberalism and Marxism, and their social-economic-political expressions, capitalism and socialism. It would have helped if the world had not had these two over-sized and over-powerful countries with their intolerant and universalising ideologies at this particular point in human history, so rich in both potentially beneficial and highly dangerous innovations. Of course, some other countries might then have taken their place; after all, the US had predecessors. However that may be, the fact is that these countries exist as key political actors on the world scene, that they do act according to the programmes written into them through those ideologies, and use these ideologies to understand the other one; that this makes for highly dangerous collision courses; and that it does not help to wish it otherwise. We somehow have to make it otherwise. But first one has to try to understand what is going on.

Much has been said about the similarities and the differences between the United States and the Soviet Union, leading to symmetric and asymmetric views of them. Obviously there are both symmetries and asymmetries — theories of "two superpowers" and theories emphasising the differences. The line here will be to try to pursue both lines of analysis, striking a balance between symmetry and asymmetry. So let us start with some of the similarities. They are both *newcomers on the world political scene,* to a large extent brought into prominence by the First World War, which made the US a world power and gave birth to the Soviet Union. The Second World War confirmed the US as the world's economically hegemonic power, and the political-military leader of the "free world", and made it possible for the Soviet Union to build an empire far outside its own borders — in the sense of imposing upon other countries its unmistakable social imprint, not necessarily in the sense of exploiting them. Thus, both of them have a particularly unfortunate (for the rest of us) experience in their recent past: *wars may be devastating, but they also offer great opportunities,* and more so the bigger they are. Wars may pay, consolidate the capitalism of one, the anti-capitalism of the other. Wars also cost; but this price has been so much higher for Russia/the Soviet Union that all symmetries dissolve in the face of *the suffering of the people on Soviet soil; and that is a key asymmetry.*

Before that, however, both of them also had an *expansionist period into vast "unpopulated" territories,* meaning territories populated by peoples of other cultures, other races, other socio-economic formations (hunter-gatherers). *Expansionism was combined with exterminism,* both in the US pioneer and the tsarist pioneer cases. Both of them drew the experience that their capitals were centres from which forces could emanate, radiate outwards, conquer, domesticate, subjugate, kill and plunder, bending others to serve one's own purpose. And both of them secured their borders in the last century by annexing great parts of Mexico (the US, in the war of 1846-1847, annexing most of what today is known as Texas, New Mexico, Arizona, California, Nevada and Utah, for $15 million) and of China (Russia, in the unequal treaties of 1858); both of them have had policies in this century of pacifying neighbours through penetration (the US is reputed to control 70 per cent of Canada's economy; the Soviet Union probably controls more than that of the Mongolian economy and politics, not to mention many of the Eastern European neighbours, but the latter benefit by being technically more developed).

To all of this should also be added the point that *both of them are Western, in the sense of occidental countries.* And the ideologies they are the carriers of, well-known for their differences, also show considerable similarities. Both of them are secular offsprings of Christianity, Protestant/Catholic in the West and Orthodox in the East, liberalism being a legitimate offspring in the sense of being acknowledged by institutionalised Christianity; Marxism being illegitimate, both rejecting and being rejected by most established Christianity (but having made some kind of concordat with the less explicitly verbal Orthodox Church in Moscow). Both ideologies are fascinated by economic activity, having the industrial entrepreneur and the industrial worker as their historical heroes, respectively. Both of them perceive the nation state as the unit of major transformation, meaning sustained economic growth in the first case and sustained revolution in the second. Both of them claim universal applicability, and the carriers of these ideologies see it not only as their right but indeed as their duty to make their ideology prevail as a system of belief, and as a concrete socio-economic-political formation to the last corner of the world: one in the name of Humanity, the other in the name of History. And they also agree that they are not only *exclusive,* in the sense that there is only room for one of them in the same niche in space and time, but they are also *exhaustive* in the sense of being the only ideologies worth discussing in the world, the rest being anachronisms or, even worse, "romantic dreams". Like Christianity they both become aggressively missionary, because they are universalist and exclusive of other beliefs.

Clearly, any country that sees itself as the carrier of an ideology, prescribing in detail what a society should look like, feeling that it is a duty and not only a right to spread this system to the ends of the world, represents a threat to other societies. Other societies or people might agree, but they should come to that as a conclusion of their own deliberations, inner contradictions and historical processes, not by having the blueprint for their society imposed upon them from the outside. *Two countries of that type, each one with a universal and intolerant ideology, become a threat not only to each other and to other societies but to the world as a whole as they obviously will be on a collision course, particularly when they are so convinced that tertium non datur,* there is no third alternative. Countries of this type are not only a threat to peace, but also to development by *imposing development programmes on others,* by limiting the range of development alternatives down to only two, free market and centrally planned economies, with all that implies. And this from countries that are themselves highly mal-developed examples of their own prescriptions! I repeat: the world would be a better place without system protagonists of this size, meaning, for instance, that the world would be a better place if the United States were dismantled into 50 components and the Union of Soviet Republics into at least 15 (the biggest of them, the Russian Republic, should then be subdivided further).

So, what is the "East-West conflict" about? Clearly, *issue number one is this superpower urge to have societies around the world that are essentially copies of themselves;* a reproduction by cloning to put it that way. Let us refer to it as the problem of having a "compatible regime" in another country; one that is friendly or at least not unfriendly, similar or at least not dissimilar. That gives four major possibilities

1. A compatible regime is highly unlikely;
2. A compatible regime is about to get into power, or an incompatible one to become compatible;
3. A compatible regime is firmly established;
4. A compatible regime is about to lose power, or to become incompatible.

Clearly, this calls for four different types of action. In the first case even superpowers are usually not so stupid that they try to intervene, except for reasons to be discussed immediately below, when basic interests are at stake.

There is some kind of sense of internal historical processes, that not all countries are "ripe", and there may even be some respect for self-determination. But in the second case they are more than willing to help, and in that case by *subversive* activities, sending advisors, material and non-material development assistance as midwife activity. Then, the third case is similar to the first case: the superpower is at rest, not because the case is hopeless, but because no activity is needed. It is needed, however, in the fourth case: this is the case for open intervention, for *"superversive"* activity, at the call of a compatible government in distress for life prolongation. Thus, as other countries trace an historical course through these four phases there will be intermittent superpower activity inside their territories. Again, it should be emphasised that to these two superpowers, steered by ideologically committed people, in the occidental missionary tradition, what they do in such cases is not so much a right as a duty, even a heavy and holy one. It is usually a mistake to believe that they do not themselves believe that their action is justified by higher principles — at least in the longer run.

This becomes a conflict *between* the superpowers when both of them are involved in the same country: it is a conflict *within* their imperial systems when only one of them is involved. And then it may be both at the same time: when those in power in a country sympathise with one superpower and those in opposition (but wanting to get into power) sympathise with the other, everything is set for superpower conflict in the area, even if the superpowers do not deem the area important enough to risk a direct confrontation. This is a rather well-known and unfortunate aspect of post-Second World War history, immediately calling for a third development alternative — neither United States *blue* nor Soviet Union *red* — so that superpower polarisation is not translated into political polarisation with accompanying class contradictions, and *vice versa*.

This will be explored in some detail later; here it only serves to emphasise the linkage between the so-called East-West conflict over peace and war, and the so-called North-South conflict over development. The development models pursued by the superpowers become — of course — supermodels. The two conflicts become inextricable.

Then there is conflict issue number two: not to spread ideology or to reproduce one's own social formation, but *material; to secure certain basic interests.* I take these basic interests to be *economic-political* in the case of the United States, essentially the classical tasks of securing access to raw materials of "strategic" importance and market/capital outlets for the tremendous production capacity of that country; and to be *geo-political* in the case of the Soviet Union, essentially to secure a belt of compatible neighbour-states around the Soviet Union that may serve as a buffer in case of one more invasion (just as the Soviet Union itself is a buffer for Russia). Of course, the United States is also interested in this, for which reason it would never permit really incompatible regimes in the two neighbouring states, Mexico and Canada, and, as mentioned already, secured itself by pushing the border with Mexico considerably further south and by having a firm grip on the Canadian economy. Though it has not succeeded in "destabilising" Cuba, it is not because it has not tried, including a major invasion (1961 — Bay of Pigs). And the policies in Central America and the Caribbean (Nicaragua, Grenada) are clear; partly also for fear of Soviet deployment of middle-range missiles. Moreover, the Soviet Union also has certain economic interests around the world centred on its peculiar form of raw material imperialism: long-term contracts with client countries to buy their brand of export commodities at favourable but guaranteed prices, then waiting for the prices to go up, and also there is the matter of the arms trade. But the immediate geo-political considerations relative to the neighbours seem much more important for the Soviets.

The net consequence of this is that the Soviet Union is mainly a threat to its neighbours and uses the means of expansion it has inherited from the tsarist regime; land-based army invasions, where the tanks have substituted for the cavalry of earlier periods, of course supported by navy and air force if needed. And the United States has pursued its interventionist tradition from the very beginning of its existence, guided by substantial material interests, having oceans on either side, relying much on the navy, later on the airforce and ultimately on missiles; supplementing with forces for land operation, the marines and ultimately the army, when necessary.

Combining conflict issues nos. *one* and *two*, over values and over interests, the United States' and Soviet Union's belligerent behaviour becomes comprehensible. The US will tend to intervene when economic interests (short-term, but also long-term) are threatened *and* a compatible regime is about to come into power or go out of power; the Soviet Union will tend to intervene when geo-political interests in neighbour buffer states are threatened *and* a compatible regime is about to come into power or go out of power. It is when both conditions obtain at the same time that belligerent action will be very likely indeed. But one of the conditions may also be indicative of danger. Needless to say, both superpowers will try to legitimise their intervention not in terms of material economic or security interests but in terms of the ideology they represent. Like all major occidental faiths, with ideologies of progress, linear or exponential, they try to see themselves as engines moving humankind towards higher levels of development, operationalised as higher economic growth and capital accumulation/turnover in the one case, more collective control over production and regime turnover — revolution — in the latter.

From what has been said so far it follows that the *Soviet Union is essentially a regional power*, since her neighbours (there are many of them) by definition are in the same region, the Euro-Asian land mass. It is highly unlikely in the near future that the Soviet Union will fight a major war in America, south or north, in Africa or in Australia/Oceania. And it also follows from what has been said that *the United States is a global power* since the country has spun economic webs, controlled partly or wholly by her, all over the world, having material interests in very many places. Strategic raw materials and essential markets are not located everywhere, but the US defines what and where they are, thereby legitimising interventions. Particularly important are the two key parts of the world where the young United States rooted her imperialist endeavours through a very simple technique: by stepping into the shoes of a dying empire, the remnants of the Spanish *conquista*, in the Caribbean, and in the Philippines. All that was needed for the US was a relatively minor push against the Spaniards in both places, at the turn of the century, with the war against the Philippine population being considerably more protracted and bloody. The Caribbean is on the doorstep, neighbours in a certain sense. South-east Asia is certainly not, and this is where the United States has fought one of the most bloody, unjust and, in addition, unsuccessful wars in recent history — the Indo-China wars. The concern with the Persian/Arab Gulf is more recent, legitimised by an alleged dependence on the area for the supply of oil. Needless to say, this could very well be a cover for more ideological or broader economic concerns. The same applies to the Soviet geo-political interest: it could also be a way of legitimising ideological or broader socio-political concerns.

To repeat: the Soviet Union is at present essentially a threat to her neighbours, while the United States is a threat to many countries around the world and is perceived as such. This explains what to the United States has always been a mystery: why is the US so unpopular around the world? The US is unpopular in the Third World because no country feels quite safe, and before Afghanistan, Soviet interventions were seen as a European matter — and essentially as an Eastern European matter — affecting a handful of countries only, largely unknown in the Third World. There is much Third World cynicism here, neglect of Eastern Europeans who have been so overshadowed in history by the more successful and much more imperialistic First World Europe. But it is hard to blame the Third World for having its own interests and security more in mind that that of Eastern Europe. However, some of this changed a little with the bloody, repressive, and already quite protracted and unsuccessful Soviet intervention in Afghanistan in December 1979 — although it is within the neighbour concept. Seen that way, the Afghanistan invasion represents nothing new in Soviet policy.

What follows from this if one wants to guard oneself against intervention? In the Soviet case it is obviously better not to be a neighbour — the same also applies to the US case, but for reasons mentioned above that issue was more for the 19th rather than the 20th century. There are 12 of these direct Soviet land neighbours, from North Korea in the extreme east via China, Mongolia, Afghanistan, Iran, Turkey, Romania, Hungary, Czechoslovakia, Poland and Finland to Norway in the extreme west. In addition, Bulgaria and Pakistan are very close — and Japan (even the US!) are ocean neighbours: altogether 15. Clearly, the Soviet Union has not intervened in all of them, and has even withdrawn from two that were occupied after the Second World War: the northernmost part of Norway (including Spitsbergen) and Finland — in either case probably because in the judgment of Moscow the chances of a credible compatible regime coming into power were slim indeed.

In Azerbaidzhan, Iran, a very friendly regime came into power in 1945. The Russians overstayed, and when they left it was due to US pressure. But they withdrew from two more countries in Europe that are indirect neighbours (neighbours of their neighbours): Denmark (the case of Bornholm) and Austria (through the 1955 *Staatsvertrag*), both profoundly bourgeois countries where the chances of class contradictions "maturing" in such a way that the communist party might come into power with some kind of support were extremely remote. It might also be mentioned that so far they have not invaded another indirect neighbour, Yugoslavia, in spite of the regime turning unfriendly. In other words, it is simply not true that the Red Army clings to whatever it has once invaded, four cases constituting rather important counter arguments against a thesis of the ever-expanding Soviet army with her armada of tanks rolling west and south unless it is stopped by the only power it understands: that which

comes out of the barrel of a gun. That they had to be forced, through
threats, out of Iran confirms rather than disconfirms this: in Azerbaidzhan
both conditions for Soviet invasion were satisfied. And they have stayed on
in Eastern Europe, legitimised by the Yalta accords. Like the US, the
Soviet Union is aggressive, but not unconditionally aggressive.

In North Korea, the Soviet Union, to a large extent to their surprise, got
a compatible regime through the division of Korea after the Second World
War; in China they found a compatible regime in 1949, after the October 1
triumph of the revolution. In Mongolia a friendly, highly compatible regime
was already installed in 1921. Pakistan was and is at a distance. In
Afghanistan an intervention has taken place since 1979 under condition (4)
above: a compatible regime losing power, *or* becoming less compatible. Iran
may have been judged as far from mature in class contradictions, the same
has probably been the case for Turkey, but here membership of the NATO
alliance may also have served as a deterrent. Bulgaria and Romania have
both been relatively clear cases of type (3), with a friendly regime firmly
installed — Romania perhaps not being a completely reliable ally but
certainly not a threat either. Hungary (1956) and Czechoslovakia (1968)
were clear cases of type (4) and got their intervention; Poland (1980-83) is
still an ambiguous case but has so far not become a case of type (4). Finland
has probably been judged as being of case (3) type after the brutal Winter
War of 1939-40 and the brief interlude as an Axis power; being
"compatible" if not friendly in the Marxist/Socialist sense. To summarise:
of the 15 countries there remain the following problems: Japan, China
(after 1958-60), Pakistan, Afghanistan, Turkey and Norway — five very
different models of problems. In addition, any one of the other 10 — with
the possible exception of Bulgaria — may become a problem some day as
the "friendliness" is with the regime, not the population.

No doubt it is historically ill-advised to be a geographical neighbour of
the Soviet Union — but there is nothing one can do about it except when the
Soviet Union ultimately, like all other empires, contracts to a more modest
size — Moscow together with surroundings from which it once originated.
What I have tried to indicate, however, is that to be a neighbour is only one
condition for intervention, neither sufficient nor necessary. The other is the
nature of the regime. The conclusion is obvious: the best defence against
the Soviet Union is to have a society that does not produce the type of
conditions under which Soviet-oriented communist parties come into
power. And the best way of obtaining this, in turn, is to conduct politics in
such a way that class contradictions are either abolished or blunted, and
social justice, equality and equity, and freedom, become major guidelines
for domestic politics. In other words, the general welfare-state politics of
social democracy, whether under the auspices of a party of that name or
not, seems to be the best defence against a Soviet intervention — not
reliable in the case of neighbouring countries (Czechoslovakia 1948), but
probably quite reliable elsewhere, where security interests are less
overriding. That national autonomy is compatible with peaceful co-
existence with the Soviet Union is shown by the case of Finland — a
neighbouring country.

A corollary of this is that the most dangerous politics would be repressive conservative politics, sharpening class contradictions, maintaining, even producing social injustice, inequality and inequity; leading inevitably to revolutionary movements that may look to the Soviet Union for support. Under conditions of economic growth West European capitalism looks more attractive, on the average, than East European socialism; under conditions of economic crisis that may all change. It should be remembered that there is a social science approach focusing on capitalist societies in crisis: Marxism. They expect crisis to come and to represent a danger as well as an opportunity. If a country in capitalist crisis is also a neighbour of the Soviet Union, only very heavy militarisation will be held capable of staving off both the internal revolt and the possible external Soviet aggression (the cases of Turkey, Pakistan, and, during the Shah's regime, also Iran — in other words the CENTO powers). In short, it is what happens inside the country that matters most — and militarisation is usually only a short-term solution since it may also tend to push the society closer to a revolution.

What should one do in order to avoid US intervention? Rule number one: try not to have raw materials in which the US might be interested (or, if you have some, dig them up and sell them as soon as possible). Rule number two: do not offer the country as a major market for US products, including US capital. It should be noted that the first condition is also geographical, but a question of physical and economic geography rather than of mere positioning on the world map, relative to the superpowers. Thus, Chile would have been much better off without the guano, the nitrate and the copper mines. As one Chilean expert once expressed it, "if, in addition, uranium should be discovered in our soil, that is the end". Again, we are up against a condition about which it is difficult to do anything except, perhaps, to steer production patterns in such a direction that these raw materials become less, not more, significant (in some cases the threat of destruction of the mines etc. may also deter an invasion). Needless to say the Third World countries are here caught in a major dilemma: the more important the raw materials the more foreign currency can be obtained, and quickly, for whatever purpose. And the less important the raw materials the less significant the country becomes as a pawn in superpower politics; the more it can hope not to be paid too much attention to, but the less liquid capital it will have. Rich (elites) and dependent, or poor (elites) and independent — a cruel choice.

Then there is the political condition. In order not to be invaded by the United States the regime should either be stable and compatible or stable and incompatible, that is clear enough. But for a regime to be stable it has to have either popular support — the short term solution — be extremely authoritarian or totalitarian, or possibly both. And that gives us immediately the four types of countries to which the United States represents no immediate threat: authoritarian, capitalist countries like the numerous military dictatorships in the Third World supported by the United States; democratic, capitalist countries like most of those in Western Europe; relatively popular socialist countries with major internal revolts highly unlikely (like Yugoslavia, Bulgaria and Cuba, as the US had to experience after the Bay of Pigs invasion of April 1961); and highly authoritarian socialist countries, for instance like the Soviet Union itself. But societies are in a flux. Conditions change, they may move in and out of these categories — and the transition phases are dangerous. In addition, there is always present the possibility of grandiose misperception, in spite of (or perhaps because of) the patient work of the intelligence agencies in gathering information about these regimes: the underestimation of the support of the Cuban people for the Castro regime, of the Vietnamese people for Hanoi, and so on, are good examples. What the US is most afraid of, of course, is the transition from an authoritarian capitalist country to a popularly supported socialist country — the Cuban trauma from 1958-61; in other words, from a less stable, friendly capitalist, to a more stable, unfriendly socialist. If the socialist regime becomes one of repression, even terror, the US might be more optimistic about the outcome, particularly if the ruling elites develop a strong appetite for material goods and adequate habits of corruptibility. Such countries may be adequate trading partners in their never-ceasing search for Western technology. Soft socialism, supported by the population, is far more dangerous (Nicaragua in its first years).

Conclusion: very much of the key to the East-West conflict lies in the internal conditions of countries — in their development. And in this there is some basis for optimism: economic, social and human development pay, in the longer run at least, in staving off the hand of an aggressive superpower.

2. The Second World War legacies of nazism and fascism

This is not an effort at recapitulating the history of the Second World War, but it was the worst war in human history and it is also fundamental for understanding the current tangle of world conflicts. The point of departure is clear. On the one hand there was the world capitalist system, much of it still in its colonial phase, but with three countries conceiving of themselves as entitled to a position at the top of that system, and without colonies: Germany, Italy and Japan, the Axis powers. On the other hand there was the Union of Soviet Socialist Republics, the USSR, and attached to it its neighbour, Mongolia (since 1921). Seen from this angle the world of the 1930s had three conflicts: between the capitalist world system and the single socialist country, already expressed in the interventionist wars (1917-22: 14 countries participated in them); the emerging conflict within the capitalist world system between those on top and those wanting to get there; and the still largely unheard of conflict between colonial powers and the suppressed peoples in the colonies — clearly articulated only in the largest of all the colonies, the Indian subcontinent. Two vertical conflicts on the capitalist side, and then a horizontal conflict between capitalism and socialism, the outcome of which would be very clear if the entire capitalist side were united: the decline and fall of the Soviet Union.

However, this was not what happened. The three latecomers on the international scene, Germany, Italy and Japan did not conceive of the world only in terms of capitalism versus socialism. Anti-bolshevism was certainly a major aspect of their ideologies, expressing itself at home in irreconcilable struggle with local communists. But, in addition, they also had to find ideological expression for their key ambition, that of arriving at the top of the world capitalist system. Since they could not turn against capitalism as such, they had to conceive of the countries at the top of the system in another vein, by adding two other aspects to their ideological armoury: anti-semitism and the "anti-plutocratic" attitude — being against the rule of money as such. But in addition to this they were also highly authoritarian at home and racist abroad, conceiving of themselves as above the lesser peoples surrounding them. Any alliance with colonised peoples on a more lasting basis would therefore be out of the question.

One might say that given this total failure to make alliances in any direction with the three other groupings on the world scene, the result of the Second World War was already given: the Axis powers were going to lose. Had only anti-bolshevism been the ideology, perhaps adding to it anti-semitism, the rest of their world outlook would meet with no particular resistance in the leading circles of the leading world capitalist power. They then might even have been able to partly shoot, partly bargain themselves into positions more compatible with their aspirations.

In retrospect, with the advantage of some hindsight, how would one expect the Soviet Union to react? Of course they would try to make alliances with one or more of these three parties inside the world capitalist system, particularly as their Marxism would lead them to think in terms of capitalism versus socialism. Understandably, the first approach would be to try to obtain some guarantees through pacts, even alliances, with the have-powers on the capitalist side, against the emerging have-not-powers, the Axis. This was (as expected?) rejected by the have-powers, perhaps not so much because of the terrible reputation the Stalinist Soviet Union had obtained through the Moscow purges and other phenomena, as because of the deeply ingrained suspicion against a country rejecting the basic tenets of capitalism — including rejecting free trade and with it the basic pillar of capitalism as an economic faith: the ideology of comparative advantages.

Then came the relatively quick expansion of Nazi Germany (Saarland 1935, the Austrian *Anschluss* March 1938, the incorporation of Sudetenland September 1938, the annexation of Memel in March 1939); the expansion of Italy (Ethiopia 1935, annexation of Albania April 1939, then turning towards Greece); Italy's alliance with Germany in the Pact of Steel of 1939; and the expansion of Japan (starting with the annexation of Formosa in 1895 and Korea in 1911, not to mention the war against tsarist Russia 1904-5, then continuing with the "Manchurian Incident" of 1931, making it into a Japanese protectorate, Manchukuo in 1933, and then the invasion of Central China and the coast of China 1937-39). What could the Soviet Union possibly do? This may not be sufficient excuse, but nevertheless some kind of explanation for three major moves made by the Soviet Union in 1939-40: the Molotov-Ribbentrop Pact of non-aggression, the pressure on Finland to cede territory so as to make Leningrad more defensible, ultimately leading to a Soviet invasion (the Winter War 1939-40), and annexation of Finnish territory up to the present, and the division of Poland and annexation of the Baltic States and Bessarabia. In

1941 this was followed up by signing a non-aggression pact with Japan. An exercise in *Realpolitik,* indeed.

Hitler had to be rather much of an ideologist, and with a low sense of *Realpolitik,* when he nevertheless engaged in *Operation Barbarossa,* issuing the directive in December 1940, and invading the Soviet Union on 22 June 1941. If he had not done this, but turned exclusively against the top capitalist powers in the West, together with his Japanese and Italian allies defined by the Tripartite Pact of 1940, the world might certainly have looked different today. For one thing, the Soviet Union could have been waiting behind its buffer-states acquired in the way mentioned, waiting for more balanced capitalist powers to bleed each other to death. Since this process inevitably would weaken colonialism, as it later did, the Soviet Union could also, quietly or quickly or both, reach out for the third possible ally: the colonised peoples themselves. Later on they tried to do that, to some extent, sometimes more, sometimes less successfully, Soviet politics in the Third World being rather mixed in its achievements. In all probability the Soviet Union might have come out of this type of conflict formation highly victorious.

When history did not take this turn, it was hardly because Hitler was contemplating this possible outcome and found it unacceptable. Rather, from early on he had had his intention of satisfying German colonial aspirations not towards the South, in Africa as his predecessors had done, but towards the East, *Ostmark, Ostland.* One half of Poland and one half of Czechoslovakia incorporated into the German Reich were not enough. Of course he could not proceed further without beating the giant country to the East, releasing his enormous military power and his exterminist death machines, not only against Jews but also against Slavs. Of 11 million Jews, he managed to exterminate 6 million (55 per cent); of maybe 100 million Slavs he wanted to exterminate on Soviet soil, he managed 20 million (20 per cent). He left two peoples behind with the mostly deeply engraved NEVER AGAIN in recent human history, perhaps ever: the Jews and the Soviet peoples, leading to the consolidation of Israel as a state and to the fortification of the Soviet Union, with all that implies. A heavy legacy indeed, for Arabs and East Europeans, for all of us.

The Axis powers went ahead, and the almost incredible weakness of the neighbouring countries, meaning both governments and the population, showed up in the equally incredible success of those three countries, militarily speaking, till the tides started turning in the second half of 1942 (Midway, El Alamein, Stalingrad). By this time the European countries were divided in six groups, as follows (see *The Times Atlas of World History*):

1. *The Big Three of the Allies,* Soviet Union and the United Kingdom — and then the United States outside Europe. France and China managed to join this group, which was later to provide the permanent members of the UN Security Council, with the success or problem for China not solved until 1971. But during the war there were only *two* countries really fighting on European soil, the Soviet Union and the United

Kingdom, with only *one* of them, the Soviet Union, fighting a land war on its own soil.

2. *Countries used by the Allies:* These were the three islands on the periphery of Europe; Iceland, Malta and Cyprus — to which one might add Gibraltar, but then Gibraltar was neither then, nor today, a "country"

3. *The Big Three of the Axis:* Germany, with Austria and Sudetenland annexed; Italy with Albania annexed — and then Japan outside Europe.

4. *Countries used by the Axis, as satellites:* Finland, Czechoslovakia, Hungary, Romania, Bulgaria and Croatia (with some other parts of Yugoslavia). It should be noted that parts of the Dalmatian coast were annexed by Italy, and that Bohemia-Moravia was incorporated into the *Reich.*

4. *Countries occupied by the Axis:* Norway, Denmark, Netherlands, Belgium, Luxemburg, France (the latter first divided into occupied and unoccupied (Vichy) France; later occupied in its entirety), Poland (divided, the German part incorporated), Yugoslavia (except for the part mentioned above), Greece (first occupied by Italy, later on by Germany).

6. *"Neutral" countries:* Sweden, Switzerland, Ireland, Portugal, Spain, Turkey. The Axis prevailed over the Allies in Europe in this period, so these countries were "neutral towards" the Axis rather than towards the Allies.

This is a very crude description, and on purpose we should not go into more detail. Suffice it only to point out that what today are known as Czechoslovakia, Poland and Yugoslavia, were all three divided by the nazi onslaught. It might also be pointed out that Norway and the Netherlands, satisfying nazi Germany's "Aryan" standards, were to be more integrated into the German economy, but that otherwise the occupied countries were probably essentially to be pacified, possibly even neutralised but tilting to the Axis; that the satellites were puppet states; and then there was the vast Eastern territory to the East of the new German borders, really earmarked for German colonisation, whose native population would become illiterate "Helots". Parts of this were occupied during the war for some time, but it will be thought of here as a permanent battlefield; treated in a way even worse than all the other countries in Europe. Operation Barbarossa was no mistake, it was basic to the entire design.

Where else in this vast territory with all together 29 countries (today there are 30 countries in Europe after Germany was divided into two) was there real resistance going on, against the Axis powers? Of course there was some type of resistance everywhere, but certainly more in some places than in others. If one should point at one common denominator of the resistance movements inside the Axis dominated countries, in all three categories, then it would be very simple: *communism*. In the Axis countries and the Axis satellites it is probably fair to say that communists were dominant in the resistance; in the countries occupied by the Axis they played major roles, particularly in Czechoslovakia (where they were defeated by the Germans), Yugoslavia (where Tito's partisans were supported by the British) and in Greece (where the communist EAM rose against the British); and then in France and Poland — but in these countries non-communist resistance was also strong. In addition, France somehow managed to give the impression of being a belligerent power continuing the battle from the outside, against Germans, and not only against the quislings.

Why do I try to recapitulate all this — simply because it has to be taken into account in understanding what happened afterwards. The Big Three were victorious and on 11 February 1945, Stalin, Roosevelt and Churchill were able to sign the Yalta agreements. The war having been so devastating, there was a clear demand not only for reparations, but also for revenge — perhaps particularly from the country most devastated by the war, the Soviet Union. Of course it mattered where the troops of the Big Three were standing when capitulation came on 7-8 May 1945, and the only major adjustments after that date were that the Western Allies were given access both to Berlin and to Vienna, the conquest of which had been none of their achievement but that of the Red Army. But this was not merely a question of where the armies stood geographically, but also a question of sharing the victory.

And here comes the major asymmetry: the Soviet Army was *occupying* Axis territory, with the addition of Poland and Yugoslavia; the Western Allies had a different role in addition to helping beat nazi Germany and beating fascist Italy: that of *liberating* countries occupied by the Axis. The Italians were as clever as the French: they managed from 1943 somehow to transform themselves from an Axis country to a country occupied by nazi Germany, thus being able to greet with a welcome the liberators when they slowly made their way up from Sicily, through Southern Italy to the North. The French managed to transform themselves from occupied to self-liberators. So, with only the key exception of Germany, wherever the Western Allies came they could be greeted with a welcome; only relatively minor groups had something major to fear.

Not so with the Soviet Union. The Red Army was standing on the soil of hostile regimes, to a large extent also hostile populations. They had shared the anti-Bolshevism of their nazi masters; some of them profoundly anti-Russian and anti-Soviet out of bitter experience. Whereas the Allies in the West hinged on to the majority of the populations and hence had no difficulty in praising ideas of parliamentary democracy, the Ally in the East could only hinge on to minorities that were both communist and in the resistance (or at least not collaborators), and would have to embrace other notions of political development if they were to remain influential in those areas. And they certainly wanted to: adding to the two reasons pointed out above (the ideological value of spreading communism; the geo-political interest of buffer states) came a third one: that of reparation and revenge over Axis countries and their satellites.

Some reflections have been made above about resistance movements in the occupied countries. The reason for pointing to this factor is obvious: *such resistance could legitimise a more independent stance later on,* independence of the liberators that is. From this circumstance alone one would predict that independent policies might be pursued by France and Greece in the West (as these were liberated by the Western Allies) and

Poland, Czechoslovakia and Yugoslavia in the East (liberated by the Eastern Ally); and Albania. And so it turned out later, even much later. The full implication of this in the case of Greece may not yet be known.

For what happened after the war soon became clear. *Hitler's "New Order" Europe was to a large extent reproduced in Cold War Europe.* The split among The Big Three defined the rest of the story. Germany was divided, so was Berlin — both still are. This pattern was reproduced in Austria, but the country got out of this unenviable situation through an act of neutralisation. The United States and United Kingdom, through their "special relationship", became the nucleus of a Western alliance. France with that ambiguous status somewhere between liberator and liberated, and all the other liberated countries in the West, were drafted in 1949 as members of the North Atlantic Treaty Organisation. Given that Canada also had a special relationship with the United States, this explains the whole NATO alliance membership when we add that Iceland continued as a base within NATO and that Portugal and Turkey, for different reasons, were recruited into the Alliance from among the "neutral" countries.

In Eastern Europe the Soviet Union created the Warsaw Treaty Organisation in 1955, after Western Germany had become a member of NATO, and put into the Alliance the *Axis satellites* that had been occupied by the Red Army — with the exception of Finland (possibly for the reasons mentioned in the preceding section) and the obvious exception of Croatia, that in the meantime had become part of Yugoslavia again (meaning Tito's Yugoslavia) — and the countries that were under *Axis occupation,* Poland and Albania. The latter two, with Czechoslovakia, saw and see themselves as having participated in their own liberation, Albania leaving the Warsaw Treaty Organisation already in 1961; the other two being "restless", to put it mildly. But in addition the Soviet Union was also to have problems with Hungary and Romania, two non-Slav countries that had been in the Axis system but did not feel sufficient reasons why they should be subservient also to the Russians. Only two relatively faithful parties remained: Bulgaria, always grateful for Russian aid in the liberation from the Turks, and East Germany/DDR, a country turned against itself, creating out of the communist fight against nazism/fascism between the wars the spiritual basis for the new state, with varying degrees of success.

In short: *Europe of today is to a large extent Hitler's creation.* And this goes very far, even deep into the structure of the Alliances that constitute the conflicting parties in the Cold War conflict formation.

At the very centre are the two Germanies, beaten into submission, rejecting nazism, but at the same time reproducing major parts of it. In the DDR the single party state, dictatorial rule, no free trade unions; in the BRD an even worse aspect of nazism: *exterminism* as a possible approach in international politics (through the readiness to consent to the use of nuclear arms), collective self-immolation through readiness to sacrifice all in case everything else goes wrong ("lieber tot als rot" being the maxim that can be derived from official West German policy). Then there are all the liberated countries in the West and all the occupied countries in the East — of course the latter had much less of a say relative to their occupant than the former to their liberator. And in the middle there are the neutrals.

How does this look on the other side of the world, around the third Axis power, Japan? Actually, surprisingly similar. After China, Japan continued the conquest, south towards Hong Kong and then Indo-China; from there onwards into what today are the five ASEAN countries: Thailand, Malaysia, Singapore, Indonesia and the Philippines. Even Burma was conquered, and great parts of Oceania. A very weak region indeed.

But then comes the big difference. With the exception of Thailand all of these countries were colonies, which means that Japan could present herself in a double role, not only as a conqueror but also as liberator, under an "Asia for the Asians" formula, letting it be understood that some Asians are more equal than others in a highly paternalistic setting known as the "New Order" for East Asia, the Great East-Asian Co-prosperity Hemisphere. Already, in Cairo in 1943, the Allies announced as their goal Japan's unconditional surrender, and they had read their history: Japan had to give up all the territory she had acquired after her 1895 conquest of Taiwan. But colonialism was dead in that part of the world, as the colonial powers soon had to realise when they tried to come back again to fill the gap after Japan was defeated.

Where had the resistance against Japan been? Of course in China, Korea and Vietnam — and in all three cases mainly from communist groups, symbolised by three famous names: Mao Zedong, Kim Il Sung and Ho Chi Minh. There was less resistance from non-communist groupings, many of them incorporated in the Japanese enterprise. The same applies to Hong Kong and to the ASEAN countries, whereas Burma seems to be an exception with considerable independent resistance, and not necessarily of the communist kind.

Again this can be used in understanding better the Cold War conflict formation. Japan became a necessity for the United States. There was no way in which she could undergo the transformation from conquered country to liberated country as there was practically speaking no opposition to the Japanese military regime inside the country. Nor were the Japanese particularly apologetic about their past. They simply had to be accepted as they were, and with them much of the system built by the Japanese and reincorporated into the world capitalist system in neo-colonised form, both neo-colonization and reincorporation to a large extent of Japanese making. That this later on became so economically efficient that it came to be a most dangerous challenge to Western economic supremacy in general, and the United States in particular, is another matter. Suffice it only to say that the countries that had resisted Japan most were not incorporated: communist China, communist Korea, communist Indo-china, and neutral Burma. The regimes might undergo changes in their policies towards world capitalism, but they certainly cannot be said to be fully incorporated.

Once more the same thing: we live in a world marked by the conflict between the two systems and the interests of the two superpowers, but largely structured in its detail by the legacy of Second World War nazism and fascism, both in Europe East and West and in East Asia. At the same time we live in a world where the borders of brutality have been pushed so far that almost anything goes, with the defence that "Hitler was even

worse". Unspeakable brutalisation to the point of extermination/
exterminism, and world geo-politics defined by the Yalta agreements: this
is the legacy. Hitler, Mussolini and Tojo did not achieve their goals. But
they certainly managed to leave an imprint on the way the major world
conflict formation took shape. Is it not about time to move on and close that
chapter?

3. Conflict dynamics between and within the alliances

In the two preceding sections the East-West conflict has been traced back
to two rather fundamental issues, one of values and one of interests, firmly
anchored in the two systems, and to something more situational: the
Second World War and its aftermath. In the present section the step will be
taken from structure of the conflict to the conflict process, from conflict
genesis to conflict dynamics — laying the basis for the final section about
conflict resolution.

Conflict dynamics: that is the history of the whole period after the
Second World War up till today, usually referred to as the "cold war" in
the Northern part of the world, and as a long, seemingly endless succession
of rather hot wars (often referred to as "local wars" by people from the
North) in the Southern part of the world. It is certainly not the intention in
this section to try to repeat what has been done in many excellent surveys
of this topic. Rather, the intention is to try a more analytical approach to
East-West conflict dynamics.

In order to do that let us take as a point of departure that no resolution
was found to the two issues already discussed in the early post-war years,
meaning 1945 to 1949. And not only that: both parties behaved more or less
as the other party had expected according to their ideological models of the
world. Thus, both of them expected the other party to be expansionist, to
embody expansionist capitalism and expansionist communism respectively.
One might add: one species of the Occidental genus can easily recognise the
other. Or, to be more specific: East expected capitalism, particularly when
in crisis, to develop fascist characteristics and hence to become totalitarian
and also belligerent; West expected communism, and not only in crisis, to
develop totalitarian characteristics, to be dictatorial and repressive at
home and expansionist abroad, "to divert attention away from domestic
problems."

In addition to these *underlying paradigms*, both parties had experienced
in recent history extremely *traumatic events*, including surprises. For the
Soviet Union these events can be summarised under two headings:
"Interventionist Wars 1917-21" and "Operation Barbarossa 22/6/1941"
(Hitler's surprise attack on the Soviet Union) — as a sequel to Napoleon in
1812; the Japanese 1904-5 and the Kaiser 1914-17. Both of them could be
interpreted, with considerable justification, within the paradigm of
understanding already developed. And the United States and the West in
general also had had traumatic experiences, also to be summarised under
two headings: "the failure of appeasement policies — Munich 1938 —
combined with nazi Germany's salami tactics in Europe" and "Pearl
Harbour 7/12/1941: the Japanese surprise attack on the US". Neither nazi

Germany nor militarist Japan were communist powers, hence a linkage had to be established in order to fit these traumatic experiences into the underlying paradigm for the understanding of communism. The linkage was established through the idea of "totalitarian regimes": it could be argued that both nazi Germany, militarist Japan and the communist Soviet Union were totalitarian, hence species of the same kind, consequently experiences were transferrable, they were relevant. But it should be noted that this thinking is considerably less tenable than the linkage established between paradigms and traumatic experiences in the Soviet Union. The West is cheating intellectually more than the East. However, both the US and the Soviet Union are rather different from the nazi Germany each side uses as a model to understand the other.

Thus they entered the Second World War aftermath: the West looking with utmost scepticism at the dictatorship in the East, the East looking with utmost scepticism at the capitalist powers in the West. The common enemy had been defeated, the bonds of alliances were not forgotten, but they tended to fade into the background. All that was needed were the *confirming events* that would establish the validity, once and for all, of the way they conceived of each other.

And, of course, there were confirming events. The Yalta agreements had led to a certain division in Europe and other places, to a legitimation of spheres of interest. One may say that the spheres were located in Europe, the Middle East and the Far East, and this is where the confirming events best known in the West took place.

In Eastern Europe, Czechoslovakia and Berlin did not fit into the Soviet model of how societies should be constructed: Czechoslovakia was a socially oriented democracy, industrialised, and could in no way be seen in its totality as an Axis country; the three Western sectors of Berlin were part of the Western social construction. So the two basic confirming events took place relative to the "dagger against the soft underbelly" (the soft underbelly being the Ukraine) and the "bone in the throat": the communist *coup d'état* in February 1948 in Czechoslovakia and the Berlin blockade 1948/49. As a result, Czechoslovakia was "lost", Berlin was not — but paradigm confirmation had taken place.

This was then repeated outside Europe in the case of Iran in 1946: the Soviet Union did not withdraw from Azerbaidzhan except after being threatened, possibly with atomic weapons. And then, on top of this, came the third confirming event in the Far East: the North Korean attack on South Korea in June 1950, North Koreans later being joined by Chinese "volunteers" and South Koreans by "United Nations Forces" — from the United States, United Kingdom, France, Benelux, Greece, Turkey, Canada, Australia, New Zealand, Colombia, Philippines, Thailand, Ethiopia and South Africa.

Let us then look at this from the other side. Which were the confirming events seen from the East? In Europe it is probably fair to say that Greece was the major example: British troops had been used already in 1944/45 to help the government put down revolutionary forces, this continued from 1946 to 1949, also with US troops. Maybe this corresponded to Czechoslovakia for the West. Maybe world history would have been simpler had these two countries exchanged positions.

But then comes what the West has difficulties understanding. The East also observed another phenomenon: that all over the world the West did not conceive of colonialism as having come to an end, but tried to reassert their colonial dominance: French troops in Algeria (1945) and in Indo-China (1946-54); Dutch troops, later on assisted by British troops, in Indonesia (1945-49); US troops in the Philippines (1946-54); French troops in Madagascar (1947-48), British troops in Malaya (1948-59). All of these were very clear signals that Western capitalism still had its colonialist character, and that the West used force to suppress struggles for freedom.

Then came the Korean War, 1950-53. I do not think to the East that this war is really seen as initiated by the West, using South Korea as a pawn. But it is certainly seen as a war that was used as a pretext by the West to intervene. More particularly, it seemed so to China — a country that had already lived through two revolutions, one "bourgeois" (1910-11) and one communist (1949) — which was deeply convinced that interventions would take place. The Western intervention in South Korea of course triggered off a strong reaction to prevent any interventions into China proper. At that time the Soviet Union and the People's Republic of China were allies, and the Soviet Union probably interpreted the events in the light of her own traumatic history as an invaded country. In other words, the Korean War became joint property, serving some of the same geo-epistemological and political functions for both East and West.

As a net result of all this issues Nos.1 (values) and 2 (interests) became even more crystallised. Moreover, it became clear that they were not going to wither away immediately, and they called for some kind of *military build-up*. Of course, that takes many forms:

military preparation: the whole cycle from military doctrine via software and hardware production to military deployment and back again to doctrine;

alliance formation: organisations of states based on the principle that "attack on one is attack on all" — possibly also "attack by one is attack by all";

militarisation: giving priority to the goals and processes of the military sector over the civilian sector, particularly over the bureaucratic-corporate-intelligentsia complex, BCI, leading to the formation of strong MBCI-complexes.

Each of these three forms of military build-up leads to conflict issues, as indicated in figure 2.1.

In this figure the three military issues are seen as derivatives from the basic conflict issues, even if this is not, strictly speaking, correct — the real situation is never that linear. Then, there is an ordering of the issues in terms of three generations of conflict; the first generation being the basic conflict issues, the second generation over military preparation, and the third generation over alliance formation and militarisation. And this is where a very basic distinction enters the picture: between *inter-party* conflict issues and *intra-party* conflict issues, conflicts *between* East and West and conflicts *within* East and West. The first two generations are

Figure 2.1   East-West conflict dynamics, I — the conflict issues

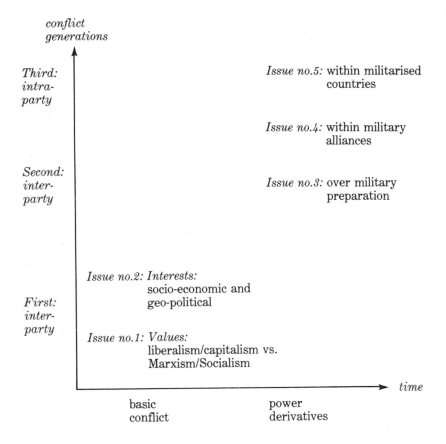

*conflict
generations*

*Third:
intra-
party*

*Second:
inter-
party*

*First:
inter-
party*

Issue no.5: within militarised
countries

Issue no.4: within military
alliances

Issue no.3: over military
preparation

Issue no.2: Interests:
socio-economic and
geo-political

Issue no.1: Values:
liberalism/capitalism vs.
Marxism/Socialism

time

basic   power
conflict   derivatives

then seen as inter-conflicts and the third generation as intra-conflicts; within the alliances, within militarised countries.

But this in no way means that there is a simple theory to the effect that over time the East-West conflict, itself a bundle consisting of these five components, has moved from inter-party conflicts to intra-party conflicts. On the contrary, these two aspects of the total conflict formation are not seen as mutually exclusive. At any given time the total "situation" may be low or high on both. Over time one may get a complex trajectory. One example is the image given in the figure below where the period after the Second World War is divided into four phases, the first three, it so happens, approximately lasting 10 years:

Figure 2.2   East-West conflict dynamics, II — the phases

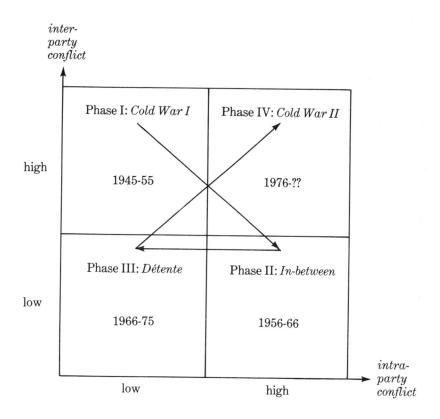

The word *image* should be stressed: this is meant as a guide only, not to be taken too seriously. The real world is always more complex, but as a rule of thumb it is put forward for a deeper understanding of East-West conflict dynamics. These dynamics we now have to examine in some more detail.

The general thesis about the first phase would be that it was used for conflict articulation and military build-up, getting the machineries into position on both sides, ready for action, for use (which does not, incidentally, necessarily mean war — "use" also includes the threat of war). Using the major incidents in that period, symbolised by the words "Berlin" and "Korea", the following diagram reflects the organisation that grew out of the first phase (see figure 2.3).

These are seen as the basic features of the conflict organisations — no effort has been made to trace all the bilateral ties to Third World countries.

Figure 2.3   East-West conflict organisation, first phase — the pyramids

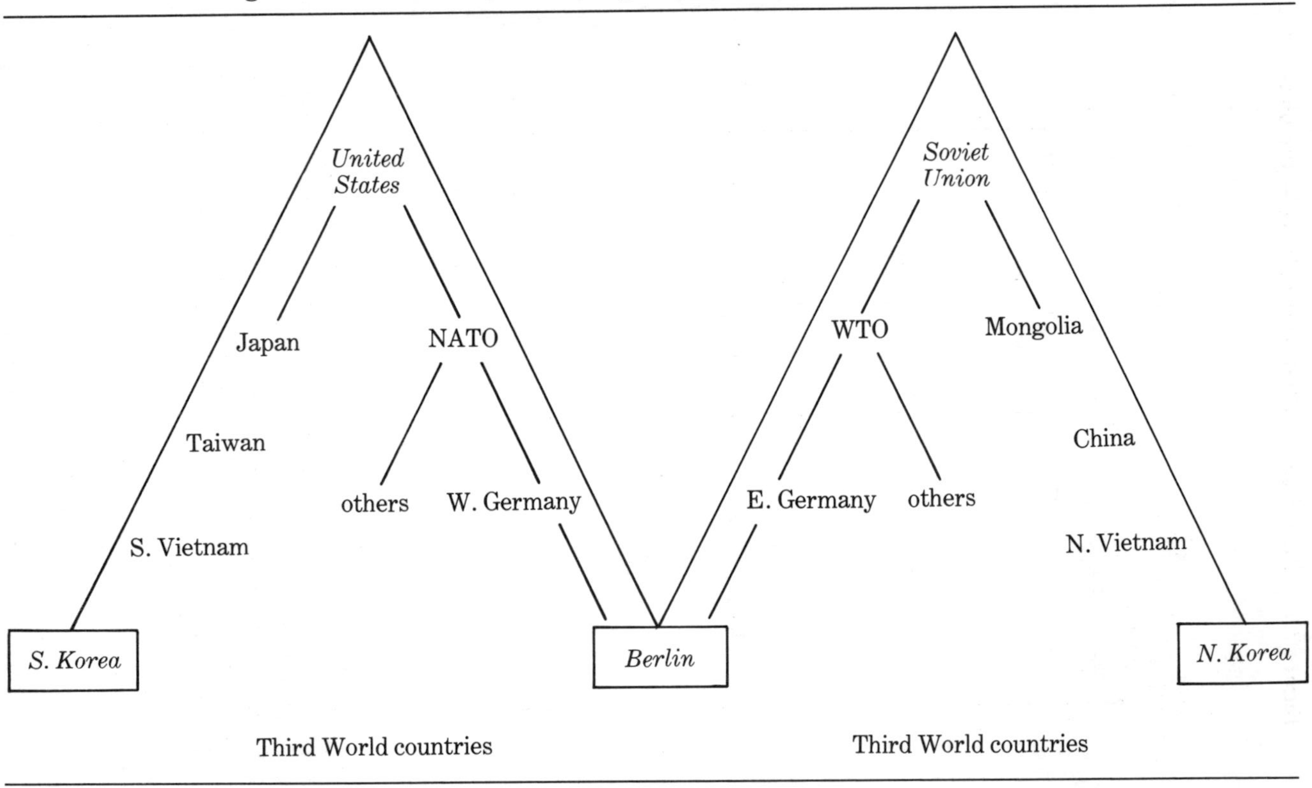

United States — NATO — W. Germany — Berlin
United States — Japan — Taiwan — S. Vietnam — S. Korea
NATO — others
Soviet Union — WTO — E. Germany — Berlin
Soviet Union — Mongolia — China — N. Vietnam — N. Korea
WTO — others

Third World countries

Third World countries

Two pyramids took shape. On the top of the pyramids were the major victorious powers from the Second World War, the United States and the Soviet Union, later to be designated as superpowers. Under them came, in Europe, the two alliances, NATO from 1949 and WTO from 1955 — both of them preceded by other organisational forms. The two Germanies received their legitimation as *bona fide* states, members of the alliances, split (but also in a curious form united) by Berlin.

But the United States and the Soviet Union were not only concerned with North America/Europe but also with East Asia. In more "civilisational" terms, not only the Occident but also the Orient became stages for the East-West conflict to unfold itself. The Soviet Union was already an East Asian power, with power in Mongolia; the United States became an East Asian power not only through the conquest of the Philippines but also through the Pacific War and the conquest of Japan. The China, Vietnam and Korean issues crystallised this further as indicated in the figure: the two superpowers had already for a long time taken sides in the civil war/revolution in China, they had taken sides in the liberation/revolution in Indo-China (from French colonial rule) and they had divided Korea between themselves along the 38th parallel. But whereas the Chinese and Indo-Chinese wars were long-lasting processes, the Korean War suddenly exploded, like the Berlin blockade, and for that reason became a major incident crystallising the conflict further. Actually, the figure should be folded so that North and South Korea meet, thereby illustrating better the global nature of the East-West conflict and making the presentation less euro-centric, in this case even "berlino-centric".

The figure, however, could also be read in another way, reflecting the Chinese way of looking at the world. On top is the "First World": the superpowers. Then comes the "Second World", the industrialised countries, meaning the NATO and WTO countries and Japan. And then comes the "Third World", the Third World with some countries drawn into the East-West conflict organisation in a very direct manner, "aligned"; and others being more closely attached to it and still others being more or less outside, "non-aligned". This is not only the North-South issue projected on the East-West issue, it is also the strong-weak, centre-periphery axis in a very broad sense. Chinese theory puts the superpowers on top as hegemonic powers — but, as usual, fails to place China herself.

However, ones does not build pyramids of this kind, gigantic conflict organisations, without costs and cracks. In the following list of major post-Second World War events in table 2.4 the inner dynamics of the two pyramids becomes clearer, as expressions of issues nos.4 (conflict within alliances) and 5 (conflicts within countries).

In no way is this a complete list, but the most important events and processes are probably included. It should be noted that it does not include such East-West confrontations as the Berlin 1948/49 crisis, the Korean War or the 1962 Cuba nuclear crisis; the focus is on intra-party conflicts. Of course, in those conflicts there is always an admixture of inter-party conflict, particularly evident in the Indo-China wars. The list, in additiion, does not include efforts to expand the pyramids, for instance through Soviet indirect intervention in Angola (Cuban forces), in Ethiopia (also

Table 2.4 East-West conflict dynamics, III — major intra-party events and processes

EVENTS

	WEST		EAST
1948	Yugoslavia not joining	1948	Yugoslavia withdrawal
1951-53	Iran Intervention	1953	East Berlin intervention
1954	Guatemala intervention	1956	Hungary invasion
1956	Suez invasion	1960	Albania withdrawal
1958	Lebanon invasion	1958-61	China withdrawal (Ussuri incident 1964)
1958-61	Cuban revolution (Bay of Pigs invasion 1961)	1961	Berlin Wall
1965-66	France less integrated in NATO	1965-66	Romania less integrated in WTO
1965	Dominican Republic invasion	1968	Czechoslovakia invasion
1964-75	Indo-China wars	1972	Egypt withdrawal
1970-73	Chile intervention	1979	Afghanistan "titoism", "khomeiniism"
1979	Iran revolution	1979-??	Afghanistan, invasion and war
1979	Nicaragua revolution	1980-??	Poland military rule intervention, invasion?
1980-??	Central America military rule intervention, invasion?		
1983	Lebanon invasion		
1983	Grenada invasion		

PROCESSES

	WEST		EAST
1965-75	Third World imperialism unmasked	1965-75	Gulag repression unmasked
1968-70	Student, youth movement	1968-70	Student, youth movement
1980-??	Green party, system challenge, women's movement	1980-??	Solidarnośc, system challenge
1981-??	Peace Movement, system challenge	1981	Peace Movement, system challenge
1980s	SYSTEM CRISIS (seen as economic)	1980s	SYSTEM CRISIS (seen as political)

Cuban forces) and in Kampuchea (Vietnam forces). It only focuses on the cracks in the systems: countries or peoples trying to get out; superpowers trying to repress.

Let us now look at the table with two perspectives in mind: *homology* and *synchrony* — in other words that these two systems, these two pyramids, are so similar in their construction that they should also be relatively similar in their cracks (homology), even to the point that the cracks should take place in a relatively time parallel fashion (synchrony). Of course the table is prepared in such a way as to make these two phenomena stand out, hopefully not more than historical reality would justify.

Thus, at the very beginning there is a focus on something easily forgotten: in 1948 Yugoslavia not only withrew from Cominform and became independent from the Soviet Union. Just as importantly, Yugoslavia did not join the Western system and still has not, except for a relatively high level of economic integration. Interestingly enough, Yugoslavia wrote itself indelibly into history in two ways in that very same year, one event and one non-event, thereby laying the basis for the non-alignment movement, a historical achievement. It was later on joined by Nasser's Egypt and Nehru's India in the Belgrade Conference of 1961, followed up in Cairo in 1964, Lusaka in 1970, Georgetown in 1972, Colombo in 1976, Havana in 1979, New Delhi in 1983 — one conference in Europe and two in each of the three continents of the Third World.

Thus, looking at the list in Table 2.4, it is clear that phase I was characterised by a high level of intra-party cohesion. There was Iran and East Berlin and Guatemala, but they were nevertheless relatively minor events. But then, in 1956, phase II is ushered in with the Suez and Hungary invasions. In the case of Suez it was Israeli, British and French troops against Egyptian troops; the US not only abstained but actually intervened to stop the war. Nevertheless it was a clear case of problems within a party rather than between parties. And the same was certainly the case for the invasion of Hungary by Soviet troops.

However, there was more to come. There were cracks in the Middle East in the sense that the Western forward position, Israel, could be threatened through developments in Lebanon (and Jordan) — hence the despatch of US and UK troops. On the Eastern side, Albania withdrew from the WTO due to a dispute over the Flora base. Much more importantly, however, the United States "lost" Cuba through the Cuban revolution, later trying to recover it through the Bay of Pigs invasion; the Soviet Union "lost" China through Chinese withdrawal (expulsion of experts, etc.), still later on expressing itself in the Far East in the Ussuri incidents. These were rather dramatic events for the two superpowers. To lose China was to lose quite a lot, the country with the biggest population in the world and the third largest land area. To lose Cuba did not count much in terms of population and land area, but it was very close to the United States and the first country successfully rejecting capitalism in the Western hemisphere.

Then there was the Berlin Wall crisis — unparalleled on the other side — against the people voting with their feet. But would the alternatives — the GDR collapsing leading to a world war — have been better than the wall?

But there was more to come: France became less integrated in NATO by

withdrawing from the military integration and expelling the NATO
headquarters from France (also US bases), and a corresponding
development took place in Romania. According to well placed sources, the
Romanian development had its origin in the invasion of Hungary in 1956
when the secretary general of the Romanian party at that time, Gheorghe
Dej, was invited to Budapest to celebrate the installation of Janosz Kadar.
He found empty streets instead of a triumphant working class, and was
deeply shocked. Determined that this should not happen in Romania he
argued for the withdrawal of Soviet troops, against WTO manoeuvres on
Romanian soil, and against Romanian participation in WTO manoeuvres.
This was then confirmed by his successor Nicolae Ceauşescu. Both France
and Romania have taken quite independent stands in foreign policy. Both
of them, however, have also made it very clear that they do not challenge
the system advocated by the superpowers: France remained capitalist,
some nationalisations notwithstanding; Romania remained socialist, some
commercialisation, particularly in connection with agriculture,
notwithstanding.

To this phase also belongs the invasion of the Dominican Republic and the
invasion of Czechoslovakia, although the latter chronologically speaking
took place in the next phase. But then it may also be argued that the East
has a general tendency to be behind, something also indicated by the
circumstance that the treaty formation came six years later. Like in the
case of the West, it was preceded by more bilateral ties, and these bilateral
ties still may be said to dominate not only the WTO but also NATO as an
organisation. Again, there are basic problems within — with the invocation
of the Monroe doctrine and formulation of the Brezhnev doctrine.

The third phase, the *détente,* was charcterised both by low level inter-
party conflict and low-level intra-party conflict. I think it can be argued
that one single person was, if not a sufficient condition, at least a necessary
condition for this phase: Charles de Gaulle. What he did was to find a
formula whereby his subjective view of French national interests (shared
by most French, I presume) and more objective views of what promotes
peace in Europe, could be reconciled. His formula did not only include a
high level of autonomy relative to the United States, of course based on
active participation by the French in liberating themselves and fighting
nazism in the Second World War, or at least based on the myth to this
effect, more effectively propagated by de Gaulle himself than by anybody
else. His approach also included the idea of promoting security through co-
operation rather than, or in addition to, deterrence, a view highly
compatible with French interests, as he must have known that the US
would be lagging behind in adapting that kind of philosophy. All of this,
then, was to be capped with an independent French nuclear force, the
famous *force de frappe.*

The formula stuck, 10 years of détente were ushered in, lasting till what
was very properly referred to as the *Final Act of Helsinki,* 1975. No doubt
the inter-party tension was low in this period, even to the point that the
East-West conflict seemed to have disappeared. The credibility of either
party going to war in Europe over any bone of contention in that area was
low, and the final act of Helsinki cemented this feeling, giving to the East a

confirmation of the geo-political *status quo*. To the West came the possibility of treating the Soviet Union and Eastern Europe as an external sector of Western economies — providing raw materials in general and energy in particular, as well as various products at a low level of processing. Capital goods could be exported there and investments in "joint ventures" could also be made. (This asymmetry was later to show up in the "debt crisis"). In other words, the first and second "baskets" of the Helsinki negotiations were perfect expressions of the geo-political and geo-economic interests of the two systems, as explored in 2.1 above. But then there was the problematic third "basket" focusing on human rights, on the free flow of persons and ideas. It will be argued in the next section that it was correct of the West to press for this, but it will also be argued that the West not only would have to be prepared to accept a counter-pressure for human rights that are more social and economic in their substance, but to see this as an equally legitimate pressure, also in the interest of peace.

Before we now proceed to the fourth phase let us try to ask an important question: if the East-West conflict somehow disappeared in this period, being less on people's minds both as inter-party and intra-party conflict in Europe, then *what happened in this third period?* Actually, these were 10 extremely eventful years in world history, but that is seen more clearly by looking further down in table 2.4, under processes. *There were the Indo-China wars*, outside Europe, but very much on everybody's mind. They served to shape the whole generation, say those between 15 and 35 years of age in that period; they will never forget it. *Western Third World imperialism was unmasked*, and for that reason what happened in Latin America and other places was much better understood. This had its clear parallel in the East: *Gulag repression was also unmasked;* like Third World imperialism it was not exactly a new phenomenon but dating far back, to before the Second World War. But the attitude to it was now shared by almost everybody, including in the Soviet Union itself. The Western attitude to imperialism in the Third World has not yet evolved that far, as will be argued later. In other words, the two systems received major blows, they became more illegitimate than ever before. World public opinion started requesting of them that they should divest themselves of such phenomena, and an enormous literature became available. Two names stand out in this process of deligitimation of the two systems: Daniel Ellsberg on the Western side. Alexandr Solzhenitsyn on the Eastern Side; neither of them particularly loved by their respective establishments, both of them today living in the US.

Another important process took place in this period: the *youth and student revolt*. It started in South America in the early 1960s, spread to California in 1964, then to China as the phenomenon initiating the Cultural Revolution 1966-69, and then all over Europe from 1968 onwards, with the exception of the Sovet Union where it certainly did not get off the ground. It was an expression of basic discontent with systems. This is not the place to try to analyse it, suffice it only to say that in the East-West system the challenge took the form of rejecting the older generation in power by adopting a Marxist stand in the West and a liberal stance in the East — rather obvious strategies for student generations. The successes were small relative to the *feminist revolt,* a historical and probably irreversible non-violent revolution — perhaps less necessary in the East.

The establishments in both camps must have been longing for the good old days of Cold War I, and for the inbetween phase II. Certainly this has been one factor in the complex web of relationships leading to Cold War II, the present phase, here seen as starting around 1976. It is probably still too early to arrive at any good judgement about how this present and very dangerous phase actually came into being. It has now become known that the plans for a new, qualitatively different generation of nuclear missiles, known under the names of Cruise (Tomahawk) and Pershing II, actually started in 1976. It is also well-known that the SALT II treaty was not ratified by the US Senate. The United States as a whole had suffered not only the humiliation of losing so totally the Indo-China wars. The country had also gone through the Watergate process. By people outside the system this was hardly seen as a confirmation of democracy, but as a way of diverting attention away from the genocidal and ecocidal war in Indo-China, towards some relatively trifling incidents in a country filled with such phenomena, yielding a pretext for sacrificing a despised president. However this may be, I think the verdict of history will be that the United States carries considerably more responsibility for Cold War II than the Soviet Union. After all, those major changes in US strategy introduced by the Carter administration (presidential directives 59 and 58 with more emphasis on counter-force weapons for fighting nuclear wars — against precise military targets and the administration on the other side — than on counter-value weapons for deterrence) and the schemes for prepositioning in Denmark and Norway and rapid deployment forces in other places, not to mention the development leading up to the so-called double-track decision of NATO on 12 December 1979, were unmistakeable. Of course, there was the Soviet invasion of Afghanistan on 27 December 1979, but there are reasons to see this as an intra-party more than an inter-party action, and as related to the general Soviet tendency to see neighbouring states in terms of their national security interests. Moreover, it came later than most of the events and processes in the West.

Anyhow, we are now in the thick of this phase. The tension of Cold War II, the nervousness, the *Angst,* is as high as during Cold War I, but in addition there is tension within the systems. The United States "loses" Iran and Nicaragua, and tries to recover Iran through the abortive effort to rescue the US embassy personnel detained in Tehran — an action so inappropriate to the avowed goal that it probably should be seen in another perspective. The United States "loses" Nicaragua through a revolution and tries to recover the country by all kinds of efforts to destabilise the Sandinista regime. And then the same phenomenon in three other Central American countries with military rule and all kinds of superpower inventions, including "advisers" but so far stopping short of invasion (autumn 1983). How long will that last?

The events on the Eastern side are remarkably parallel. What actually happened in Afghanistan in 1979 is not yet quite clear: it probably had something to do with "Titoism", and something to with "Khomeiniism". But, regardless of the interpretation, the next outcome was an invasion, and what seems to have become a very long-lasting war. I have not juxtaposed it to the Vietnam war, as is so often done in the press, for the simple reason that it is highly unlikely that it will ever again attain the genocidal and ecocidal magnitude of the Indo-China wars. But it is the third of the Soviet invasions in neighbouring countries and possibly not the last (autumn 1983).

Poland in a certain sense corresponds to Central America. Something close to a revolution took place, there was military rule and Soviet interference, certainly also including "advisers". Both for Central America and for Poland the possibility of superpower invasion has been indicated. I have always felt that a Soviet invasion was unlikely provided the political processes following the Gdansk launching of the Solidarność movement in August 1980 did not lead in the direction of withdrawal from the WTO, nor challenge the basic wish of the communist party to have a "leading role", at least formerly. The second of these traffic rules was not adhered to, hence the threat of invasion became more real. But military rule from December 1981 was interposed as an alternative to what at that time seemed to be the only two possibilities: civil war or invasion. If one accepts that these were the only alternatives, a short military rule was probably the least evil.

Here there is a difference relative to Central America where there is civil war against the military rule — the only "alternative" would be even more repressive military rule. These possibilities being exhausted, invasion would become more likely as the revolutionary movement progresses. But the danger of invasion should not be completely disregarded in the Polish case either.

At the same time certain fundamental processes are evolving further. Solidarność as a movement was and is a fundamental challenge to the system in the East. So is the Green movement, and more explicitly its political arm, the Green parties, to the system in the West. At the same time, and closely related to this, there is the strong peace movement in the West capable of getting between two and three million people participating in street demonstrations already by the autumn of 1981. This movement is then to some extent paralleled in the East, but perhaps more directed against issue No.5, militarisation of society, than against issues Nos.3 and 4, not to mention Nos.1 and 2 (Fig 2.1). But it could also be argued that these basic issues are exactly what the Green movement in the West, and the Solidarność in the East, are about.

And then there is the basic phenomenon underlying so much of this and putting its general imprint on phase IV dynamics: the socio-economic crisis in the West and the socio-political crisis in the East (which isn't to say that there is not also a political crisis in the West and an economic crisis in the East). Very much can be said about these crises and that will not be done here. Suffice it only to say that the West is now in fundamental economic difficulties, probably partly because the North-western corner of the world has to a large extent been outpaced by the South-eastern corner of the world. Firstly this was by Japan, then by the mini-Japans (South Korea, Taiwan, Hong Kong, Singapore); then by the other ASEAN countries (the Philippines, Indonesia, Malaysia and Thailand); and in the longer run possibly also by the socialist countries in that corner of the world (the

People's Republic of China, North Korea and Vietnam). A second good reason why the Western system is in difficulties is the problems it has with all its forms of exploitation: exploitation of nature runs up against depletion and pollution problems, not to mention the ecological movement; exploitation of the internal proletariat is opposed by trade unions, social democratic and socialist parties; exploitation of the external proletariat — the Third World — goes against all the phenomena grouped together under the heading "New International Economic Order"; and exploitation of people in general through demands for higher productivity entails the civilisation diseases, cardio-vascular diseases, cancer, mental diseases — including general alienation and lack of meaning in life, ultimately also including suicide as a way out. And then finally, not to be forgotten, the military expenditures mainly stemming from the East-West conflict are so high that the capital investments in the civilian sectors are seriously curtailed, impoverishing society further.

What would correspond to this on the Eastern side, what is the nature of the crisis there? Maybe one could say that there is, indeed, a general disenchantment with the system. The farmers are against the system because they want bigger private plots and more possibilities of marketing their products — certainly very much short of total privatisation of agriculture, but favouring a better mix. The workers are against the system because they are against monopoly control and for that reason seem to want some kind of trade union protection against exploitation by the state and the party. However, they are not going to learn about this from Poland, a country to a large extent hated by the Soviet Union, among other reasons for its participation in the Interventionist Wars where Poland wanted all of the Ukraine as a part of Poland (and actually got a lot, but lost it in 1939).

Furthermore, the intellectuals are against the system because they want more freedom of impression and freedom of expression, and are denied both or at least one of them. The socialist bourgeoisie is also against the system because they want better consumer goods, less shoddy, more up to the standard they find in the West. And then there are the "minorities" that together constitute a majority: they are against the system because they want more autonomy inside the system. This also applies to the countries in Eastern Europe and probably to all countries in the pyramid dominated by the Soviet Union: they want more autonomy. It also applies to many or most of the communist parties (euro-communism). In short: disenchantment everywhere.

To these phenomena, however, can be added a more general factor: whereas under Stalin hardly any of them was articulated, and whereas under Khrushchev they were articulated singly, they seem now, under Brezhnev and Andropov, to be articulated in a more combined manner. Action groups relate to each other, there is a contagion effect from one issue to the next. In a sense this is not so strange since over all of them one might write the same general slogan: *give us more self-management*. They are all reactions against excessive repression, centralism and state-ism; and this process, once started, is irreversible. It can be halted, but not reversed.

Thus, we are dealing here with two systems in profound crisis. Looking through the list again one might even say that the crises seem to expand not only in domain, all over the world, but also in scope and in depth. Moreover, the contention with which we started seems to have been borne out: there is a certain homology and there is a certain synchrony. It is a little bit like two twins: they are born, they grow up, they reach puberty, menopause (for women, and also for men!), old age and ultimately death — in a relatively parallel fashion. Ordinarily we do not see these phenomena in one of them as being the cause or effect of the same phenomena in the other; we see them as expressions of an *Eigendynamik*, autism, a self-contained evolution. But of course there is also a certain mirroring effect: one superpower stops autonomous movements within its domain, the other one thinks it has to do the same in order to maintain balance of power. Both perspectives are valid, only the first is so easily forgotten.

The basic question, however, is the following: what is the life expectancy of such systems? Of course there is no clear answer to this question, we simply do not know. The only thing we know for certain is that it is not infinite: no such construction has lasted forever. One might also say, looking at the list, that it looks as if we are dealing with systems that have become too big, have over-extended themselves, have more problems within than without, and we would come to the conclusion that the life expectancy is relatively short.

But that only leads to another question: how do such systems react when they are approaching the end of their viability? Let us return to Figure 2.2 according to which we are now in the worst phase with both intra- and inter-party tension high. Let us also assume that the present phase cannot possibly last more than 10 years, like the other phases. So, what comes next? Back to Phase I, by managing the international tensions? Perhaps more likely: the systems come sufficiently close to a war to be scared, reverse their course, stabilise, concentrate on the internal tensions. Back to Phase III, a total reversal? Only by a tremendous act of will, like back in the mid-'60s. For this to happen at least two conditions have to be satisfied: some alternative policies have to come up, both for inter- and intra-party conflicts — the present book offers some examples of such alternatives. But there also has to be a political situation, such as looking into the abyss of war — alluded to above — or some new North-South conflict that makes the East-West conflict pale in significance. Or: a tremendous and effective pressure from the peace forces. *Or else:* the process of Figure 2.2 shoots out of the four boxes — the war that must not come. If that should happen, a major factor might be the inabilty to handle the intra-party conflicts — and a shared interest in concealing the two crises through a major war.

4. Is conflict resolution at all possible?

Let us now turn back to the roots of the conflict, the values and the interests, issues Nos.3, 4 and 5 obviously being parts of the escalation process of the conflict into the realm of threat and use of force. As has been argued in the first chapter, even if these three issues should be settled

Nos.1 and 2 would still be there and could any time again generate escalation. In fact, in a sense they constitute the evil soil out of which these weeds seem to grow so well. Something has to be done about that soil, making it less capable of giving rise to such developments. Is this at all possible?

It does not look too promising. Both issues are embedded in the deep political culture of the two systems in general and of the two superpowers in particular. They both tend to see themselves as *the* two systems, "market economies" and "centrally planned economies". In both systems there may be rich and poor, more or less developed countries usually measured in terms of level of industrialisation. But these are seen as societies that are "undeveloped" or "developing", not as alternative social formations. In other words, the hardliners on both sides would tend to see the world in terms of only two possible goal-states, their own. It is "all me, nothing you" or the other way round:

Figure 2.5   Images of social-global socio-economic formations, I:
Blue vs. Red

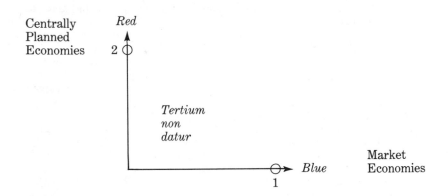

In position 1 the *Blue* system, based on market allocation of production factors and market distribution of goods and services, on capital accumulation and turn-over, and on power to corporations dominates the social-global socio-economic formations alone. There is nothing to the red system, based on planning for allocation and distribution, on state accumulation (in the sense of the general aggrandisement of the state, and power to bureaucracies). In position 2, however, the Red system dominates the society and/or the world alone, and there is nothing to the Blue. What we have said above is that positions (1) and (2) reflect rather well how the hardliners of both systems view the world: it is either you or me. Where do they get that idea from?

I think essentially from Occidental religions, with their strong emphasis on *universalism* (validity for the whole world) and *singularism* (validity of only one system). In other words, Occidental religions conceive of themselves not only as mutually exclusive (and exclusive of other religions) but also as exhaustive: as they are valid for the whole world there is no need for any other faith. Whether the devotion is via Israel, as selected people, and the Divine Prince, to Yahve; via Jesus Christ, as the Son, to God; or guided by Mohammed to Allah, universalism and singularism are the basic points — with the important exception that Judaism at some time gave up universalism and became the particular faith of the Jewish people, a tribal religion.

Liberalism and Marxism as the ideologies underlying the blue and the red systems respectively have taken over the assumptions of universalism and singularism, and since this is in the deep culture and often not even clearly seen by the adherents we are in a most unfortunate situation. To clarify this situation let us make a very small excursion into conflict theory. Let us imagine another conflict that looks somewhat similar and see what resolution, or perhaps rather dissolution, possibilities there might be for that conflict. Let us imagine that there are two brothers, who agree perfectly on one thing, they both want to be King of Milan: if necessary using a battle and military victory as the decision mechanism.

Figure 2.6   Images of lordship over Milan

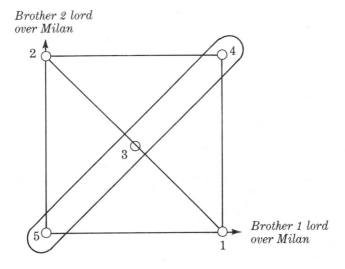

In position (1) Brother 1 lords it alone over Milan; there is nothing to Brother 2 — in position (2) it is the other way round. But it is easily seen that there are at least three clear alternative possibilities to these rather classical monarchic outcomes. Thus, there is position (3); a compromise whereby they would divide Milan, for instance along the river Po, one ruling to the North and the other one to the South of that river. Then there is position (4) which is considerably more imaginative, similar to the biconsular solution for Rome some time ago: the two brothers rule together. Of course, like position (3) this means a re-definition of the situation since the point of departure, the struggle for outcome (1) *or* outcome (2) clearly was in terms of either brother ruling Milan, and all of Milan, *alone*, to the total exclusion of the other brother. Positions (3) and (4) mean that they both have yielded, contenting themselves with less than they were originally heading for, possibly seeing the situation in a broader context, even to the point where this "less" *may* become "more". For, after all, a compromise might become a stable solution different from a victory that has to be reinforced and re-confirmed at considerable costs. A co-operative solution involving ruling together might turn resources that otherwise would have been used for defence against revanche or a new attack into constructive activities solidifying the position of both brothers, at the same time. And then, on top of this, there is also position (5) where neither brother lords it over Milan. Authority may be exercised by a third person, or even by the inhabitants themselves — through abolition of the monarchy, for instance.

It should be noticed how the entire focus on a conflict of this type changes the moment attention is switched from the traditional (1)-(2) diagonal to the diagonal connecting positions (3), (4) and (5). It should be noticed how the choice of focus on diagonals depends on the political culture. In a monarchic successor system of the either-me-or-you type the focus is obviously on the first diagonal; the moment one escapes from that basic framework one can switch to the other diagonal.

Correspondingly, if one accepts that the East-West conflict is a question of positions (1) *or* (2), with one of them being "good" and the other one being "fundamentally evil", then the logic of the East-West conflict will continue unabated. So, let us try to repeat what has been done above for the case of the brothers wanting Milan, introducing positions (3), (4) and (5), even giving them political colours (see figure 2.7).

Here three other socio-economic formations enter the picture. They are clearly related both to Blue and Red. First, there is position (3). The *Pink* option, often referred to as social democracy or democratic socialism, some kind of mixed economy with neither market forces nor planning forces dominating or fully developed. Then there is postion (4), the *Yellow* (or Golden!) option with full articulation of both the Blue and the Red. In the view of the present author this is typical of the Japanese economy and imitated by several countries in that geographical region (today also by some blue countries). And finally there is position (5), the *Green* option with neither national and transnational corporations nor national and transnational bureaucracies much articulated, with more emphasis on the local level, on the production/distribution capability of people in smaller groups such as communes, villages, families, peer groups, etc. But this is not the place to develop that theme.

I think very much of the East-west conflict depends on the extent to

**Figure 2.7   Images of social global socio-economic formations, II.
Blue-Red vs. Green-Pink-Yellow**

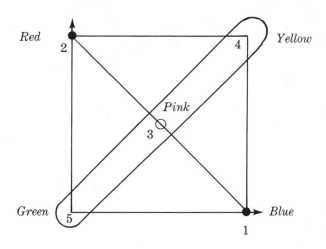

which people all over the world, and not only the hardliners among the blue
and the red, conceive of the ideological conflict: only in terms of the (1)-(2)
diagonal or also the (3)-(4)-(5) diagonal. It is probably correct to say that
social democracy has had a mediating function both in the sense of opening
people's eyes to a third way, and in the sense of leading people within that
formation, key social democrats, to take on mediating roles. This can
probably also be said of the greener countries in the Third World. But it
cannot be said, at least not so far, of Japan or of the "mini-Japans", partly
because they are located in a field of extreme tension in the East-West
conflict (often forgotten by Europeans), and partly because they are so
strongly dominated by the major victor in that area after the Second World
War, the United States. What one might like to see for the future would be
an alignment of the socio-political forces in positions (3), (4) and (5), the
pink, the green and the yellow, to some extent pitting them against the blue
and the red, but then more constructively by telling the world: "look, there
are alternatives! There are so many other things we can do, look at us, not
only at the blue and the red . . ."

In reflecting on this, one should by no means underestimate the
tremendous compelling force not so much of the liberalism/Marxism as of
the underlying Occidental assumption of universal/singularism. For
simplistic minds it is so reassuring when these two ideologies exhaust the
ideological universe and are mutually exclusive. But this assumption is
exactly what the thinking underlying Figure 2.7 purports to negate. They
are not seen as exhaustive, there is also the green option. They are not seen
as mutually exclusive as there are also the pink and yellow options,

differing in the degree to which the blue *and* the red are realised within these formations. Thus, one approach to social democracy would be "functional", letting some of the economy be run according to the market logic and the other part of the economy according to the planning logic. Then, another approach would be more "structural", letting the whole economy be run by boards and trusts where both "private" and "public" interests are represented, with all of them partly playing on the market, partly having access to public funds on the condition of paying attention to some planning directives. Obviously, a further development of the second alternative would push the system into the yellow corner. The parallels with the Milan story are obvious, underlying them both is the same basic figure of thought in conflict theory — incidentally a very underdeveloped field in social science.

The translation of perspectives such as these into concrete politics can only take place if helped by concrete events and processes in the real world, not the paper world of which the present book is a part. Needless to say, the military power of today is concentrated in positions (1) and (2) in Figure 2.7. But the allegiance of people, inside and outside, to a system does not only depend on military power, but also on how the systems are performing along social and economic dimensions. It would also depend on how the alternative systems are performing. Socio-economic and political crisis for the blue and the red, combined with a positive performance for the other systems, would be a decisive factor in the longer run. However, it should not be underestimated how the blue has somehow managed to incorporate the green and the pink and the yellow, seeing them as shades of blue when they succeed, as insufficiently blue when they perform badly. So again we are back to the problem of images of the world, of what kind of typology people in fact have, not only of how the systems are performing in a more objective sense.

It may be objected that these are long range perspectives, and I would agree. Not in the sense that the crises are for the future; they are already there both in the blue and in the red systems, for everybody to see. But the alternatives are not necessarily viable, and if they are viable, they are not necessarily seen as alternatives: as mentioned above they tend to be seen as shades of blue. More importantly, however, crises do not necessarily lead to conflict resolution, as argued in the preceding section. They may lead to just the opposite: agression as crisis response. From this the important conclusion can be drawn that the positive approach of creating alternatives to the blue and the red may be more peace productive than the negative approach of letting the crises unfold themselves even to the point of major war. In addition, to condemn the two major systems to historical oblivion rather than giving them the chance of improving themselves may be very satisfactory for those who do not adhere to these systems, but also very dangerous — a theme now to be discussed.

Let us therefore lower aspirations somewhat and look at more short range measures. By that I do not necessarily mean what in the jargon is known as CBM, "confidence-building measures". In this there is an element of Madison Avenue public relations: behave so that the other person develops confidence in you, justifiably or not. Moreover, the measures seem to be mainly focusing on what above has been referred to as issues 3, 4 and 5. I would be thinking of something else: of trying to identify precisely what it is that is provocative in the other system, going beyond the generalities of "universalism/singularism" to the level of concrete politics. What is it in one party that makes the other party frightened, in fact so frightened that they engage in arms races and other types of behaviour that come out of a deep sense of frustration, of *Angst?*

Of course, there is nothing new in this kind of approach. Just as we have the concept of hostile image or *Feindbild,* we also have the notion of how such adversary images can be built down. But again one should proceed with care: it is not really a question of "images" — that is also an example of the public relations approach. We are concerned here with reality, with one party trying to understand what makes the other party justifiably afraid and being so concerned about these anxieties that he prefers to abstain from such provocative action. In other words, the focus is on reality, not on image. And the reality is that one system is liberal/capitalist and the other is Marxist/socialist. Hence, if the point of departure is that the system of the other side is *in and by itself* provocative, even "fundamentally evil", then one is in fact declaring war on the other system since nothing but its eradication can be satisfactory in the sense of being non-provocative. An attitude of that kind cannot but lead to increased tension since the other side is not likely to perceive itself as "fundamentally evil" and join in that crusade against evilness, meaning against itself.

And that is already the first conclusion: a willingness to accept that the other system is different, to accept its right of existing however much one might wish it differently and however much one might believe that over time the other system will come one's own way. In other words, "peaceful co-existence", tolerance.

The second conclusion is less elementary and more problematic: to identify those dimensions about which one may nevertheless be entitled to say: "This is not essential to your system, moreover I find it most provocative". Two such aspects can easily be seen although whether the cut-off point is where the other side may justifiably claim to be provoked is open to discussion. One of these dimensions has to do with external behaviour, the other with the internal dynamics of the systems.

The *external* aspect is easily defined: the tendency to intervene in other countries' affairs, militarily and/or politically, even to invade. It has been pointed out in the preceding section that there is a certain parallelism here between the two systems. There is also a parallelism in the sense that each intervention confirms the image the other side has of that system, as basically aggressive, dependent on intervention in order to maintain the system. West Europeans make the basic mistake of assuming that only what happens in Europe counts and find, rightly, more interventions from the Soviet Union in Eastern Europe than from the United States in Western Europe (although some of this can be traced back to the difference in status of the two superpowers: one was more of an occupant, the other more of a liberator, after the Second World War). But in a world society Europe is but a part. Superpowers are responsible for actions anywhere, and will be held to account for what they do everywhere, even if it is outside the centre of concern for Euro-centric people. And most Europeans, including Soviet Russians, are Euro-centric.

Where is the cutting point? I think it is justified to request that the superpowers at least refrain from military invasion, regardless of the number and authenticity of invitations to exercise "brotherly assistance" that they may receive from governments in dire difficulty. Whether it takes the form of midwife activity to give birth to a new regime (subversive activity) or the form of life prolongation in order to keep an old regime in power ("superversive" activity) the net results are the same: an artificial dimension is brought into the internal dialectic of another country and all countries on the other side feel provoked and nervous. Will it also happen to us?

On the other hand, we live in a world where the free flow of persons and ideas should be encouraged. Ideas are as strong as military weapons. The objectionable behaviour should not be subversive or superversive activity as such, but military and parliamentary ways of doing it, directly supported by the countries on the other side — and not only by the superpowers. The provocative effect may also be there when a lesser power engages in such activities outside its own border.

However, it must also be recognised that the superpowers have certain legitimate interests. The Soviet Union has a legitimate interest, given its historical experience, in the safety belt mentioned. But that interest only goes to the point of devising systems whereby it is guaranteed that the neighbouring country cannot be used as a platform for an attack against the Soviet Union. So, maybe we simply have to recognise that the superpowers have an interest in neighboring countries not being in any way themselves potentially aggressive, nor being in any way at the disposal of potentially aggressive countries — be that with alliances, bases, intelligence co-opertion, communication co-operation in general, etc. Interestingly, the stronger the power, the more nervous it seems to become.

Similarly, it can be argued that the United States has a legitimate interest in trading with other countries. Its system is, in fact, to a large extent based on this interest, even if the foreign sector of the economy is a relatively small proportion of that enormous volume. Perhaps it can be argued that this is to some extent also the case for the Soviet Union. But recognition of the interest in trade is certainly not the same as recognition of a right to intervene when a country for one reason or another wants to steer a more self-reliant, or even self-sufficient course, a green course, in some or many or even all types of goods and services. Moreover, nor is that any reason to accept exploitative practices. Consequently, we are thrown back to what have been seen as major traffic rules in international relations: the principle of "non-interference in internal affairs" and the principle of "mutual benefits". The problems of definition are tremendous, but if a trade pattern is clearly disadvantageous to another country, meaning to large sections, even the majority of the population, then the right of abrogation must somehow exist. If it does not, there is a clear case of exploitation.

Concretely, this means the following: whereas a zone of neutrality can be seen as a legitimate interest around a superpower for the time being — certainly not as a long term goal in international affairs — a zone of willingness to adjust trade patterns to the interests of a superpower is not. Why insist on asymmetry between geo-political and socio-economic affairs? Perhaps essentially because geo-political affairs are even more basic. There is so much at stake, human survival both in the individual and collective sense. Differently with trade: trade really for "mutual benefit" is of course to be welcomed by everybody, particularly when a good definition of "mutual benefit" has been arrived at. But, whereas neutrality is a state of affairs, a trade relation is an ongoing process which over time can prove to be beneficial, but also to be detrimental. It becomes like traffic rules in a society: it is reasonable to demand of a citizen that he does not attack or prepare attacks or help others attack other citizens; it is unreasonable to demand of him that he should also interact with other people on their premises. The first is a demand to abstain from behaviour detrimental to others; the second would have been a demand to engage in behaviour that might even be detrimental to oneself. If one fails to see this difference some blindness may have crept into the social consciousness, possibly caused by an unswerving faith in "free trade" because one has always been on the sunny side of it.

Let us then turn to the *internal* aspects of the sytems. What is it in the socialist system as it has developed in the countries of "really existing socialism" that provokes the countries outside? Leaving the possible answer, "socialism itself, as such", to ideological die-hards, I think one is left with a very important answer: the infraction of human rights of the first generation, the civil and human rights. However, I would not see these infractions as deriving from "socialism" as such. It is true that a system of planning leads or at least *may* lead to an accumulation of state power because of the equation of the state with the provider for basic needs of all kinds, material as well as non-material. But I do not think that from this it follows that human rights have to be infracted. I would rather refer to that tendency as "Stalinism". It deprives people of fundamental freedoms of expression and impression, of assembly, of travelling and communicating and being travelled to, and communicated with. This deprivation of freedom even goes so far as institutionalisation, putting people into concentration camps and/or prisons, and/or turning the country itself into something reminiscent of prisons and/or concentration camps. In the most extreme case not only the basic need for freedom is at stake, but the basic need for survival as such: the case of death penalties, even mass execution, even mass extermination.

The basic reason why Stalinism is provocative to the outside derives from one very simple observation: *if they can do this to their own people, even to people in neighbouring countries* (the "safety belt") *then they can also one day do it to us.* It is bad enough that they do it to themselves, but people have all through history shown a great ability to tolerate the suffering of others provided they are far enough away socially, in space, and in time. It is the possible suffering of *me* and *us, here* and *very soon* that is provocative. And at this point, of course, the notion of "communism" as inherently expansive, precisely because it presents itself as

universalist/singularist, enters: one day it may come to us, we are
somewhere in their scheme of things.

From this I draw the simple conclusion that one of the major
contributions the Soviet Union can make to peace in the world is the
continued fight against Stalinism. What happened at the 20th Party
Congress in January 1956 when Stalinism as such was condemned was a
very important step. But the roots of the evil are deep, and not so easily
extracted, as any Soviet citizen, high or low, will readily testify. It may
probably be measured in degrees and there are oscillations. When it goes
up the West feels provoked, when Stalinism goes down there is a tension
relief in the West. The insistence on human rights by the West, hence,
should also be seen as a struggle for peace, as a way of exercising pressure
to build down a major source of tension. Whether that is best done under
pressure from the outside, or through the political work from the inside
without such pressure, is another matter. Probably both.

What would correspond to this on the Western side? What is the most
provocative aspect of the capitalist system? Again, it can be argued that it
is not accumulation of capital as such, but something that easily follows in
its wake. And that something also has to do with human rights, but this
time with the second generation of human rights, the social and economic
rights. In the wake of uncontrolled accumulation of capital under
capitalism follows the negation of the basic human right for material well-
being, the negation known as "misery". Concretely it means hunger, or at
least to be malnourished, it means being unsheltered and unclad, illiterate
and suffering unnecessarily from diseases. The condition is very
widespread in the periphery of the capitalist system, but also found close to
the core of that system itself.

Then, there is the concept of crises of capitalism, when the system shows
signs of malfunctioning even at the core. This shows up in many ways, one
of them is unemployment which may exacerbate conditions of poverty,
even misery. All of this is clearly against the second generation of human
rights and might lead to declarations of solidarity any bit as justified as the
declarations of solidarity with the victims of the direct violence of
repression referred to above as "Stalinism". The argument above,
however, was that people have a great capacity for tolerating suffering
that is sufficiently far away. Hence, can one with any justification feel that
a crisis of capitalism is provocative, is it not strictly speaking an internal
matter?

I think it can be seen as provocative. I do not think one has to be anything
like a 100 per cent Marxist (whatever that might mean) to agree that
*capitalism under crisis, and particularly in deep crisis, will tend to develop
fascist aspects*, and that although many of these aspects are internal and
take the form of increased repression, particularly of the working class,
some of them are external and will take the form of increased aggression.
Ultimately it may even lead to a war through complex mechanisms. One
may, and one should argue, that Germany between the two world wars of
this bad century was a special case, and nazism an even more special case:
nevertheless these mechanisms are recognisable in the pattern of events
from the early 20s to the early 40s. The most disastrous consequences of

those events were suffered in the East, not in the West: it was in the East that nazism searched for colonial territory.

Hence, I draw the conclusion that anything the West can do to prove to the world that they are capable of mastering these crises, and not at the expense of anybody through direct or structural violence, is a contribution to peace. My own experience, however, is that it is easier to have Soviet elites admit that Stalinism was provcative than to have US elites admit the same for capitalist crises in general, and unemployment in particular. There is a tendency to see such phenomena as usually external, not intrinsic to the system, and even if they should be more inherent in the system, they are then seen as internal matters. A war is not seen as caused by such phenomena, only as being related to them by chance. Such views, however, can easily be shown to be somewhat historically naive. But even if one should not accept data or theory to the effect that there is a link here, one should at least accept that the other side feels provoked and take that as a basis for improving contemporary international relations.

At this point it is possible to summarise. If both superpowers could keep their external and internal behaviour somewhat under control it would help tremendously. More particularly this means to stop, or at least build down considerably the pattern of military intervention, be that in "safety belts" or in areas of socio-economic interest. It would also help if they stopped exploitative practices, or at least made it relatively easy for countries that want to withdraw from such practices to do so. Further, it would help if they could prove their ability to control the worst excesses of their systems, here referred to as "Stalinism" on the Eastern side and "fascism" on the Western side. I think it is correct to link the former to excessive power given to the state (and the party-military-police complex in particular), and to link the latter to the role of excessive capital accumulation by the corporations, that become rigid in addition to being greedy, and incapable of adequate crisis management.

It may well be that the best cure in the Eastern case would be to open up society more, put fewer things under the control of the state, release some market forces, not only to bring about some of the efficiency of small-scale capitalism, but also to make for a more pluralistic society. It may also be that the cure for the Western evils is just the opposite: to increase public control over private enterprise and to increase the control by the pubic over that "public control". But then it may also be that there are other solutions, unknown today. And it may be that what has just been said are only the prejudices of a left-wing social democrat from a Nordic country, unhappily in love with the political party which he left because of its support (so far) for one of these two alliances, and through that for one of the superpowers, and through that for one of the two systems — in spite of its own alleged faith in bridge building, non-alignment and a third system, *Pink*. It does not matter, the important point is to identify the major sources of provocation. If in addition one took one step further, and devised those policies whereby countries might even help each other become less provocative, through dialogue, an enormous step forward would have been taken. Willingness to recognise this oneself is important, and I think the Soviet reaction against Stalinism should be seen in that light. So, why not call on the US Congress to denounce the crimes committed in the Indo-China wars, for instance? And the Soviet Union to do the same for Afghanistan — and the United States to do the same for the misery induced by its system, abroad but also at home. The list is long, this is for the future. But sooner or later the future will be here. And sooner or later those two systems, with excessive power given only to capital forces or only to state forces, will yield to something more balanced, more advanced, more human. Hopefully sooner rather than later.

3

Balance of Power

1. On the general theory of balance of power

There are only two of many views one cannot have on this difficult subject:
that balance of power always deters wars, and that it never works.
Obviously, there are many cases in history, more than we can possibly
know, when a potential aggressor has given up in advance because the
other party was too well prepared. And many cases, more easy to get at
because they are more dramatic, when an attack took place because there
was a "vacuum" on the other side. But then there are all the cases —
difficult to verify — when attack did not take place although there was
excess of capability to do so, but because there was no motivation to attack.
And then, again more easy to get at and interesting — attack takes place
even when the other side is stronger. In the latter case David might
sometimes win over Goliath, which proved David actually was stronger. In
other cases the minor power might go to war with other goals in mind than
victory. And that is one of the most frightening prospects today: there
might be circumstances where, to some very powerful people, losing a war
is the lesser of two evils. There may be something that is even worse —
such as losing honour (Germany in World War I?), capitulating before an
economic boycott (Japan in World War II?) or seeing one's whole system
collapse because of inner dissent and failure to achieve the goals promised
— very real possibilities for both superpowers.

In short, the issue is complex. To explore it let us leave the East-West
conflict behind for the moment in order to touch ground with it later on,
and consider the general theory of balance of power. Unfortunately, some
definitions are needed — even some simple formulas.

By "power" we shall in this context mean "force", *destructive power*,
carried out through threats and eventually through destructive action,
keeping in mind that there is also ideological power, carried out through
appeals to ideas and ideals, and remunerative power, carried out through
promises, and eventually through delivery of goods and services.
Destructive power ultimately implies delivering "bads", "disservices".
And they are of many kinds; human inventiveness in this field of *how to
destroy* is considerable, as amply documented through human history. The
list includes the *piercing/impact* weapons (crushing, piercing, tearing),
incendiary weapons (flames, heatflux, oxygen consumption), *high
explosives* (blast, high veolocity fragments), *chemical/toxic* destruction

(poisoning), *biological* destruction (contagion or other ways of inflicting diseases biologically), *radiological* destruction, not to mention the way in which all of this is combined in *nuclear* destruction, (blast, thermal radiation, primary and secondary ionising radiation and the electromagnetic pulse) and, not to forget: *psychological* destruction, how warfare and the threat of warfare is working on people's minds. In addition to this there are also always the *new* weapons, in the preparation process — such as laser and particle beams today.

Let us then ask: *what is it that can be destroyed?* If we divide the targets, as was done in 1.2 above, into human beings, human settlements (human society, with structure and culture) and then the environment, we get three types of weapons. To this we add a fourth category: weapons directed against the *means of destruction* themselves:

1. *homicidal,* even *genocidal weapons* targeted on *human beings* (for instance neutron bombs);
2. *sociocidal weapons,* targeted on *societies* (weapons aiming at "decapitation", destroying administrative centres, economic boycotts);
3. *ecocidal weapons,* targeted on *nature* (for instance, area denial weapons);
4. *weapons targeted on weapon systems.*

The first three types of weapons are usually referred to as "counter-value", whereas weapons targeted on other weapons are referred to as "counter-force". Needless to say this entire distinction is more logical than empirical as weapons do not in general discriminate that neatly. All weapons of mass destruction tend to be *omnicidal*.

But this is only the destruction side of the balance of power. The other side, equally important but certainly not discussed enough, is the *level of invulnerability of possible targets*. This is the capacity to negate the destruction, blunting the impact of destruction so that weapons either do not destroy, or the damage is so limited that self-sustained recovery within a reasonable time-span is possible. One can make human beings relatively invulnerable, at least for some time, by putting them into underground shelters (civil defence); one can make weapons relatively invulnerable by dispersing them, making them mobile, putting them into hardened silos or in the oceans, in submarines. Nature has its own mechanisms of invulnerability through renewal; its own resilience. But like all types of invulnerability it is a question of degree, it may prove insufficient beyond certain levels of destructiveness. Particularly valuable things, including more or less self-appointed elites, can be hidden away in bunkers; but there is no civil defence for the whole population against direct nuclear hits, only (partly) against secondary radiation, fall-out. And nature, particularly the biosphere, is also highly vulnerable and can more easily be destroyed than protected by human beings.

A society can be made considerably less vulnerable if it depends less on foreign trade (particularly in such essentials as food, energy, health inputs and arms); is less centralised so that administration and production cannot be knocked out through a couple of well directed hits; by having a technology that is not too "sophisticated", meaning that it can relatively easily be made inoperative through well directed action. A good example of the latter would be the now famous electro-magnetic pulse (EMP) that comes as a by-product of an atomic device exploded above the ground, having among its many effects also that of demagnetising data-banks, thereby making modern "information society" inoperative. Administrative data will disappear in many countries, so will banking information, control systems for trains and aeroplanes, and — quite importantly — navigation and command systems for submerged submarines, including those carrying the ultimate means of destruction. Much work is now being done (glass fibre optics) to make communication systems less vulnerable to that side-effect of nuclear weapons, particularly in a surprise attack.

But there are other aspects to vulnerability of a society. A society may also disintegrate because of inner contradictions, when skilfully utilised by an external aggressor. Any society has certain rifts, more or less in the open, along the dividing lines of class, race, ethnic groups, age and gender, lifestyles, geographical borders, etc. Sometimes the rifts criss-cross, sometimes they are aligned, in the latter case the society is particularly vulnerable. There is always the danger that the less privileged part under the existing order may make a deal with the enemy, in exchange for a better position in a future order.

All this is rather obvious. But it becomes less obvious when we try to make use of this type of insight to define that rather hazy concept, "balance of power". Let us simplify and say that we have only two parties in a conflict, $Party_1$ and $Party_2$ and that they possess an arsenal of arms or means of destruction with the level of destructive power of D_1 and D_2 respectively. Only the most naive people in the field would today think of calculating balance of power by comparing D_1 and D_2, arriving at the conclusion that there is a balance of power when one can say

(1) $D_1 \simeq D_2$

meaning that D_1 is "roughly equivalent" to D_2 (everybody would agree that it is not a question of exact mathematical equality).

Obviously this equation is only interesting when the two parties have only one weapon system each, the same one, so that the *qualities* are the same, and balance is a question of comparing two *quantities* of the same kind. The least one would have to do is extend this to more than one weapons system unless there is some agreement as to how this can become one-dimensional:

(2) $D_{1i} \simeq D_{2i}$, for each weapons system i

However, what one has to discuss if one wants to be anything like realistic is a somewhat more complicated formula:

(3) $D_1 - I_2 \simeq D_2 - I_1$

where I is a measure of invulnerability.

The search is for a rough equivalence between the *actual* destructive power which is the *potential* destructive power, D (e.g. as measured in tons of TNT and corrected for the precision of delivery) minus the level of invulnerability of the other side, I (again with the distinction between one-dimensional and many-dimensional analysis). The problematique is as ancient as warfare itself. It is the piercing power of a lance *minus* the invulnerability brought about by the knight's armour; the destructive power of a bomb minus the invulnerability brought about by hardening, hiding or dispersing whatever it is the bomb is supposed to destroy; human beings, weapons, etc.

This serves to identify a major intellectual flaw: most of the current debate about "balance of power" is about potential destructive power, not about actual destructive power. And one reason for that again is not disagreement with (3) but that destructive power is much more easily talked about, let alone measured, than the level of invulnerability. It is clear from the list given above that much of the latter is fairly intangible, and at any rate difficult to operationalise, such as the level of centralisation in a country. And yet, military commanders at all times, particularly the clever ones among them, operate according to equation (3) and certainly not only according to equation (1). The clearest application of this would be the effort to find points of very high vulnerability on the other side so that much real destruction can be brought about, even with considerably less means of destruction than the adversary. Actually, this was David's trick against Goliath!

Let us now look more closely at this. A country feels threatened by another country, known to possess means of destruction at the level D_2. The question is how much of a bite this level of destruction has, and that is a question of level of invulnerability, I_1. Let us simply define as *security* the following quantity:

$$(4) \quad S_{1,2} = I_1 - D_2$$

It should be noted that this is the security of Party$_1$ relative to Party$_2$. The security relative to Party$_3$ might be different since Party$_3$ might have another kind of destructive power, asking for other types of invulnerability. Security is here simply defined as one's own invulnerability minus the capacity of the other Party to destroy. I think that it is a fairly reasonable definition of security: it means the capacity to come out of a conflict unscathed, in other words the probabilty that human beings, society, nature and also one's own defence system will survive. One may later on decide to change them, but then out of one's own will. If the invulnerability level is insufficient, then one is *insecure*.

But this means that equation (3) above, the first attempt to understand "balance of power", can also be written in the following way:

$$(5) \quad I_1 - D_2 \simeq I_2 - D_1 \text{ or } S_{1,2} \simeq S_{2,1}$$

In other words, the security levels of the two parties are roughly equal. This can also be put more explicitly, perhaps more dramatically and in a form that is highly important. It is an insight shared broadly by military and non-military experts in the field: *the security of one party depends on the security of the other party.* It is only when the other party feels about equally secure as I do that I have reason to feel secure. Security is a relation, not only an absolute property of one of the parties alone. The absolute property is important enough: to have an invulnerability excess over and above the destructive impact of the weapons of an adversary. But the relative aspect is equally important: balance of power means *equal security*, which means that security is something one has in common, is shared. And that gives us two goals for security policy: *as high as possible, as equal as possible.*

Some more insight into this can be derived from a diagrammatic presentation. In the diagram below, the horizontal axis stands for D, the destructive power of the other party (meaning potential destructive power), the vertical axis for I, the level of one's own invulnerability. The diagonal line corresponds to the situation where invulnerability and destructiveness just cancel out each other (the lance just about pierces the armour, the bomb is very close to starting killing) in spite of the dispersion/hiding/hardening level. Above that line one could talk about a *security excess*, where things remain pretty much as they were because the destruction only hits the armour, the shields in a concrete and abstract sense, so that complete recovery is possible, within a reasonable time frame. And under the line one can talk about a *security deficit:* destruction is wrought and more so the further one is away from the diagonal line. There is general insecurity; the danger of being *hit,* and *hurt.*

Figure 3.1   Security as the balance between level of invulnerability and destruction

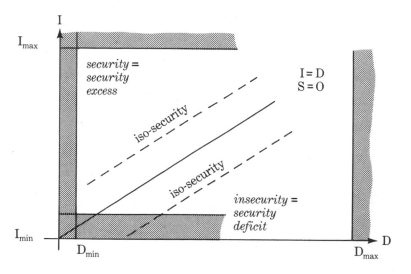

We have also tried to indicate in the Figure that there are minima and maxima to the levels of both invulnerability and destruction. The level of invulnerability is never zero (meaning that vulnerability is total), nor is the level of potential destructiveness ever zero as long as we are dealing with human beings as we know them. One might also say that the bottom corner

to the left represents a very precarious balance: the societies are
ultravulnerable and there is no potential destructiveness. Only a little bit of
change where the latter is concerned could be highly destructive.

At the other extreme of the diagram is a more complicated situation.
Clearly there is a limit to invulnerability: a society can be hardened or
protected in other ways to the point where it perhaps is indestructible, for
instance by putting it underground or by dispersing it totally in units down
to the size of individuals or families. But then it is no longer the same
society; the search for invulnerability against destruction has itself led to
destruction. Then, on the other hand, the destructive power can be of such
a magnitude that it no longer is a political instrument if it is presumed that
the purpose of a war is to bring about something of value, not a radioactive,
smouldering ruin, ultimately becoming a desert. Of course, the latter is
political if seen as the only way of preventing the other party from making
oneself into a radioactive, smouldering ruin, not only today but also in the
future. But what if both become deserts in the process? This is arguing
from an extreme situation that I still claim is relatively unlikely. In the
world of politics, with war as the famous (infamous) continuation of
politics, there certainly is an upper limit to the destruction. But the
arsenals transcend such limits.

However, regardless of how one thinks about this matter it does not
change the key argument: that security can be seen as the balance between
invulnerability and destructiveness. If this balance is negative one would
talk about insecurity rather than security: the society will become
victimised by an attack beyond a certain level of destruction. It can now be
argued, and is argued by many, that the atomic age is insecure for all
countries, that *there is no defence against nuclear weapons*. In a war
possibly not, but does there have to be nuclear war? It presupposes
unlimited willingness to drop nuclear bombs. It presupposes, in other
words, that there is nothing that stays the hand of he who has the finger
close to the button (or possesses the code that would release the ultimate
destructiveness). Of course, there are things staying that hand over and
beyond the fear of retaliation:

— who, for instance, would like to go down in history as the person who
  ordered the destruction of Paris (to mention but one example), if not as
  the home of millions of people than at least as the home of countless art
  treasures, concrete manifestations of human civilisation through
  centuries, points of reference for human identity?
— who would like to destroy a country like Switzerland which, after war,
  could be extremely useful to any country, destructive or destroyed, but
  only if it is reasonably undestroyed?
— who would like to destroy a country in the nuclear way, if that country is
  highly vulnerable, with no capacity at all for retaliation, and in
  possession of nothing of much value to others than those who live there?

If such factors make the application of the ultimate destruction less likely
then they should be added to the list of invulnerability factors, as
something adding to a country's security. And yet such factors are rarely
mentioned in security debates, and very difficult to bring into the

conference rooms in a disarmament meeting. Yet if they did not exist, we might not exist either.

This certainly does not mean that there are not conditions under which nuclear arms could and would be used. But these are conditions that cannot be made too precise, because that discussion itself might inspire counter-strategies. But the ultimate destruction is not condition free. In other words, we presuppose that the bombs are not in the possession of *totally* irrational people whose *only* goal is destruction as such. If this condition should obtain it is probably true that there is no real defence available at all, under any circumstances. One reason for this is the ease with which such people could place bombs anywhere in the world, of course not by the very cumbersome method of using ground-, sea- or air-launched ballistic or cruise missiles, but for instance by using suitcases, placing the bombs in big lockers in luggage deposits in certain places around the world (some of the bombs are sufficiently miniaturised for this to be realistic), and having a system of remote control for electronic ignition. The vulnerability of modern society to nuclear terrorism is about the same as to terrorism in general. I shall return to this later.

Under some limited assumption of rationality it would, then, make very much sense to discuss the whole problem of balance of power between $Party_1$ and $Party_2$ in terms of one simple quantity, the *security difference:*

$$(6) \quad B = S_{1,2} - S_{2,1} = (I_1 - D_2) - (I_2 - D_1) = (D_1 - D_2) + (I_1 - I_2)$$

What is being said here is that something called B, or balance, is the difference between the two security levels, which in turn is the sum of the difference in potential destructive power and the difference in invulnerability. When the difference is (close to) zero one would talk about *balance of power*; (6) reduces to (3) above. What it means is simply that the two levels of security are roughly equal; that the two parties are located on an iso-security line, and in the diagram two such lines are drawn, one in the security excess region and one in the insecurity region. Clearly, if the two countries are located on the same line, there is a certain equivalence to the level of destruction they can inflict on each other. If they are located on very different lines, that equivalence no longer obtains and there is no balance. The assumption underlying the balance of power hypothesis, then, is that this equivalence deters: "He cannot harm me more than I can harm him." This, of course, presupposes that the party that strikes first cannot disarm the other party so much that he cannot strike back with sufficient destructiveness.

One could now distingish between three cases: both parties are in the security zone, one is in the security zone and another in the insecurity zone, and both are in the insecurity zone. In the latter case, if they go to war, they will certainly both lose: their level of invulnerability being in deficit relative to the destruction that can be wrought by the other party. The peace movement often argues that this shows the irrationality of war: there is no winner, only losers. Unfortunately, however, that is not correct. To win and to lose are also relative, not absolute, entities. The question is not necessarily whether one gets out of the war enriched relative to what one was before, but could also be -- perversely -- seen in terms of whether one has managed to lose less than the other side. *The winner is the lesser loser.* And this could also be turned around for the case that they both are located in the security zone: the loser is the lesser winner. Both come out with security intact but one less so than the other. It should also be noted that this becomes more complex if we bring in the *war booty* and calculate not only in terms of differential losses but also in terms of differential gains. In a nuclear war, however, it is hard to imagine any "war booty" that can compensate for the destruction, except one: to be destroyed less oneself.

Evidently, the critical case is when one party is in the security zone and the other in the insecurity zone. As usual the situation is a complicated one as there are four independent variables that are often changing all the time: the two levels of destructiveness and the two levels of invulnerability. Thus, the insecure country may try to increase its level of security by increasing its level of invulnerability, or to push the other country into the insecurity zone through a build-up of its own destructive power. And the other party may do the same. We are then firmly in the midst of the phenomenon referred to as an arms race, or, perhaps more correctly, a security race which turns into an insecurity race because it moves into the insecurity zone.

Before we explore that in more detail, let it first be stated once again that there is no assumption that wars are launched by the more secure party, nor that the more secure party has a positive security. One could also argue that the more insecure party could launch a war in a desperate effort to break out of the vicious circle before it becomes even more insecure, or simply because it is no longer able to wait for a war it thinks will come. It might prefer the tension release to waiting and permanent inaction. Nor is there any assumption that when there is balance in the sense that $B \simeq 0$, then there will be no war.

But the condition is an interesting one since it has such a hold on the minds of men — perhaps less on the minds of women, who seem by and large to have greater capacity to see the totality of the arms situation, not taking too seriously the often ridiculous abstractions that men try to reduce that totality to. So let us look more closely at the equation we arrived at in our search for balance of power:

$$(7) \quad B = (D_1 - D_2) + (I_1 - I_2) \simeq 0$$

A sufficient condition for this equation to obtain would be:

$$(8) \quad D_1 \simeq D_2 \text{ and } I_1 \simeq I_2$$

or stronger:

$$(9) \quad D_{1i} \simeq D_{2i} \text{ and } I_{1i} \simeq I_{2i} \text{ for each weapons system.}$$

In other words, that the two levels of potential destructive power and the two levels of invulnerability are both roughly equal, even for each type of weapons (system). Equations (8) and (9) call for a rather abstract, very ageographical and ahistorical situation: two countries of the same size, with the same economic basis and social formation; both of them equipped with only one weapons system of the same magnitude (8) — or with the same weapons systems, always of roughly the same magnitude (9). The moment they have not one but at least two weapons systems the question of substitution and relative equivalence — how many tanks correspond to how many rockets — arises, and the answer becomes very speculative. Of course, one cannot assume that tanks will fight tanks and rockets will fight rockets. But adversaries in all arms races will tend to match each other system for system. It is the simplest thing to do — "to be on the safe side". In the world of facts those equivalence conditions become meaningless: wars are not fought that way. In the world of logic, however, these conditions are *very strong,* and also *easily understood* as sufficient conditions — except for their inability, even conceptually, to touch the vulnerability dimension.

Weaker conditions that can be read straight out of equation (7) would be that the destructiveness differences and invulnerability differences roughly compensate for each other:

$$(10) \quad D_1 - D_2 \simeq I_2 - I_1 \text{ (the same as equation (3) or (7))}$$

But then we are back to the old problem: granted that there is a way of measuring destructiveness, how does one measure invulnerability, not to mention compare invulnerabilities of two different societies, and compare that difference with destructiveness differences? On some physical dimensions, we can, but in general? To mention just one factor: the invulnerability of human beings obviously has not only a somatic side that perhaps to some extent can be taken care of through underground shelters; it also has a psychological, or spiritual side. There is this intangible thing called *morale,* fearlessness, fighting spirit, defiance. Rather obviously, both the Vietnamese and Afghani fighting the superpowers and their collaborators had and have a lot of it, making them relatively invulnerable to the threat of destruction and thereby able to fight their materially overpowering enemies, the United States and the Soviet Union. On the destructiveness side of the equation there is a corresponding factor: imagination, ability to make destructive power work where it hits most, including the ability to think and act "extra-paradigmatically" — outside the model of thinking and acting that has been most prevalent. Hitler went around the Maginot Line in an unexpected way, for example, and the Japanese approached Singapore from the blind angle of the guns.

I shall not go into more detail with this type of reasoning for the conclusion is relatively clear: to pursue balance of power, even rough balance of power, is to pursue an entity that, like the famous unicorn, can be conceived of but not operationally defined except by finding out empirically, through a war, whether there is a draw (highly unlikely) or one party proves to be superior to the other. But a war not only invalidates the balance of power hypothesis; a major war is what must not happen! Hence, there is something metaphysical about this pursuit. Too much insistence on equivalence along all dimensions of power will only lead to endless pursuits of a balance which, like the rainbow, recedes further and further away the more one pursues it. And the simplest approach, equivalence for the *sum* of all dimensions does not work: there is no consensus on how to make multi-dimensional power uni-dimensional.

What has been mentioned so far is not only practically and politically a problem. It is also theoretically, conceptually, and intellectually rather difficult to handle. Hence, there will be efforts to simplify the matter further, beyond what has already been explored above, and also in order to arrive at less complicated conclusions, particularly in terms of action directives. The conclusions may be wrong, but they are at least understandable!

The first approach, of course, is to focus mainly on the means of destruction, but then not in the simplistic way of equation (1) above — the bottom level of intellectual activity in this field. Actually, not even that is done: the focus is on weapons only.

At this point one introduces the factor of invulnerability, *but only in connection with the means of destruction*. The analysis switches to force and counter-force, to the capability to destroy the means of destruction on the other side, $D_1(D_2)$ and the capability of making one's own means of destruction invulnerable, $I_1(D_1)$. Whether it is done through the hardening of stationary missiles, the random dispersal of non-stationary missiles on the ground, in the sea or in the air, by making them difficult to hit through radar-absorbing coating or flight profiles below the radar range, or by other means developed and to be developed, is of less importance; these are technical details.

Thus, we arrive at the condition for *strategic balance of power:*

$$(11) \quad D_1(D_2) - I_2(D_2) \simeq D_2(D_1) - I_1(D_1) \text{ or } I_1(D_1) - D_2(D_1) \simeq I_2(D_2) - D_1(D_2)$$

which is actually the same as quotations (3) and (5), but focusing on only one aspect (the fourth) of what can be destroyed: the means of destruction themselves. That this should be of such overwhelming importance is certainly not only a psychologically convenient trick of intellectual simplification focusing on fewer and more measurable entities, with secrecy rules protecting the analysis against uninvited dialogue. The means of destruction being what they are in the nuclear age, their destruction as well as their invulnerability becomes of paramount importance. It is also easily seen why the whole approach is too simplistic: counter-force weapons can also be used as counter-value, to destroy and kill anything, even if the opposite is not the case because of insufficient precision. But let us pursue the approach further.

What has often been referred to as the "iron law of the nuclear age" was the idea that both parties should have positive and even roughly equal strategic security; that both of them should be in the security excess zone where their own strategic weapons are concerned. Put differently: after the first strikes have taken place they should both have a second strike left (the positive balance, the excess referred to) capable of delivering a devastating blow. If this were not the case, the reasoning goes, the party more in the black would attack the party less in the black, or even in the red, and attack first, meaning certainly do not renounce a first strike option (never agreeing to a no-first-use clause in connection with nuclear weapons), letting the other party live with the uncertainty that that option might in fact be used. And then it would presumaby go through a protracted nuclear war with strikes nos.3, 4 . . . n +1 till one party has its destructive power eliminated, or the process comes to halt for other reasons. The process could also be telescoped in time through "launch on warning", using weapons before they are destroyed.

So we are back to the point of departure, but now in a slightly more limited field. Again there are four variables to be manipulated for each weapon system: the two levels of destruction (meaning not only yield, but also precision — e.g. as measured by CEP, "circular error probable", the radius of the circle within which half of the missiles fired on a certain target would fall); and the two levels of invulnerability — by the methods indicated above — and other ones. Any change in *any one* of these four variables will immediately affect the strategic balance. And even if the two security balances are both negative, as reasoned above, we still have the same problem: for certain people it is not a question of winning in an absolute sense, but of losing least. It is just as well to see clearly that this is what it is about: the world has leaders in both superpowers whose mentality is fashioned by this relative idea of losing least, not by the absolute idea of how much one loses. Within a broad range, that is. There may be, even in those cowards whose personal invulnerability is secured through bunkers, an upper limit beyond which damage becomes unacceptable in an absolute sense.

Again, one can come to the conclusion that to pursue a point of balance is to pursue something metaphysical, at least as long as the *experimentum crucis* is not carried out. I would not underestimate the psychological significance of this last point. There must be a tremendous urge among some nuclear planners on both sides simply to see what actually will happen, not only through calculations, war games, scenarios, simulations — but in reality. Again, the higher the level of invulnerability provided for themselves through underground bunkers etc. (the famous presidential directive PD58 of the Carter period) the higher, probably, this urge will be. Much like sex education in a convent, I presume: just *one* little try!

On the other hand, it should be admitted that the reduction of the total balance equation to a strategic balance equation makes it not only theoretically but also practically somewhat easier to handle. There is a certain military clarity about this: the variables are more physical (number of missiles, number of warheads, yield, CEP, penetrability, amount of hardening, degree of dispersion, degree of randomness, degree of "stealth" or camouflage in approaching the other side) and the variables are administered by men who think very much the same way on both sides. The range of surprise is probably more limited, the range of destruction certainly extended. In a somewhat different world the two superpowers could have their means of destruction with accompanying invulnerability systems set up in isolated parts of the world or in space (treaty restrictions notwithstanding), targeted on each other. They might even try it out, like in a duel in ancient times, and simply test in practice who wins. In that abstract world the equations would carry much meaning, because the empirical world itself would be modelled after the equations rather than *vice versa*.

But we do not live in that world. In practice the weapon systems are inextricable from the non-weapon systems, the civilian side of society, not to mention nature itself. As a matter of fact, one of the ways in which weapons can be given a certain invulnerability would be exactly to place them in heavily populated areas, for instance on submarines in the waters of neutral countries, assuming that the other side would hesitate somewhat in killing millions of human beings in the effort to destroy a couple of missiles. And then there is the factor mentioned above: however much the *intention* may be to use counter-force weapons only against the destructive force on the other side, the fact remains that such arms can also be used against "value", against the other three targets that are worthy of being destroyed in an all-out war. It is capability that counts, not motivation. The fact that the weapons have been made incredibly precise (if all the boasting to this effect is true) does not mean that they cannot easily be made less precise. The fact that the yield can be lower where precision is higher does not mean that it cannot easily be made higher again. In short, the focus on weapons instead of on the other targets does not present a way out of the dilemma. One simply must not be lulled or misinformed by the terms "counter-force" or "counter-value" when one is talking of such large-scale and indiscriminate weapons. "Counter-value" is indeed counter value, but nuclear "counter-force" is counter force *and* counter value.

But that does not mean that the distinction is invalid for weapons not of mass destruction, in other words for "conventional weapons" — knowing full well that the latter recently have been "developed" so far as to overlap very well with the former in lethality. Hence, let us combine the types of insight developed in the approaches underlying (4) and (11) above and give a more complete expression to the notion of security:

$$(12) \quad S_{1,2} = I_1 - \left[D_2 - (D_1(D_2) - I_2(D_2)) \right]$$

The idea is the same: security is one's own level of invulnerability minus the *net* potential destructive power from the other side, which — in turn — is the gross destructive power minus what one has been able to destroy of that which — in turn — is one's own counter-force destruction capability minus the level of invulnerability of the weapons on the other side. And the second idea is also the same; at least not to have less security, than the other side; $S_{1,2} - S_{2,1} \geq 0$ (see (6) above).

The conclusion can now be stated: not only is balance of power in the strict sense impossible to define operationally; *security is also unobtainable*, in any reasonable sense of this word. Even given very generous assumptions about the level of invulnerability of humans, society and nature, these systems will not be able to withstand the net destructive power hitting them if today's armoury is really unleashed.

The popular expression, "there is no defence against nuclear weapons" then becomes true, referring to the two meanings of the word "defence":

a. the targets cannot be made sufficiently invulnerable except by destroying them;

b. the weapons cannot be sufficiently destroyed because they are too invulnerable.

To this it may be objected that even if true today these conditions may be different tomorrow. All factors in (12) may change: the invulnerability level may be increased, but then also the destructive power from the other side;

one's own capacity to destroy that capacity may be increased, but then also the invulnerability level of the destructive power on the other side. What is easier in general, to increase the power to destroy humans, society and nature, or their level of invulnerability? — certainly the former. And what is easier in general, to increase the level of invulnerability for arms or for humans, society and nature? — certainly the former, except for some selected few human beings,.the elite. The only remaining possibility would be an increase in the capacity to destroy weapons, possibly even combined with a decrease in the invulnerability of weapons, for instance by making the oceans and the underground transparent (but then weapons can be hidden under ice-caps, ice-bergs and mountains). That break-through, such as a laser-belt impenetrable to any type of missile, ballistic or cruise, air-, sea- or ground-launched — would be a break-through — indeed, it is still science fiction. If only one side has it, it would change security differentials and the balance of power dramatically by putting one side in the black with a security excess, and the other side way out in the red with its heavy security deficit. So this is, of course, where most of the research can be assumed to be going on — any treaty against anti-ballistic missiles notwithstanding. And this is where counter-measures can be assumed to be developed: not only to destroy the destroyers of weapons (anti-anti ballistic missiles — A^2BM — to counter anti-ballistic missiles — ABM), but also new approaches in launching a devastating attack, for instance, through pre-positioning on adversary territory by means of the suitcase approach (there are also other approaches).

And thus it is that the search for security leads to ever more insecurity, and the search for balance of power leads to no balance. The simplest reaction left open in such a situation is what both parties pursue, and relentlessly so: *to increase the destructive power so as to deter, if not by defence, at least by the threat of retaliation.* Increase of one's own destructive capacity, as well as increase of one's own invulnerability, both for value and for force, have the advantage that they can both be done on one's own side, maybe with complicated agreements with allies, but at least not with even more complicated, if not impossible, agreements with an adversary.

Conclusion: *the arms race* — for this is what they do.

2. Why balance of power is not stable

Let us now summarise and explore a little further some of the basic points explored in the preceding section, this time — I promise the reader — without formulas. I think the topic can be discussed under three headings:

(1) *the destructive power has become too high;*
(2) *the war systems have become too complex,* and
(3) *balance of power is not necessarily pursued.*

The old reasoning behind the Roman adage *si vis pacem, para bellum,* was "attack should not pay". The damage imparted to the attacker should outweigh any value he could obtain through the attack. This holds as far as a cost-benefit analysis holds, in other words under certain conditions of rationality. But what if the value the attacker is pursuing is not anything he can possess or bring home, as when he occupies, annexes or simply is out on a robbery expedition; but the value consists precisely in destroying? He might hate the other party so much, think it is such a threat to himself, humanity or history that destruction is the only way out, even at considerable loss to oneself. And what then, when, due to the development of modern weapons of mass destruction, this simply is possible?

Well, balance of power then becomes balance of terror; deterrence is based not on making costs outweigh gains but on making unacceptable costs to one side outweigh unacceptable costs to the other side through mutual assurred destruction. There is still a certain rationality to this as the trend of thinking is still carried by old balance of power paradigms. But that paradigm is now used to justify totally different phenomena. In the old days it might even have been used to justify combat, as when in a duel it was meticulously assured that the destructive power and invulnerability levels of the two combatants were equal so that the outcome of the fight could be interpreted as the voice of higher forces, and used to settle conflicts. Today it is used to accumulate ever higher levels of destructive power so as to make sure that the level of destruction will be comparable, not only to the point of total destruction, but also well into the region of overkill, and not only of weapons, as in well directed counter-force attacks, but of human beings (civilians as well as military), societies and nature. *Omnicide,* in short.

And that leads to two further terrifying reflections. First, the super-weapons have been rationalised by reference to super-antagonisms; to the idea that the conflict between the two systems is so basic and irreconcilable that super-weapons are needed in order to keep the other party at bay. But maybe it is rather, or just as much, the other way around, that super-weapons lead to super-antagonisms, because the destruction is so total that it can only be justified by a conflict also seen as total? Those who are planning the use of such weapons must also justify eventual use in their own minds. If they are guided by the general idea that means and ends should at least to some extent be of the same magnitude, then the end, the horror to be avoided, has to be seen as something of the same level as the horror to be used to avoid it, a war of mass destruction. It is hardly necessary to point out what kind of role the adversary has to be cast in, in order to fulfill this important intellectual and moral function: a monster, a criminal of Hitlerite magnitude, the "centre of evil" (Reagan).

Second, if balance of power is balance of deterrence, but deterrence is no longer interpreted as defence but rather as retaliation, then it becomes balance of mutually assured destruction. And this gives us some insight into how a nuclear war might be fought. That it is destructive follows from the destructive power of the weapons. That it is mutual, and even in an assured way, follows from the invulnerability of a second strike. But what about the balance? I can imagine how both parties exchange devastating blows at each other — and not necessarily according to the old first strike/second strike formula but according to the simultaneous strike formula, the launch on warning made necessary, possibly even automatic, because of the short time difference between launching and impact — then halting the war in order to find out whether the exchange was indeed verifiably "balanced" in its destructive impact. Does this or that city destroyed on their side really correspond to that or this city on our side? One can even imagine conferences convened under the "mutual and verifiably balanced" formulas, but this time focusing on something highly concrete, the amount of destruction wrought, not on something more ephemeral, like in a disarmament conference where the same formula is used.

From this, however, it does not necessarily follow that balance of achieved destruction will be used to terminate a war, as a successor to the old idea that balance of power can be used to prevent a war. First, they may never agree as to whether the destruction was really balanced. One party may feel that the other party has an edge over him and hence feel entitled to catch up, and thus the war continues. Second, even if there is balance of destruction one party may feel that he is entitled to an excess because of some real or imagined wrong that the other party perpetrated before the nuclear war started, or simply because he is entitled to an excess in any case, regardless of what the other party did. He may justify this in various ways, one of them being that in order to prevent a war in the future more destruction has to be wrought on the other side since that is the belligerent side. Regardless of the rationale, this is an obvious second formula for continuation of the war. It should be noted that both formulas have as their implication protracted warfare, not the massive all-out blow but a process, infinitely painful to all involved, over a considerable period of time — days, weeks, months, years.

But even if this model of a protracted war should not become reality, I think sufficient points have been made to show how an old form of thought, "balance of power", is lingering on far beyond its usefulness simply because it is available. It has been reinterpreted so as to fit modern conditions of warfare, but now leads to conclusions that cannot be said to be anything but perverse. As we shall see later, however, this does not mean that the form of thought is entirely invalid, only that it becomes invalid in its consequences when deterrence is interpreted in terms of *retaliation* rather than the way it was originally intended, in terms of *defence*.

The second trend of thought is based on the idea that the war systems have become too complex. There are at least four dimensions underlying this: the *number of actors* in a war system, the *number of weapons systems,* the complexity of the *invulnerability* notion, and the *role of perception* as opposed to more objective reality.

As has been pointed out, the balance of power model makes very much sense in what can be referred to as the (2, 1) case; two actors and one weapons system, on the condition that the two actors are roughly the same; no geographic, economic, social, etc. asymmetries of significance. To this should be added that the perceptions also have to be appropriate. If both think the other side is stronger, then that might prevent a war, but it is hardly a stable condition as it may not stand up against more objective data. The more complex the systems are the more discrepancies, probably, between subjective and objective reality. And it may not necessarily work as in the example: it may also be that one or both parties underestimate the other side and for that reason launch a war that might otherwise have been effectively deterred.

The importance of all these considerations can be clearly seen in the situation in 1983 with regard to the Geneva negotiations. These negotiations were purportedly about disarmament, but in order to get off the ground a point of departure had to be established. There had to be a commonly shared definition of the situation — this is the perception side. Since they are not able to deal with the invulnerability dimension they focus only on the destruction dimensions, and as a very minimum they would have to have shared views as to who are the actors and which are the weapons systems, the latter both in terms of quality and quantity. One may say that the US position is a case of reductionism down to the (2, 1) case: there are two actors, the United States and the Soviet Union; there is one weapons system, land-based intermediate range missiles. Since the definition automatically, by the range itself, excludes all land-based rockets that are not on the Euro-Asian land mass, and they presumably are not in Korea, this limits the discussion to the European "theatre". The US position then becomes a very logical one: the US has zero such rockets, the Soviet Union has a number N with a total destructive power D — it all has to be dismantled (or permanently removed from the European "theatre") or else the US will catch up with the 572 cruise and Pershing II missile launchers. A possible alternative would be to meet somewhere inbetween; 75 and 300 are numbers that have been mentioned.

One may say that the US with this negotiation stance tries to recreate arms conditions that perhaps obtained a very long time ago. The approach is conceptually very simple, but the underlying model of the world totally unrealistic. Consequently the Soviet Union's response was predictable: to bring in a much more realistic image of the world according to the (m, n) formula: m actors, n weapons systems. The United Kingdom and France are brought in precisely because they possess more or less independent nuclear forces with middle range capacity; had they been totally integrated under a unified NATO command the (2, 1) approach might have been used with NATO and WTO as the two actors. Of course, independent nuclear forces do not necessarily mean that they are directed against the Soviet Union, and this is where the difficulty with any formula beyond two actors enters the calculation: are all other actors really adversaries? Is France as much an adversary as the United Kingdom? It is clearly not a zero per cent adversary since it is after all a NATO member, and on the other side where socio-economic formation etc. is concerned, it is equally clearly not a 100 per cent adversary. Does that mean that some kind of weighting should be applied? Who would establish the weights, how would one do it — beyond the kind of games that social scientists like to engage in? The Soviet approach has been to reason according to the formula "he who is not with me is against me", putting them all together "on the other side". One may certainly object that this is not a wise political strategy since it defines France as an adversary instead of inviting France into a more neutral position, but leaving that aside one might add that the approach is more realistic.

Within that formula the Soviet Union would then tend to extend the number of weapons systems. It may stick to the middle range, but in that case not only to the land-based; it may stick to the land-based but in that case not only to the middle-range (including also the short-range); it may also include air-launched missiles. Where the US solution has the advantage of being so simple that anyone can grasp it, this approach now becomes very complex with no clear borderlines as to what should be included and what not, with the consequence that the Soviet Union both will and can change its position quite frequently whereas the United States cannot do so qualitatively, without disguarding their own paradigm, but only quantitatively. On the other hand the US position gives an unrealistic image of the world, while the Soviet position is much more realistic. One defines balance in a totally abstract world; the other one operates in the concrete world. But on that basis there will hardly be any consensus as to what constitutes balance.

And that leads us to the third train of thought: is balance of power really pursued? This can best be answered by reference to the five conflict issues developed in the preceding chapter.

The *first* conflict issue, over *values*, defines both parties as essentially self-righteous. They are the carriers of both universal and exclusive ideas and ideals, and hence have certain entitlements, even obligations. These obligations might not only be seen in terms of defence but also in terms of the right and duty to expand the system for which they are the supreme exemplars. For defence purposes rough parity might be sufficient; for expansion superiority would be indispensable. Suffice it then only to be added that even if this type of thought should not be found in any one of the superpowers, it would be hard to convince the other superpower that that is not the case, ideologised as the conflict is. The Soviet Union sees capitalism as a *necessary evil* in History; but the US sees communism as an *unnecessary evil* — a dramatic difference which may underlie US striving for superiority.

The *second* conflict issue, over *interests*, leads to similar considerations. It boils down to a question of specific military action in order to defend or secure specific interests, here and now. In order to do this the safest move is to attack a much weaker party, even a party weakened by having some kind of status as an ally and for that reason presumably not prepared for an attack from the protector himself. The consequence of this is the whole history of superpower interventionism, including interventionism by France and England. Against the other superpower this becomes too dangerous. But a judicious exercise of threats might still be applied; the skillful use of force would make real use unnecessary, limiting it to threats. But in order to make the threat (also nuclear) credible there has to be an element of excess; to "prevail" presupposes "strength", and "strength" is another word for superiority. It means unbalanced power, power unchecked by power on the other side. And the most extended superpower, the US, will be the one striving most for superiority.

The *third* conflict issue is over the *strategic positioning* itself. Balance of power is for deterrence; if deterrence fails, so the reasoning goes, there will be a war and a war will be won by the stronger party, by definition. If one were absolutely certain that balance of power in the sense of parity would really deter, then a positive balance in the shopkeeper's sense of superiority would not be necessary: as there is only a probability not a certainty that "parity" deters, an excess of power becomes necessary. An excess may also be needed to compensate for vulnerability. Whether one or both parties reason like that, the result is the same; an arms race, either because both sides seek to exceed the other, or because one tried to exceed and the other to catch up. And thus the US gets about 2,000 bases around the world, the Soviet Union about 500 and France 200-300 (some of these not more than landing rights for planes, though).

The *fourth* conflict issue, over *alliance-formation*, tends to push the system in the same direction, towards increases in destructive power. The reason is simple: added to the problems of establishing a balance between the adversaries, be that in the sense of parity or superiority, come the problems of establishing balances within alliances. An alliance is in principle a system for mutual protection. But if the benefits are to be shared, including arms profits, then it stands to reason that the costs are also to be shared, and this means not only financial and other costs, but also the risks in connection with unintended and intended wars. "Sharing costs and risks" becomes a key formula for understanding what takes place. In the old days this meant that if one alliance member had something the adversary coveted, a piece of land, a geographically advantageous position, raw materials, industrial capacity or whatever else might be the successors to the cattle-and-woman-type booty of olden days, then other powers would come to the rescue. Today that power of rescue itself, as in the case of land-based missiles, becomes not what adversaries might covet but what they fear most. *The logic of warfare would not be steered so much by what one hopes to gain, as by what one hopes to avoid. Raketen sind Magneten,* rockets function like magnets, hence they are risk factors, hence they have to be distributed relatively evenly between the members of an alliance. More generally and more precisely expressed: in order to equalise the risks, the distribution of targets worthy of a nuclear attack has to be relatively equal. This in itself might only lead to the distribution of the launching sites, not to a further growth in their number and destructive power. When, nevertheless, growth tends to be the consequence, this is partly because of all the other factors mentioned and partly because the leading power of an alliance also wants a sizeable excess over and above the other members, even above the other members combined. Adding it all up, one might say that the disciplinary function within the alliance is well exercised through a judicious distribution in the rate of growth of the destructive power potential, with the leader clearly on top. For an alliance with 15 members (NATO) this would be more of a driving force than for one with only seven (WTO).

The *fifth* conflict issue, deriving from the *MBCI-complexes* (military bureaucratic-corporate-intelligentsia-complexes), as has so often been pointed out, would also tend to push the system towards higher levels of destructive power. In their pursuit of parity or superiority the military will tend to develop new strategies. The intelligentsia, in this case the researchers for the military establishment (of hardware, software or both), will tend to devote their intellectual ingenuity to the development of new weapons systems, "modernisation". Bureaucracy will tend to be interested in more power for itself, and corporations in more profit. It is very easily seen how these four can co-operate so they really become a complex:

Figure 3.2   The MBCI-Complex

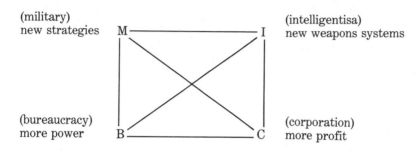

(military)
new strategies   M ———————— I   (intelligentisa)
new weapons systems

(bureaucracy)
more power   B ———————— C   (corporation)
more profit

In very concrete cases one can trace a causal chain at work within this web of relationships. It may start with the military developing some new strategy, ordering corresponding weapons from the intelligentsia, which in turn is hired by a corporation that sees the chance of making big and quick profits, all of this overseen by a bureaucracy (a defence department with affiliates) which becomes ever more powerful by having more money and more life-and-death issues to handle. Or it can start with the power motive, the profit motive or simply as has often been pointed out, with the intellectual innovation motive: new weapons are developed in search of new strategies rather than *vice versa*. But any effort to reduce this complex to one or two causal chains misses the basic point: we are dealing here with a family of very related phenomena pushing in the same unfortunate direction, towards higher levels of destructive power. It is exactly a complex, and most developed on the US side because of the corporate profit (and employment) motive. In addition there is the internal US arms race, between the army, navy and air force (and the marines).

For all five factors mentioned under this third and last train of thought it may be objected that these are circumstances leading to increase in destructive power, not necessarily to imbalance of power. Precisely because they may be assumed to be operating in both superpowers and their alliances, the five factors *may* be compatible with balance of power, only this balance becomes a non-static one, a moving, dynamic balance, but nevertheless some kind of equilibrium — as is well known from mechanics. This may be correct, but it should be pointed out that the first three factors point to the significance of having an excess of power, not only more power. It should also be pointed out that any concern with real *balance* relative to the adversary would have to be superimposed on these five factors, themselves automatic and very strong. The balance of power concern is certainly not built into them; the question is whether it is ever strong enough. On all five counts the US side seems to give evidence to the contrary: deliberately or not, superiority is being sought, with no idea of upper limit.

Conclusion: *the arms race continues.* The pursuit of balance of power becomes not only like the search for the unicorn; it starts looking more like an effort to square a circle. As is well known from mathematics, there is no difficulty in conceiving in an abstract sense of a square that has the same area as a circle, but it cannot be constructed geometrically, because of certain mathematical qualities of pi = 3.14 ... (it is a so-called transcendental number). That makes the pursuit *under current conditions* even more metaphysical. The realists become the idealists; those who talk most about the balance of real power become those furthest removed from the realities of this world.

3. The chances of a major war

The arms race continues, but will it lead to a major war? Of course nobody can answer with any certainty, but we can at least have a look at the data from the past, back to early in the last century. The data are relatively convincing: *arms races have a tendency to end in war.* A US peace researcher, Michael Wallace, made a study of 99 cases or "situations" of "serious dispute or military confrontation", in the period 1820-1964. These were cases of conflict, otherwise there would not have been "dispute or confrontation". He had a look at the 10-year period prior to the participants involvement in this dispute or confrontation, calculated an arms race index as the product of the "rate of arms race growth for pairs of contending states", and then investigated what happened: an escalation into war, or a non-escalatory outcome. He had 26 of the former and 73 of the latter, and 28 arms races and 71 situations not preceded by arms races.

The correlation is highly convincing (Yule's Q = 0.98); one rarely gets such correlations in the social sciences:

Table 3.3   The relations between arms race and escalation into war

	war-escalation	*non-escalation*	*SUM*
arms race high	23	5	28
arms race low	3	68	71
SUM	26	73	99

(*Journal of Conflict Resolution*, March 1979).

Of course, it does not follow from this that it is correct to regard the arms race as a cause and the war as the effect. "Condition/consequence" might be a more appropriate terminology, reflecting correlation rather than causation. For obviously there is an underlying factor: a *conflict,* with a probably increasingly intense awareness that the other party stands in the way of the realisation of one's own goals. For whatever reason — be it that one thinks war is inevitable and would like to have the upper hand or the other side is by nature aggressive and will attack, particularly if it feels superior — an arms race takes place, and it ends with a war as the aggressive consequence of having one's own pursuit of some political goal frustrated: a pre-emptive war, or simply a war in order to reach a coveted goal. Or, as is so often the case, in concrete historical situations: arms races for *all* these reasons, wars for *all* those reasons. Moreover, the reasons for arms races, and for the wars, do not have to be the same.

Of course, one cannot simply use these data to arrive at conclusions about individual cases from aggregate, statistical analysis. But the conclusion nevertheless has an off-hand plausibility: *if* there is an underlying conflict, and *if* an arms race has been going on, and *if* a "situation" then arises involving "a serious dispute or military confrontation", *then* there certainly is a danger of war. We are living under such condtions today; we have been for some time, as a matter of fact.

From this, however, it does not necessarily follow that the only way to avoid war would be by not having an arms race. It could also be by having a positive balance of power in favour of a non-aggressive country, in other words the theory that the US today seems to have of itself, "only a stronger America can prevent a holocaust" (Ronald Reagan). There are actually two versions of this argument: the objective *policeman* beyond any suspicion, strong enough to control any aggressor around the world, and the theory of the *race champion*, to be the one who simply wins the race, exhausting the other party into conceding defeat, admitting inferiority. There are, however, rather severe problems with both versions.

The first presupposes that the other party accepts the implicit division of labour between a superior policeman and an inferior potential delinquent. Superpowers seeing themselves as harbouring ultimate truth are highly unlikely to conceive of the world in such terms. They will rather tend to see themselves as the carriers of something objective, of Humanity in the case of the liberals/conservatives and History in the case of the Marxists, not simply as the carriers of subjective self-interest. And they would hardly concede that this could apply to the other party, as and even more rightly so than to themselves. To see it that way would undermine the whole basis for their *Weltanschauung,* for the deeper layers of their world ideology. They would rather see the other party as fundamentally aggressive, and misled because of his serious misconceptions of human nature/human history. Consequently, if either of them should try to appoint itself as policemen the other one would certainly only see it as one more way of legitimising armament or re-armament, as a way of getting the upper hand with a positive balance in their favour, something that immediately would have to be compensated for by stepping up the armament level on one's own side. At the very least this would call for parity, not submitting to the other as somehow more "legitimate". Nobody will cast himself in the role of delinquent.

Then there is the race champion theory: one country or superpower is richer than the other and gets ahead in the arms race. The other party, not so rich and somewhat behind in technology, has to respond both in quality and in quantity, until it is outdone technologically or is on its knees economically and gives up. Of course, given the asymmetry in technology and economy one party may get ahead of the other, but that does not mean that the other party admits defeat. On the contrary, it could stimulate that party to develop even more diabolical weapons, something totally unheard of before, so as to redress the balance. Thus, if the US should have placed 200 MX missiles on those famous race tracks trafficking between 23 silos each, giving a total of 4,600 places from which they could be fired, the obvious response on the Soviet side would be to make 4,600 precise missiles, each one targeted on one of the silos. (If this is against SALT provisions, then there is no difficulty finding some evidence that the other party has also done something against those provisions). Further, if the US deploys Cruise and Pershing II launchers that can be fired from trucks, and those trucks seem to be deployed in certain districts rather than others, then the obvious answer would be to develop strategic arms with the explosive power of a doomsday machine, putting the missiles out of action regardless of where they should happen to be, within an area of many square kilometres. The first approach would call for increased precision, the second for increased yield — in both cases the result is a continued arms race. And that, of course, is also the obvious outcome of the deployment of 464 Cruise and 108 Pershing II missiles in Western European NATO countries: a corresponding escalation on the Soviet side, as they tend to see their own SS20s as responses to Pershing I, Trident and Polaris (and as modernisation of SS4s and SS5s, just as these are seen as responses to Thor and Jupiter, the old middle range missiles the US stationed in the Southern NATO countries, and later on removed). The two parties would simply not see the history of the arms race the same way. Why should they? And who can judge who is right?

What then about the argument that one of them might give up, not because it is militarily inferior in a technical sense that can be compensated for through more armament, but simply because it is incapable of more armament for lack of resources? The answer seems to be that those resources will be found, and that the population in general would be willing to contribute the surplus needed to enter into that type of production if adequately stimulated by their leaders. Since the leaders, not only in the Soviet case, but for all practical purposes also in the US case, dominate very effectively the means of information in this field, there is little reason to believe that they would not be able to mobilise not only mass sentiment but also mass sacrifice in order to continue the arms race. Nationalism, patriotism, even chauvinism will prevail over dislikes for leaders, if the alternative is submission to conditions dictated by the other side. At this point both sides will tend to over estimate the degree of dissent on the other side, and the degree of sympathy the working class in the US would have for the Soviet Union, or the dissident class in the Soviet Union for the US.

But if the balance in the sense of *parity* is not stable, as argued in the preceding section, also when it is dynamic as opposed to static, and *if* the balance in the sense of *superiority* is not stable as just argued here because the other party will not submit, and *if*, further, the opposite of balance — meaning arms races — tends to lead to war, *then* we are back to the main train of thought in this section: how likely is that major nuclear catastrophe? There are many ways in which this can be discussed. If the focus is on the chances of a major nuclear war then one dimension would have to be the *scope* of the war in terms of the type of weaponry employed (conventional, tactical nuclear and strategic nuclear; down to the amount of megatonnage employed and its dispersion so as to be able to discuss the destructiveness), and another dimension would have to be the *domain* of the war, meaning the range of areas affected. The latter is usually done in terms of another tripartite division into Third World, Europe/East Asia and superpowers. And then the reasoning would make use of the following figure:

Figure 3.4   Scenarios for a major nuclear war

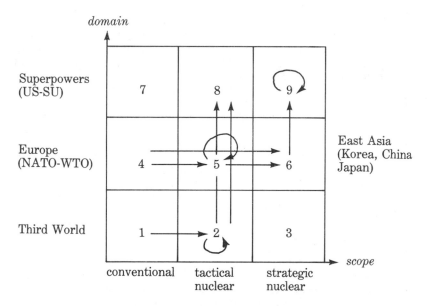

There are actually three lines of thinking underlying this set of scenarios. First, there is the general agreement that the superpowers have established rules of conduct so as to carefully avoid direct violent confrontation, be that with conventional, tactical nuclear, or with strategic nuclear arms. They know too much, they are too convinced that the other party will escalate and/or retaliate in kind so that they would not go beyond the more general threatening stances that they hold to be necessary in order to make the ultimate use of nuclear weapons credible, knowing well that they also increase the tension considerably, almost intolerably. Hence, the reasoning goes, a strategic exchange between superpowers would come at a late, possibly even the latest stage of a major war, not in the initial phase. This argument, then, also leaves out nuclear war by accident, indicated by the circular arrow in box 9 in the table, the likelihood of which is very difficult to assess.

If we accept this type of argument the problem is whether a major nuclear war can come about in other ways, through escalation in scope and/or domain. And this is the second line of reasoning: an escalation in *scope* is likely, particularly if a war should start in Europe, but also if it should start in the Third World. In the European case the tactical nuclear weapons (defined as weapons used to complement or supplement conventional operations) are so close to each other, and the decision-making can be made at such low levels in the hierarchy, that the escalation from conventional to tactical nuclear (once the top level green light to go nuclear has been given) looks not only likely, but almost automatic, like a launch on warning (in Asia this would be somewhat different since it is at least assumed that North Korea does not have tactical nuclear weapons, nor Japan). Of course, there is also the possibility that such exchanges might come about through accident, perhaps particularly because lower echelons in the hierarchy are involved and might be more vulnerable to psychological or other types of malfunctioning. But this may also be a class judgement: when lower levels start a war it is a mistake, when higher levels do so it is politics. On the other hand, the more decision-makers, the higher the probability of irrationality. But, however this may be, the assumption is that use of strategic nuclear arms (meaning by that weapons with impact beyond usual combat objectives, such as major destruction — the distance between site of launching and site of impact being insignificant in this connection) might easily result. The doctrine of limited nuclear war is held to be untenable by very many: there will be escalation to strategic levels.

And then there is the third line of thinking: escalation in *domain*, from Third World to Europe/Asia, from that area to the superpowers themselves. Since the Third World is seen as not possessing strategic weapons, or at least that they will not be called into action at an early stage, the general trend of scenarios is from the lower left regions of figure 3.4. to the upper right regions.

The reasoning behind the assumptions of escalation in scope and escalation in domain is not watertight. That a conventional war in a Third World area could lead to the use of nuclear weapons is probably correct. If one of the parties already possesses such arms and is about to suffer a major defeat, the arms would probably be pulled out, even used. This may also be true if they have strategic weapons at their disposal. The question is what the transmission mechanism from there to the European and the superpower theatres would be. There are such transmission mechanisms, but they are not entirely automatic. Thus, if a tactical or strategic Third World nuclear war should take place in North or West Asia (in eurocentric terminology the latter is often referred to as the "Middle East") then the geographical vicinity to nuclear arms deployed in the European theatre would itself constitute such a transmission mechanism. Particularly important here might be the Comiso base in Sicily and its proximity to Libya, and also to this part of the Third World in general, all of it well within the range of land-based cruise missiles. But naval considerations might make a war in northern Europe equally likely, because of the strategic significance of the Kola peninsula and the alleged feasibility of naval nuclear war.

But then there is the other transmission mechanism: not geographical linkage, but political linkage. Third World countries, even when not formally parts of alliances, and even when formally declared non-aligned, are usually backed more by one superpower than by the other. Equidistance is rare in this world. If one Third World country is threatened by nuclear defeat from another then a superpower protector might step in, either to deter or possibly to avenge nuclear destruction. But if one steps in the other one is also likely to step in, and even if they use a Third World theatre there is by then an exchange at the tactical nuclear level between superpower weapons — in other words an escalation from box 2 to box 8 in the diagram. Again a linkage that is probable, although not entirely automatic.

Somewhat more problematic to the present author is the assumption that there has to be escalation to strategic weapons, and particularly escalation to strategic nuclear war between the superpowers themselves. I would rather be inclined to think that there is, or would be, some kind of bond between the superpowers of common interest making them abstain from strikes at each other; in other words limiting the war to European (and East Asian) theatres. The target density in general, and the population density in particular, being what it is in these theatres, strategic weapons of major magnitudes may not even be necessary/useful; short-range weapons might do and would not serve as a warning that strategic weapons have been launched. The advantages to both superpowers are obvious. But the advantages to the European nuclear powers are none, meaning to the United Kingdom in particular — and to France — they may risk being very severely hit under this kind of tacit agreement. The logical response would be to deflect the attention away from themselves as targets, and in that case towards the superpowers again. So imagine that the British and/or French submarines launch missiles at the Soviet Union which is, after all, the only country from which they themselves can be hit if Eastern European countries at the most have tactical nuclear arms at their disposal (or so it seems). What would the Soviet Union do in that case? Direct a more devastating blow at these two countries, or make an all-out attack on the United States? They might do both, for instance, because they might not even know who hit them. The nuclear warhead might not carry the address of the sender. And in that case would it not be in the interest of the United States to prevent such attacks from taking place — for instance by having US submarines chase the French and the British ones? A bizarre world indeed, but this is the world in which we live.

My own conclusion is that we do not know: we have no empirical evidence, and theoretical arguments would tend to point in both directions, limited war and unlimited war. That one of the superpowers rejects the theory of limited war and pledges itself to an unlimited response is an indication that the theory may be wrong, but not a proof. In other words, the reasoning leading to an all-out war is not quite watertight. But it would be rather perverse to see some belief in some limitation as being "soft" on nuclear weapons in general and nuclear war in particular: there would still, easily, be hundreds of millions of Europeans and East Asians sacrificed, and others as well (fall-out).

Back to Figure 3.4 again: how does the situation look? Down in Box 1 we have the kind of conflicts we are used to: the Third World has overwhelmingly been the theatre for the "local" wars since 1945, so we have developed a high level of tolerance for that type of war. Wars in box 4 are not quite unknown either: Poland, DDR, Czechoslovakia and Hungary are examples of one type, Greece and Ulster another, Cyprus a third — but all of them have been relatively limited. Proliferation of nuclear arms makes escalation into box 2 a likely possibility in the relatively near future, clustered around such conflict centres as Israel, Central America and the Persian/Arab Gulf area. The populations in the NATO and WTO countries will probably learn to live with that kind of Third World disaster also, even with strategic nuclear wars, as they have learned to live with enormous amounts of structural and direct violence perpetrated on the poor populations in those parts of the world. As long as it does not hit any of us directly, it is to be deplored. But that is it.

Both geographical and political linkage will make it very likely that sooner or later a situation arises where the conditions stated in the beginning of this section come true: there is an underlying conflict (meaning the first two conflict issues over values and interests between the two systems), there has indeed been an arms race going on, there is a "situation" involving a "serious dispute or military confrontation", and the powder keg may be ignited. And that powder keg is us, potentially all of us — leaving us with the possibility that neither scope nor domain may be maximum. A miserable comfort indeed.

However, the assumption behind what has been said so far is that a direct war between the two superpowers is unlikely. I am not so sure one can believe in that assumption. Whether a direct war (box 9) is more or less likely than a war that comes about because they have been unable to regulate the arms race and/or confrontations in the Third World and/or the European/East Asian areas, is another matter; I certainly do not know. But it should not be assumed that wars could only come about through accident or escalation in scope and domain, as discussed above. Let us look at the factors that might make a direct superpower superwar likely; the key factor making it unlikely — the suicidal character of such a war being well known.

The *first* factor is, of course, that there are those who believe that the war may not be suicidal, it could be "merely" genocidal for the other side through a paralysing first strike, whether it is to prevent, pre-empt or simply in order to try to eliminate the other side, for instance because he is seen as the "centre of evil". Precisely because the destructiveness is so enormous, deterrence invites a first strike (with MX +, or SS18, or large numbers of Cruise/Pershing II or SS20) because launching a first strike is seen as a lesser evil than suffering a first strike.

The *second* factor relates to this. There seem to be those, again in the United States, who are of the opinion that communism is not only an evil but a *totally unnecessary* evil that could and should be eliminated, even if it should cost many US lives ("20 million" has been the famous estimate of one US security advisor, with the understanding that it may be worth it). The Soviet Union is seen as the factor standing in the way of liberalism and capitalism. To disregard this as only "words" is as irresponsible as were those who had the same attitude to the policies advocated by Hitler in *Mein Kampf,* for instance in connectionwith colonisation of *Ostland, Ostmark.* It should be added that such views have not been heard from the Soviet side, and also be emphasised that from the Soviet point of view capitalism is evil, but a *necessary* evil in the historical scheme of things. Communism will survive capitalism, be present at the funeral. But capitalism will die from its own inner crises — a first-strike is not only immoral, it is also unnecessary.

The *third* factor is precisely that, and this is what causes the present author most nightmares: that the superpowers should both prefer a superwar to two parallel supercrises, unmasking the two systems as inadequate. However, there is no need for an hypothesis to the effect that they might *both* see a superwar as the lesser evil because of a certain crisis coincidence; that collapse because of war is preferable to system collapse. It is sufficient that *one* superpower feels this way, and it would have to be the one that is superior, i.e. the United States.

The *fourth* factor relates directly to this and is the old theory of relation between economic cycles and war cycles. An economic system based on markets rather than plan will sooner or later get into an over-production crisis. In its wake follows unemployment and all the other symptoms of economic crisis. To stimulate production again there is the possibility of finding new markets and of launching new products, but in a highly competitive world market with new major actors (Japan, mini-Japans, ASEAN countries, etc), and world-wide protest against exploitation, this may not solve the problem. An arms race helps: AWACS to Saudi Arabia recycles eight billion petro-dollars; the B1 bomber saves Rockwell. But only one thing is sure to solve the problem: sufficient destruction of capital so as to create a demand for reproduction and get the wheels turning again. Many people will be killed in the process. But people reproduce and production is so automated that workers are less necessary — what is needed are consumers, later on. After the war unemployment will then disappear, production will pick up, demands will be met, there will then be an overshoot and eventually a new overproduction crisis — and all is set for the second cycle. Evidently, this factor relates to the capitalist more than the socialist system. A planned economy may be sluggish and inefficient, but precisely for that reason does not get into over-production problems.

The *fifth* factor relates to the strategic situation. The 572 launchers to be stationed in Western Europe are for missiles that can reach the Soviet Union, with ranges of 1,800km for Pershing II (the Russians say 2,600km) and 2,500km for the Tomahawk cruise missile — promoted by the US Air Force and the US Army respectively. The SS20 to which they are supposed to be the answer cannot reach the USA. The dislocation towards a European war theatre is clear; this make the war *somewhat* less risky for the United States, *somewhat* more risky for the Soviet Union, *extremely* more risky for the Europeans, and particularly for those with Euro-missiles on their soil. This could make Europeans want to get rid of the rockets, in other words make them more likely "allies" in the sense of being willing to participate in a first strike option. Western Europe is vulnerable in the extreme and cannot survive a first strike. The only chance is to shoot first; even that is probably insufficient. Hence, what the United States has achieved or is achieving is not only a dislocation of the war threatre, but — possibly — also a dislocation of the responsibility for the first reckless step. Of course, Western Europe would never do that alone; it could only be as part of a well co-ordinated general strategy. The point made here is only that the deployment of land-based Euro-missiles changes the motivation pattern among the Europeans from supporting spectators to active partners — and that was, in all probability, the intention.

The *sixth* factor is the way in which the Soviet Union is now being put under pressure. A tremendous economic pressure is on, forcing them into an armament burden that takes away, perhaps, as much as 70 per cent of the annual capital investment (about double the rate of that of the US). The country will be encircled by as many as 7,500 cruise missiles with an alleged accuracy of 100 feet pointing at it, and a strategy of "decapitation" (destroying all political, administrative and major economic centres) is announced. At the same time there are problems along the borders of the Soviet system; there are system crises and cracks. Sooner or later the Soviet Union may make the mistake that could serve as a pretext. An invasion of Poland might be a mistake of that type; at the very least it could serve to solidify the Western alliance and hence be as much desired by the US administration as the Soviet Union would try to avoid it! But the Soviet Union *might* also cross the borderlines indicated by the US out of spite. To make the point more clear: any Soviet indication that invasion of Nicaragua mght be a *casus belli* could be a factor making a US invasion of Nicaragua more, not less likely — out of spite.

The *seventh* factor is the impatience that comes with increasing tension. The impatience must sometimes become unbearable for those who are at the centre, on either side. Contingency planning, with all the options they are capable of imagining already tried out in manoeuvres or simulated in other ways, are insufficient as psychological surrogates. Deterrence is only meaningful if it is credible, and it is only credible if accompanied by big and threatening words and facial expressions and actions, sufficiently often. Moreover, it cannot be made too precise: any list of conditions under which the nuclear deterrent would be used might give too many good ideas to the adversary, and might make one too predictable since there would be an implicit promise that if an attack came in any *other* way, then the deterrent would not be used. Consequently the tension under a strategy of deterrence can only increase, and the increase has to be inflationary: yesterday's threats already sound trite, there has to be threat escalation to sound credible. How long can people in the centre of this "game" stand the tension without, in the end, a desperate act for tension relief?

The *eighth* factor brings in the following question: under tension, who is likely to shoot first? Of the night burglar or the house owner switching on the light, both seeing the gun in the hand of the other, who is more likely to shoot first? I would argue: he who is more vulnerable, the big, burly one standing in the limelight, rather than the tiny, slim one in the shadows. Who is more vulnerable, US/Western Europe or Soviet Union/Eastern Europe? Unfortunately the former, the party with the most belligerent record in this post-war generation and the most threatening postures and the greater capacity for a first strike, because of its armoury and strategic positioning.

The *ninth* factor is the way in which the disarmament option is systematically being destroyed. As will be indicated in the next chapter, "the game of disarmament", to use Alva Myrdal's very apt phrase, is played in such a way that it cannot possibly succeed. Both superpowers are responsible for this, the United States probably more than the Soviet Union. But the fact is that the option seems closed, or is, at best, very slim indeed.

None of this means that somebody tomorrow will say "It is GO, Caspar". But the clouds are dark, indeed — and the probability of a direct and major nuclear war, most probably initiated by the US, is well above zero.

4. Is balance of power at all possible?

With the gravity of the present situation in mind let us look for some bright spots. These matters are relatively complex. And yet it is absolutely mandatory that as many as possible try to come to grips with them, not only in the sense of seeing more clearly what goes wrong and *what will always go wrong,* regardless of political will among the parties, but also in the sense of training oneself in finding ways out of the impasse. The following is *one* approach. It can be done without the very simple formulas that are used, but then it becomes quite unwieldy. Hence, some symbols, even formulas will be used again, in a short summary.

The point of departure is *security,* the probability of "system maintenance", meaning that the society will only change due to its own, endogenous forces — not through force, or threat of force from the outside. Imagine we have two societies, P_1 and P_2, and that the security of P_1 relative to P_2 is $S_{1,2}$. And let us start with a simple point of departure: a *definition:*

$$(1) \quad S_{1,2} = I_1 - D_2 > O \text{ and } S_{2,1} = I_2 - D_1 > O$$

the security level of P_1 is its invulnerability level, I_1, minus the destruction than can be made by P_2, here called D_2. Clearly, there is only security insofar as this entity is *positive;* if it is negative there is negative security, or *insecurity.* Of course, it does not mean that D_2 *is* unleashed, it only means that I_1 offers insufficient protection should it be unleashed.

The problem with (1) is that in the age of weapons of mass destruction in general, and nuclear weapons in particular, *there is no (passive) defence against the destruction.* Or, put differently: necessary and sufficient invulnerability is only obtainable through total change of the society, e.g. by putting humans, the human-made environment and the environment underground, or on another planet. But in that case invulnerability has become a caricature, destruction of society has been brought about by threat from the outside, but carried out from the inside. *And even so it might not help:* missiles can be made to drill a hole down and explode when "value" is encountered, just as they can be made to drill a hole up and retaliate. Obviously, some other approach is called for.

The other approach, of course, is to say that "I am insecure, my only hope lies in making you insecure to":

$$(2) \quad S_{1,2} = I_1 - D_2 < 0 \text{ and } S_{2,1} = I_2 - D_1 < 0$$

However, this is not enough: the other party is also insecure, but may be *less* insecure than oneself, suffering lower losses in an "exchange". So, what they both want is actually more security than the other party; they want a security difference in their own favour, a positive balance, $B_{1,2}$, or $B_{2,1}$:

$$(3) \quad \text{Party}_1 \text{ wants: } B_{1,2} = S_{1,2} - S_{2,1} > 0$$
$$\text{Party}_2 \text{ wants: } B_{2,1} = S_{2,1} - S_{1,2} > 0$$

Clearly, this is impossible; they cannot both have a security balance in their favour. They cannot both have superiority, but they can both have parity, meaning:

$$(4) \quad S_{1,2} = S_{2,1}$$

or, multiplying by -1:

$$(5) \quad D_1 - I_2 = D_2 - I_1$$

meaning that they can cause about the same level of destruction to each other. This condition is better known as *balance of power,* only that is actually *balance of terror* given the level of destruction of today's weapons. Invulnerability (civil defence) is of little or no avail against them, but should be subtracted for the sake of completeness, and because such programmes are increasingly likely.

What has been done above is not quite so trivial as it may look. There are two points:

— that security is a *relational,* not an absolute quality; it is how the security of P_1 relates to the security of P_2 that matters;
— the only solution is (relatively) *equal security,* which — with the definitions used above — turns out to be identical with the conditiion known as *balance of power.* That simplifies the matter.

However, the problem with what has just been said is that it does not help much. Even if the condition for stability should be equal security (the parties are on the same iso-security curve) the problem still remains that the absolute level of security is *negative,* i.e. *insecurity.* A war may still be "won", but only in the sense of losing less than the other party — yet with terrible losses. Obviously, this is unsatisfactory, hence another approach is brought in through the distinction between destruction that is *counter-value* and counter-force, and *invulnerability* of *value* and *force.* The idea is simple enough: "I cannot make my values (humans, human-made environment, environment) invulnerable, but I can possibly destroy the means of destruction". The answer to this is well known: try to make the means of destruction invulnerable. If we refer to the level of destruction of D_2 by P_1 as $D_1(D_2)$ and P_2's level of invulnerability of his means of destruction as $I_2(D_2)$ — and similarly from the point of view of P_2, then we get *the following eight variables to take into consideration in any study of security:*

Table 3.5   Common security: the eight key variables

	Invulner-ability value	Counter value	Counter force	Invulner-ability force
$S_{1,2} = I_1 -$	$\big[D_2 -$	$(D_1(D_2) -$	$I_2(D_2)\,)\big]$	
$S_{2,1} = I_2 -$	$\big[D_1 -$	$(D_2(D_1) -$	$I_1(D_1)\,)\big]$	

We now assume that both P_1 and P_2 are trying the following:

Axiom I: To make the *absolute* security positive, *or* as high as possible;

Axiom II: To make the security *difference* positive, *and* as high as possible.

In other words, I do not assume that they are striving for balance of power in the sense of parity, but in the sense of superiority; still, in other words, that there is no co-operation. I further assume that the only way to make them co-operative is to show them that their goal is unattainable.

Since passive defence (vulnerability of value) is ineffective, P_1 tries to subtract from D_2 by destroying $D_1(D_2)$. P_2 tries to subtract from this subtraction by making D_2 more invulnerable, $I_2(D_2)$. The strategic arms race, naturally, shifts from counter-value to counter-force but with the same logic, that of equation (5), but also (1) through the efforts to make arms invulnerable. It is a Chinese boxes kind of logic and can be continued: P_1 can try to destroy the invulnerability, $D_1(I_2(D_2))$ which will lead to an effort by P_2 to make the invulnerability invulnerable, $I_2(I_2(D_2))$, and so on, and so forth. So, what is the conclusion?

As long as the following two axioms hold, the conclusion is clear: it does not help either.

Axiom III: For *value* invulnerability can never compensate completely for destruction.

Axiom IV: For *force* destruction can never compensate completely for invulnerability.

Put simply: It is easier to destroy value than to protect it; it is easier to protect force than to destroy it (completely). But this means that the two parentheses inside parentheses will never be equal to, or even come sufficiently near to, D_2 and D_1, respectively. Unprotected $D_1(D_2)$ may be, perhaps, like $0.9D_2$, but with protection $D_1(D_2) - I_2(D_2)$ may be like, say, $0.5D_2$ — in other words far from good enough. Already one Hiroshima bomb is one too many — and humankind does not accept the type of geno-fascist lingo engaged in by some representatives of one superpower.

Hence, the conclusion is that this does not work either. Let us therefore try something new with the hope of seeing some exits. Let us introduce the old distinction between offensive and defensive weapon systems, and simply define them in the following way:

> *defensive weapons* have such short range and limited impact area that they are essentially only useful on one's own territory;
> *offensive weapons* are those weapons (systems) that are not defensive.

The definition hinges uniquely on objective capability; there is no element of subjective motivation in it. With offensive weapons aggression is *possible;* whether, in fact, they will be used for aggression is another matter.

Let us use the symbols d and o for defensive and offensive respectively. This changes the content of Table 1. More precisely, what is called D_1 and D_2 — counter-value destruction — becomes D_1^0 and D_2^0; for these are offensive capabilities, by definition. And counter-force and invulnerability-force splits into two, for offensive weapons and for defensive weapons, so that we get:

Table 3.6   Community security: the 12 key variables

	Invulnerability value	*Counter-value*	*Counter-force*	*Invulnerability force*
$S_{1,2} =$	$I_1 -$	$\left[\; D_2^0 \right.$	$\begin{array}{l} - [D_1^d(D_2^0)- \\ - [D_1^0(D_2^0)- \end{array}$	$\left.\begin{array}{l} I_2^0(D_1^0)] \\ I_2^d(D_2^0)] \end{array}\right]$
$S_{2,1} =$	$I_2 -$	$\left[\; D_1^0 \right.$	$\begin{array}{l} - [D_2^d(D_1^0)- \\ - [D_2^0(D_1^0)- \end{array}$	$\left.\begin{array}{l} I_1^0(D_1^0)] \\ I_1^d(D_1^0)] \end{array}\right]$

The whole point is simply this: there is a branching-off process in counter-force activity, a defensive branch, and an offensive branch; on both sides. There is the effort to fight the weapons (force) of the enemy on one's own ground and on his; and naturally his efforts to make his weapons invulnerable when they operate offensively, $I^0(D^0)$ ($I_2^0(D_2^0)$) and $I_1^0(D_1^0)$ — and when they are still at the home base, $I^d(D^0)$.

For the most important case, D being nuclear-tipped missiles that are offensive, these four symbols stand for the following:

$D^d (D^0)$ stationary laser shields, short range anti-ballistic missiles (ABM);

$I^0 (D^0)$ MRV, MIRV, decoys, very short warning time, forward base supersonic speeds, cruise trajectories, stealth, numerous other features;

$D^0 (D^0)$ very high precision or yield, silo penetration, anti-submarine warfare (ASW);

$I^d (D^0)$ mobile, dispersing, numerous, hiding underground and hardening, on submarines, under ice-caps.

Defensive counter-force, to be worthy of the name, has to be short range (or stationery) with limited impact area, which means a high level of precision. Offensive counter-force does not operate under such limitations, is long range and could also have a vast impact area in order to destroy all the offensive capability there is. High precision and penetration capability, however, is generally seen as more efficient. Offensive invulnerability means invulnerability of offensive forces over the other party's territory; defensive invulnerability begins at home and ends at home. The last decades are the history of switching from one approach to the other, and of new technologies within each of these four possible approaches.

Let us have a look at the situation of P_2:

Figure 3.7   The strategic "game", as seen by Party No.2

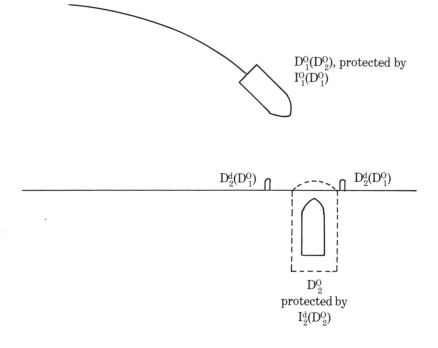

$D_1^o(D_2^o)$, protected by
$I_1^o(D_1^o)$

$D_2^d(D_1^o)$ $D_2^d(D_1^o)$

D_2^o
protected by
$I_2^d(D_2^o)$

There is an incoming, hence offensive, missile from P_1; it is counter-force, and protected. It is aiming at an offensive missile which is protected in two ways: through defensive invulnerability and through defensive destructiveness, e.g. silos and anti-missile missiles. This can also be put into a table, using the offensive-defensive distinction, and the destruction-invulnerabililty distinction:

Table 3.8   **The four approaches in a strategic "situation"**

	destruction approach	invulnerability approach
offensive approach (from P_1)	$D_1^0(D_2^0)$ "active offence"	$I_1^0(D_1^0)$ "passive offence"
defensive approach (from P_2)	$D_2^d(D_1^0)$ active defence	$I_2^d(D_2^0)$ passive defence

It is the balance of these quantities that decides what ultimately happens; the net balance in the end, of D_2^0, is what is left for a second strike.

Let us now use this scheme of analysis to try to explore five questions, all of them crucial to the whole peace and security issue:

(A) The first strike/second strike distinction.
(B) Characterisation of some offensive weapons systems.
(C) The 1972 ABM Treaty.
(D) Is this approach to security and balance of power at all viable?
(E) Is some other approach to security and balance of power viable?

(A) The first strike/second strike distinction

A typical first strike weapon would be low on $I^d(D^0)$ and high on $I^0(D^0)$ since its task is to destroy by being used first, hence it can afford to be (but does not have to be) badly protected at the point of departure, but well protected at the point of arrival. It has to be highly destructive, presumably of force since it would be dangerous to use a first strike not to try to eliminate the offensive capability on the other side — which means that it has to be high on precision, and reliable (single weapon reliability or compensation for unreliability by high numbers). The yield is less important (see table 3.9).

A typical second strike weapon would be high on $I^d(D^0)$, can be low on $I^0(D^0)$ since its task is to survive an attack, and hence has to be well protected at the point of departure, but can afford to be (but does not have to be) less well protected at the point of arrival. It has to be highly destructive, presumably of value more than of force since this would be the promised retaliatory attack that is supposed to serve as a deterrent — which means that it has to be high on yield but does not have to be that reliable; there is enough to destroy. Precision is less important.

It should be noted that if a missile is highly protected at the point of departure, in other words has a high level of "survivability", then there remains at least the option that it can be used as a second strike weapon. If it is poorly protected, then there is no choice: *use it first or else lose it!* For this reason poorly protected missiles, such as the MX in Minuteman silos or the SS18, or Pershing II and Tomahawk cruise missiles, as well as SS20s, are among the most provocative, and hence destabilising.

Table 3.9   **"Idealised" first strike/second strike characteristics**

		First strike (counter-force)	Second strike (counter-value)
Passive defence	$I^d(D^o)$	can be low	must be high
Passive offence	$I^o(D^o)$	must be high	can be low
Active offence	D^o	precision, reliable yield	less reliable

It should also be noted that when a missile has multiple war-heads, in other words is mirved, then one missile can destroy more than one on the other side. The exchange ration is greater than 1, whichever side strikes first will have more missiles left because it can destroy more than are used up. Mirving, hence, is not only a mechanism for offensive invulnerability, or "penetration capability"; it is also a way of achieving a better trade-off, and hence highly provocative, and hence destabilising.

Thus, *in the construction of the system there is already the main message;* the system carries a genetic code, so to speak. It is quite clear today how a first *strike* and a second *strike weapon should be made. This should not be confused with first use* or second *use,* that is a question of who starts any kind of nuclear exchange. Nor should it be confused with whether the first strike is *effective* or not, in the sense of eliminating sufficient nuclear capability on the other side to make the losses that side can inflict tolerable. To achieve this a high quantity would also be necessary. These are all questions of the broad strategy of the two parties, with mixes of threats of use and actual use, time orders, etc. — only partly derivable or guessable from the nature of the weapons systems as such. The only thing that is relatively certain is that both parties will do their best not to have their own strategy determined by the other side, and try to retain strategic options.

(B) Characterisation of some offensive weapons systems

The most typical first strike weapons, not yet existing, would be highly precise and reliable missiles, highly mirved, clustered together in large numbers and poorly protected (and hence with very low survivability) close to their target (for a surprise attack). And the most typical second strike weapons would be less precise and reliable, with single warheads, highly dispersed and very well protected, for instance in a submarine, under the ice-caps.

Of the systems existing today, or forthcoming, if one is to rely on the information about them, those that come closest to being first strike weapons seem to be the MX and the SS18, because of their low survivability and high level of accuracy and penetrability, through mirving (up to 10?). Next would be the Pershing II; it has only a single war-head but compensates by proximity to target and high speed and hence short flight time, 12 minutes or less, with very high accuracy, having a terminal guidance system. If it were even more forward-based than in Western Germany, e.g. in West Berlin, its first strike character would be even more pronounced. Numbers are also very important, and even though the Tomahawk cruise missile is slower, large numbers can compensate if the goal is offensive invulnerability. But this would be more risky: some of them would be detected in time and lead to a launch-on-warning. The SS20 has a somewhat longer flight time, and even if it is mirved (three war-heads), it is more likely to cause a launch-on-warning. SS20 is also mobile, like Pershing II and cruise, but so slowly that its survivability may be questioned.

Clearly a second strike capability, based on defensive rather than offensive invulnerability, is much less provative than a first strike capability. A Pershing II, and also the cruise missiles, land-based in Western Europe, provoke without adding to security since they will invite a pre-emptive first strike. In addition they represent qualitatively new approaches to the problem of making offensive invulnerability; in German terms they stand for "Vorrüatung", not for "Nachrüstung".

(C) The 1972 ABM Treaty

Let us assume that the purpose was, as usually stated, to protect a minimum second strike capability. According to Table 3.8 there are four ways of doing this:

a. cutting down or eliminating offensive counter-force destructive capability;
b. cutting down or eliminating offensive counter-force invulnerability;
c. building up or maintaining defensive destructive capability for force;
d. building up or maintaining defensive invulnerability of force.

Four additional methods are the following:

e. building up or maintaining offensive counter-value destructive capability;
f. building up or maintaining offensive counter-value invulnerability;
g. cutting down or eliminating defensive destructive capability for value;
h. cutting down or eliminating defensive invulnerability of value.

One may say that SALT I was an effort not to carry out (a) but at least to control further armament. One may also say that (d) and (e) were going on anyhow, as well as (f) (MIRVs!). Method (h) is in effect, since the contrary (effective civil protection against nuclear weapons) was and is not feasible. What was left was (b), (c) and (g). Of these three possibilities, the 1972 ABM Treaty focuses on (g) and is an effort to cut down, almost to the point of elimination, anti-ballistic missile systems. At the same time it does the opposite of (c). Why focus on (g)? Probably mainly for the simple reason that such systems did not exist and looked almost impossible as an engineering project. To hit an aircraft with a missile may be difficult enough; to hit a missile almost impossible. Systems were developed but did not impress. The treaty can be read as a joint statement: "We have tried but did not succeed, so we might just as well outlaw the approach".

The loopholes in the 1972 ABM treaty are easily spotted:

i. *The concept legitimises offensive destructive capability*, by focusing attention on a second order problem, that of guaranteeing penetration for a second strike capability;

ii. *The concept does not focus on offensive invulnerabilty*, and hence opens the way for a qualitative arms race in mirving, decoys, short warning times, forward basing, high speeds, cruise trajectories, stealth, etc.

iii. *The concept does not rule out research on defensive destructive capability* — and since a breakthrough here (e.g. in the form of a laser-shield) would increase security considerably, any country would put that higher than adherence to the treaty.

iv. *The concept is both anti-psychological and anti-human* in demanding of people that they shall abstain from a measure of defence rather than from a measure of offence, and that they shall accept that security rests, ultimately, on the ability of both parties to sacrifice their own populations through a pact of mutually assured destruction (MAD).

Clearly a treaty of this kind is not stable and will collapse the moment an active ABM becomes feasible. It is as an anticipation of this that offensive invulnerability (Pershing II, cruise) should be seen.

(D) *Is this approach to security and balance of power at all viable?*

Of course not. Axions III and IV remain valid, and as long as they are valid some destructive force will survive, and the passive defence (invulnerability) will be insufficient to balance it. Security will remain negative. But, in addition, efforts to compensate for this by at least making the security *difference* positive (see axioms I and II) will continue. There is so much work to do. Table 3.6 calls attention to 12 key variables in the arms race. There will be efforts to increase invulnerability of force and value, to compensate for this with increased destructiveness; this will be done by both defensive and offensive means. Sometimes the other party will respond on the same variable, sometimes they will try to compensate on another variable. Had there been fewer than 12, or eight variables to stick to the offensive ones, then maybe the system could be kept stable by some co-operative agreement or some third party control. With this number of degrees of freedom of the system it becomes like a system of communicating vessels: press down at one point and it shoots up at some other point or points. Or, like trying to catch a tiger by holding on to one leg: chances are the other legs, head, body and tail will start moving rather dynamically.

In short, neither high, nor equal security will ever be attainable. To some of this insecurity we are condemned, we humans, for the rest of our lives, given the nature of our innovations. Precisely because the consequences of a war are so horrible both parties will do all they can to act according to axiom II. It is highly unlikely that axioms III and IV will undergo any drastic decrease in validity in the foreseeable future. Hence I assume that as long as this logic is adhered to the strategic arms race will continue till it is interrupted by a war. The question is whether the struggle for security, and even for peace, could be steered by some other logic.

(E) Is some other approach to security and balance of power viable?

The first assumption is, of course, that both parties see a strategic war as the worst possible evil, the way it is now seen by the peace movement and probably by most of the population in Europe. In Western Europe, for instance, a nuclear war is definitely seen as worse than a Soviet occupation, by most. However much that possibility is dreaded, most people seem to think "better red than dead" — if I am dead I can do nothing, if there are "reds" in my country *I* am not for that reason red and can still do a lot. Hence they reject a policy the implication of which is "better dead than red" — the present NATO policy of rejection of no-first-use coupled with the promised Soviet answer to a Western first use.

The second assumption would be some kind of agreement as to the goal of *common security*. Here is one attempt:

By "common security" is meant a system whereby

— *both parties have as high absolute security as possible;*
— *both parties have as equal relative security as possible;*
— *both parties co-operate to make high and equal security possible.*

It should be noted, before proceeding, that these conditions are similar, but also quite the opposite of what is actually happening in the world today. Their security is very low for both, or very high negative security, insecurity, to put it more precisely. At least one party, the US, is clearly trying to obtain superiority. And rather than co-operation, there is a plethora of efforts to outsmart the other, whether out of fear or in order to have the best position for an attack, or both. And yet the games are not that different.

Let me now make a jump in the reasoning, spelling out very quickly a set of proposals, and then try to discuss them in the light of the three key ideas for common security just given. The proposals are:

  i. *No-first-use doctrine accepted by the West* (Soviet proposal).
 ii. *Withdrawal of all foreign nuclear arms* (Egon Bahr proposal) *possibly starting with 300km border zone* (Palme Comm. proposal).
iii. *Change of military doctrine to conventional arms* (Union of Concerned Scientists' proposal).
 iv. *Change of conventional doctrine to defensive conventional defence combined with paramilitary and non-military defence.*
  v. *Increasing invulnerability of the societies:*
      more national self-reliance — stable eco-system;
      more local self-reliance — stable eco-system;
      more decentralisation;
      overcoming of cleavages inside society;
      a better quality of life.
 iv. *Fighting factors that are most provative to the other side:*

in the East: remnants of Stalinism — human rights infractions;
in the West: crisis in capitalism — human rights infractions;
between East and West — new forms of active peaceful coexistence.

The last three would be typical of the kind of thinking found in the peace movement; the first three are well known proposals currently floated at the political level. The six proposals should now be tested for consistency, including consistency with the principles of common security.

As often pointed out no-first-use does not imply the end of nuclear arms: they would still remain in the countries that produced them (at present five or six countries, possibly more). Hence, the terrible logic of Table 3.5, with its insolvable dilemma of extreme insecurity, remains.

However, the value of the approach would be to build into the countries liberated from nuclear war and arms, to the extent this is possible through (i) and (ii) above, *a new security system* based on (iii), (iv) and (v), and then attempt to do something beyond that to come to grips with the conflict itself, or at least not to aggravate it further (vi). The hypothesis would then be that this type of new security system might be seen as preferable and hence spread to the nuclear powers; they might feel the alternative system offers more security than the system based on nuclear deterrence. It should be noted that (iii) is actually a transition between (i)-(ii) and (iv)-(v) so we only have to discuss the latter.

What it means is actually very simple. Let us use the symbol D^d for the class of defensive weapons as defined above, assuming that that class is much bigger than it is today, since so much inventiveness has been put into the class D^o of offensive weapons (ICBMS, IRBMs, long-range bombers equipped with stand-off missiles and long-range hunter-bombers, tanks, just to mention some important examples). Thus, the weapons that would be used under this formula would be the defensive weapons used to destroy the other side's offensive weapons, including in this both the other side's "hardware" and "software" — the military personnel. But offensive destruction, retaliation against the other side's civilian population, civilian society or even against military installations on his territory, would be out of the question since these would be clearly offensive strategies, and the distinction between weapons that can be used to hit other weapons and those that can be used to hit civilian society is more problematic than the distinction between defensive and offensive weapons as drawn here. The reason for that is simple: the defensive/offensive distinction is tied to the notion of a geographical border which in most cases in the world, in connection with international war, is relatively unambiguously drawn, whereas no such unambiguous border line exists between military and civilian society anywhere in the world. On the other hand, the border criterion may also be too rigid: it is the overall military posture that should be unmistakably defensive.

Thus, the defensive weapons would be anti-weapons, counter-force, by and large on the assumption that they are used on one's own territory, when the enemy is in the country, up to any level, including anti-anti-anti weapons, and so on. But, in addition to this, invulnerability would certainly remain as a part of the defence concept, including the invulnerability of one's own destructive weapons. And in addition to this again would also come non-military defence, meaning defence not directed at the destruction of the intruding adversary, but at rendering what he wants for his own enrichment, or to control, useless to him — in other words some type of withdrawal.

Hence, under this concept one would be left with an arsenal looking in terms of our formulas somewhat like this:

$$(6) \qquad D^d(D^o),\ D^d(D^o(D^d(D^o)\,)\,)\ \text{etc.};\ I,\ I(D^d)$$

What would be obtained with this type of "disarmament", or maybe rather "transarmament", since there would certainly be both arms and armour involved?

First, the threat function would have been eliminated, since nothing of what is included under (6) above can be used with any efficiency abroad. It does not affect any other country's security as there is no destructive power than can be used in any other country. This is rather important since a major factor behind the arms race certainly is fear, fear that the other side's effective destructive power is higher than one's own and that the only thing to stay his finger before it pushes the button would be his fear of even more destruction in his own land. When there is no offensive power than can be directed against oneself, one's own security becomes equal to the level of invulnerability, undiminished by any destructive power. One may also put it differently, in a way more meaningful to the mathematically minded than to other people: destruction as measured by D-I becomes negative when $D = O$.

Second, there is less problem of conversion of military hardware or software. Transarmament is an easier process from this point of view than making swords into ploughshares. Military people will still be military people but with an unambiguous defensive function. Offensive arms will have to be scrapped but defensive arms would still be made. Whether the military budget would be higher or lower is a separate and important question to be looked into: some data seem to indicate that it could be lower, even considerably lower. In that case some funds should be released, possibly to be used for development purposes, within or without. As will also be indicated later, there is some positive relation between invulnerability and development, at least for some range of variation, and with some definitions of these two concepts; and that may make this type of conversion a very interesting proposition indeed.

These are two rather good arguments, and might lead one to ask the question: since this looks so rational why do not all countries have defence of this type, in other words a defensive defence? One reason for that, of course, is that many countries are not only defensive, they *are* also "offensive", meaning aggressive. Only recently did they submit to the idea of referring to their ministries of war as ministries of defence, but they continue intervening and invading abroad. A transarmament, not only of the name of the ministry but of what it administers, would draw a much sharper demarcation line between truly non-aggressive countries and aggressive ones, and that would not be in the interest of the latter, for which reason they would try to resist it. Any country that transarmed to defensive defence would unmask potential aggressors; in itself a rather important function of transarmament. However, more important in this connection is another line of reasoning.

The point is simply that most countries today, most "modern" countries that is, are so vulnerable that they cannot risk destruction on their own territory. Only highly invulnerable countries can take that risk, the invulnerability compensating for much of the destructive power. We actually get four different types of countries as indicated in the diagram below:

Figure 3.10
The relation between defensive/offensive and invulnerability

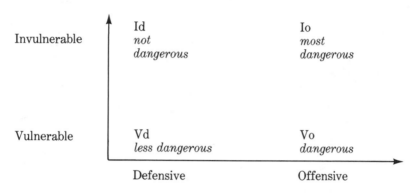

(It should be noted that this is not the same diagram as that used to define security: in that diagram own level of invulnerability is related to the destructiveness from the other party; here own level of vulnerability is related to one's own type of weapon system).

The "best" country from the point of view of a disarmament or transarmament process would be a country of the type Id: high level of invulnerability, and mainly defensive weapons (meaning low level of offensive weapons, high level of defensive weapons). Nobody else should have anything to fear from that country since it is incapable of bringing about any destruction outside its own borders, and it should also feel quite safe at home due to its high level of invulnerability, in other words not be tempted into any pre-emptive actions, to secure supplies, to divert attention away from internal contradictions, etc.

The vulnerable countries in the diagram would be thus tempted; the Vo-type (vulnerable, with offensive weapons) might carry it out because it has the capabilty of doing so. This is the type of country in whose interest it is to export the theatre of war; it simply cannot afford to have the war inside its own borders. It might export the war to the adversary's territory or, if that is too dangerous, to a third country. An adversary Vo country may do the same. One particular reason why this type of country is dangerous to its environment is that it would be tempted to strike first because of its vulnerability, making use of its offensive capacity — for instance with the hope of eliminating any second strike as retaliation from the other side.

The fourth type, however, would be the prototype of the aggressive country; making itself invulnerable at home, equipped with an offensive capability like dashing out from a hardened redoubt, striking hard, hitting many places before returning to safety back home (whether this is done by cavalry or nuclear missiles); waiting for a "retaliation" against which it is well protected. Which only goes to show, once more, how significant the introduction of the variable vulnerability-invulnerability is in any power analysis — Djingis Khan knew this.

No doubt invulnerability is tantamount to some kind of armour between oneself and the rest of the world; and a defensive weapon system means using destruction, including killing of human beings, as an acceptable option in utter distress, with the adversary already invading the country. From an ideal pacifist point of view these are not acceptable options. It would be much better to be totally open, *perhaps even using vulnerability as invulnerability,* and having no means of destruction at all — and the present author might personally prefer this. However, there is one important problem: regardless of problems of efficacy there is the problem of credibility. Very few people believe in the pacifist option, one reason being that it has so rarely been tested (Ghandi, Martin Luther King) and when it was tested one may argue that the cases are atypical. And that would of course be the third reason to favour this type of transarmament option: many people might believe in a defensive defence posture combining conventional, para-military and non-military elements.

The question to be explored then is whether this constitutes a system not only of security, but of *common* security in the sense defined above. It is easily seen that this is the case if both parties adopt defensive defence as their military posture and add to this a high level of invulnerability. They are both secure, and in a sense the problem of how equal the security is does not arise. However, there is always the possibility of cheating, of hiding some offensive capability; and/or of having it in the open, legitimated as needed for interdiction of supply lines etc. to support an attack on one's own territory. Still, with an overwhelming overweight on defensive capability it can be argued that security is not only high, but equal, or equal for all practical purposes.

More important, however, is the question of whether it is co-operative. Here are examples of co-operative tasks; there are three of them, coming neatly out of the logic presented:

— helping each other get rid of the existing, mutually threatening, offensive capability — seeking it out and destroying it;
— helping each other develop defensive capability, exchanging information, with the possible exception of concrete location;
— helping each other to become less vulnerable, e.g. by:
    promoting national self-reliance,
    local self-reliance,
    technological diversity.

To the first task the logic of a World Health Organisation smallpox eradication campaign would apply: seek and destroy (which may work for a virus; the malaria mosquito is more tricky and the campaign may strengthen it in a more immediate way). Obviously, this will only happen if offensive weaponry is really seen as a common enemy, and the thesis of the present paper is that that in turn will only happen if alternative modes of producing security have been found.

To the second task and the third task there is also a corresponding World Health Organisation logic: secondary prophylactic medicine in the sense of building strong bodies, e.g. through better nutrition and level of living in general, but also through inoculation (which would correspond to invulnerability). The countries of the world are co-operating in WHO with all its weaknesses; it is suggested that whether they co-operate or not depends on whether they see it in their own interest or not.

But this means that there might be more ways in which the United Nations could come into the picture than has been the case so far: not only detecting and controlling and, if at all possible, destroying offensive capability, but also in developing defensive capability and invulnerability. And one approach to mutual invulnerability would be through the United Nations peace forces in the Palme Commission corridor.

In short: security and balance of power are possible. But the condition remains that of getting rid of offensive capability.

4

Disarmament

1. On the general theory of disarmament

I think the general theory of disarmament has still to be written, which is not strange given the practice of disarmament has been so miserable. But that does not mean that one cannot speculate on what such a theory would look like, which would be the major chapter headings, so to speak.

The first distinction to be made would be between *goals, processes* and *indicators* of disarmament. To start with the latter: if the disarmament means the reduction of destructive power then the indicator of disarmament would be the reduction of the indicators of destructive power — one might then discuss whether this means net power or gross power, potential power or actual power as defined in 3.1. As is evident to everybody, this type of indicator has not shown any decrease in our generation, after the Second World War; hence, there must be something wrong with the disarmament goals or the disarmament process or both. Since disarmament negotiations in disarmament conferences are seen as the major carriers of the disarmament process this may be one important place where things go wrong, and that is the topic of the next section.

Let us then focus on disarmament goals — what is the whole exercise about? Here a second distinction should be made, between *military preparation* and *military action* — the release of the results of military preparation in the actual use, or threat of use, of destructive power. To simplify, let us leave out the threat aspect for the time being, and rather focus on the distinction between preparation and use. Preparation is also often referred to as "armament" and — when there is more than one party — as the "arms race", however inexact that translation may be. There may be armament without an arms race as the two parties may be engaged in parallel processes that only look like an arms race, like two runners on separate tracks in different parts of the world, but monitored by television so that it looks like they are competing with each other. Also, there may in fact be an arms race without an increase in the levels of armament (meaning levels of destruction power): it may take the form of "modernisation" while at the same time reducing the level of destruction, for instance by discarding two old warheads for each new, modern warhead deployed.

How, then, should one conceive of military preparation? Here a third distinction should be made between the various *weapons systems* on the one hand, and the *preparation process* on the other. For the present analysis we shall make use of the distinction between eight different classes of weapons systems, three of them conventional and the next five weapons of mass destruction already indicated in 3.1 above, keeping in mind the possibility of new weapons. And as to military preparation: it obviously ends with *deployment* where by the weapons are ready to go, targeted on the adversary. But before that there will be *training/manoeuvres*, before that *production/stockpiling*, with a sideline referred to as "proliferation", a particular term used in connection with military preparation for trade and secondary production in other countries. Before that again, however, there will have been *development/testing*, and before that *research*. All of this is very similar to the ordinary production and distribution process for economic goods/services in general — with training/manoeuvres corresponding to demonstration exercises and publicity for products and deployment to their display in shops etc. The use of these means of destruction would then correspond to the use of means of consumption, in other words to end-consumption itself.

However, before this happens there has to be a *military-bureaucratic-corporate-intelligentsia-complex* (MBCI-complex), with the military part of it divided into military organisation and military human power. And before that again there is the whole underlying ethos, the code or more or less explicit programme directing the whole exercise — here referred to as (military) *doctrine*. A long chain, with a strong inner logic, not easily broken.

If we now combine these two major dimensions of military preparation, the weapons systems and the preparation process, and in addition add the ultimate purpose of military preparation, military action, then we get a formidable looking table of combinations that contains the various points of attack for a possible disarmament process — in other words a table of goals of that process (see table 4.1).

In passing, it should be noted that very often military action or use of force are not considered in conjunction with the preparation process or "armament". Action, a euphemism for war or the threat of war, is seen as the subject of the laws of war; armament as the subject of disarmament. But these two goals, that of reducing the impact of the destructive power during a war and that of reducing the destructive power itself should be seen in conjunction, even as a continuation of each other since that is the logic within which they fit. They do not come in two separate compartments. It will also be seen that several important disarmament proposals today in fact deal with both at the same time (zones, no-first-use).

The ultimate goal of disarmament is *general and complete disarmament*, meaning all over the world; complete in the sense of doing away with all links in the chain of the preparation process for all weapons systems. An ambitious goal indeed, and it is not even clear that the goal is meaningful — a theme to be taken up in 4.4 below.

Looking at the preparation aspect, a distinction can now be made between three levels of disarmament goals, starting with the most ambitious: *elimination, cut,* and *freeze*. *Elimination* is the clearest and also morally the most satisfactory; it simply means total prohibition of any one

Table 4.1   The goals of disarmament: the weapons systems and the preparation process continued

	Doctrine →	Organisation Military M⊕I: Research → Human power	Development → Testing	Stockpiling Production → Proliferation	Training Manoeuvres → Deployment →	Action
conventional	Piercing/ impact					
	Incendiary					
	High Explosives					
mass destruction	Chemical/ Toxic					
	Biological					
	Radiological					
	Nuclear					
	Geophysical					

or more of the 56 combinations indicated in the table. Actually, it should be noted, lest one should imagine that this is a question of 56 jobs, that each one of them is subject to considerable sub-division, counting at least 40 different nuclear weapons systems, for instance.

The next level, the *cut*, is more modest, which should not be confused with being more realistic. It can be expressed in terms of absolute or relative numbers, cutting out so many weapons of this or that type, or such and such a percentage — for instance 50 per cent (the Kennan/Gayler proposal for the nuclear armoury, across the board). And then there is the most modest (but again not necessarily most realistic for that reason) proposal: the *freeze*, contenting itself with the *status quo*, "let us at least not proceed further with the armament process/arms race", usually hoping that the freeze may later be transformed into a cut, later to be transformed into elimination.

There is another important distinction with disarmament goals: the *geographical dimension*. The distinction would be between universal and regional disarmament goals, the latter usually referred to as the *zoning* approach. However, there is a built-in set of constraints in the very concept of a zone that should not necessarily be left undisputed. A "zone" usually implies two important traditional considerations: that the countries included in the zone are geographical *neighbours*, and that they agree simultaneously on the creation of the zone — in other words that this disarmament process is *synchronic*. Neither condition is necessary and might even be harmful to the process. Hence, one could imagine another regional (as opposed to universal) approach: the *club*, where member countries are not necessarily contiguous and do not necessarily enter at the same time — the process could be *diachronic*.

Let us then turn to the rather important action aspect. There is something corresponding to the elimination-cut-freeze dimension. However, *status quo* is rarely stated as a goal ("let us at least not use worse weapons than we used last time"). Elimination is stated as a goal, it takes the form of *prohibition* of one or more weapons systems, also referred to as *no use*. And then there is something between *no use* and *status quo*, just as the cut is between elimination and freeze: *no first use*. A mutual no-first-use pledge for all parties in a region and for all weapons systems is tantamount to a mutual non-aggression treaty.

Then, just as there is the geographical dimension in connection with the preparation aspect there is a *target dimension* in connection with the action aspect (actually, the geographical dimension also applies to the action aspect, e.g. the idea of neutral). The target dimension is an effort to withdraw some possible targets from military action. We can use the typology of targets introduced in 3.1 (also see the typology used in 1.2), but in a slightly different order and with two important sub-divisions:

> Military targets (weapon systems)
> Human beings, military
> _____
> Human beings, civilian
> Societies (human-made environment)
> _____
> Environment

For a long time the distinction between military targets and military people on the one hand and non-military targets and people in general on the other has been the basic dichotomy on which the laws of war have been founded: the former are legitimate targets, the latter not, or at least not for the most cruel weapons systems. Recently the environment has also been seen as "taboo", a consideration deriving from the vulnerability of the environment, the fact that the environment is the basis also for human existence, and possibly the notion of environmental "innocence". Total warfare has tended to obliterate the distinction between military and civilian targets, not only because of the high destructive power of modern arms making it nearly impossible, but also because the civilian sector is so obviously supportive of the military sector. The effort to set the environment aside may be seen as a last ditch approach, "let us at least maintain the basis for possible recovery", and also as an expression of a notion of freeze: "let us at least not expand warfare into ecocide" (strictly speaking this means historically "let us at least not repeat the Indo-China wars, and rather revert to the level of warfare in the Second World War").

Of course, there are other dimensions that could be introduced, subdivisions that could be made, but this will do for the present purpose. The goals of disarmament are presented, from the most ambitious, meaning universal elimination of all links in the preparation process for all weapons systems, and in addition to that prohibition of all kinds of use — to the most modest little effort, geographically limited, for one weapons system only, for only one link in the preparation process, and with a modest target denial for military action. The gap is so tremendous that one might hesitate in referring to the whole range as "disarmament goals", but we shall stick to that use of the term.

What should be emphasised, however, is that some boxes in the table are considerably more modest than others. Obviously it is more important to eliminate, cut down or even freeze weapons of mass destruction than conventional weapons. But it should also be pointed out that there is a similar differential along the preparation process axis. It is much more productive to attack the process at the early stages, the first links in the chain, than at the other end. Thus, disarmament in the sense of elimination of certain types of deployment (also called "stationing") is important; it means that the weapons systems are no longer targeted. It could be referred to as *distargeting* rather than disarmament. But the weakness of the approach is obvious: if the whole preparation process has been run through and the weapons are fully produced and stock-piled and the training/manoeuvres have been engaged in, then deployment is only a question of logistics, particularly if all the preparatory steps in terms of communication, control and command (that actually are a part of deployment) have already been taken. The last link in the process is most easily restored.

It helps a little if one more link in the process is rolled up: training/manoeuvres. It means at least that the time lag will be greater because of lack of training. As a consequence there may be more hesitation in actually using the weapons. But again the time lag is a minor one.

However, needless to say, it helps considerably more if the weapons are not stockpiled and the production process in fact has not gone beyond the development/testing level. In that case the weapons are simply not available beyond some prototypes. Hence, this would be a major disarmament goal, a major dividing line in the whole preparation process.

But it is not the only dividing line. If the capacity for research and development/testing is available then all that is missing is the go signal for production. Hence, if in addition these two links could be eliminated — in fact eliminating development/testing would already help — one would be considerably closer to a more comprehensive disarmament goal. Researchers are absolutely crucial in the whole process. They are responsible for a qualitative arms race just as the producers are responsible for the quantitative arms race. They even have a name for it: "modernisation".

However, there are still two links to go. At the beginning of the process stands the formidable military organisation itself, with its organisation including the capital that is put into it and all its human power, in sheer numbers. And closely linked to it is the bureaucratic-corporate-intelligentsia complex as far as military matters are concerned, together constituting the MBCI-complex. The power of this basic nucleus around which modern societies are built is of such a magnitude that, unless something is done about it, it will be capable of regenerating any interrupted military preparation process. In the mind of the present author this leads to the not very original conclusion that something has to be done about the MBCI complex, but given its strength, the "something" cannot be its elimination, only a freeze or at most a relatively modest cut. The approach has to be another one, that of giving it other tasks for which it is equally capable, but tasks that are less dangerous — this will be taken up again in 4.4. below, and in 5.2.

Finally, at the end of this train of thought, at the very beginning of the preparation process is the doctrine itself, the whole framework of thought from which the process derives its intellectual nourishment and moral legitimation. It is this doctrine that is underlying the type of thinking discussed in chapters 2 and 3 above, particularly in 3.1. So my second and rather basic conclusion in this connection, adding to the conclusion about the MBCI complexes, is simply this: *we shall make no headway whatsoever unless the military doctrine undergoes some change* — and it is obvious that by this I mean a change in the direction of the type of thinking developed in 3.4. This is where there will be most resistance, but also where real gains can be made.

With the aid of table 4.1 we are now in a position to situate not only existing agreements on disarmament, (see end of next section), but also to situate current proposals (see 4.2). Suffice it here only to say something about the movement against stationing of intermediate range, land-based rockets; the nuclear freeze; proposals for nuclear weapons free zones; and proposals for no-first-use of nuclear weapons.

The peace movement has focused on the first of these four issues, then embraced the next two, and is at present looking more closely at the fourth proposal. It is quite clear in which box the *resistance against the deployment/stationing of the 572 launchers* (the number of missiles is much higher) is located and that in a sense puts it in perspective: it is actually a very modest, very limited proposal. It simply amounts to the following: *at one point we have to say stop,* and this is it — thus the new peace movement started. Let it only be added that even if the movement succeeded in obtaining this goal, all that would have been obtained would be distargeting, not disarmament in any broader sense. The training manoeuvres will continue in Canada unless the Canadian peace movement succeeds in stopping them, meaning that the whole preparation process falls short of only the very last — but politically very important — step. It says something about the strength and determination of the forces on the other side when even this modest level of resistance meets with such heavy counter-resistance.

The *freeze proposal* goes further. It says: let us draw a line and stop where we are right now, let us not go one step further. This would include the movement against the deployment of the new missiles, and would then expand to all other nuclear weapons systems, and in principle all the way back in the preparation process up to but possibly not including, the research link. In other words, there is to be no further development and testing, no further production, no more training/manoeuvres. In other words, it is much more radical as a disarmament proposal.

This also applies to the *zoning proposals* of which there are currently very many. As opposed to the other two, this proposal also extends into the action aspect of military activity, declaring certain regions of the world (in the sense of a zone or in the sense of a club) to be off limits for nuclear warfare (neither as a sender, nor as a receiver), and then extending backwards in the preparation process chain so as to eliminate any deployment (preferably including communication, command, control), training/manoeuvres, production/stock-piling, and development/training. Whether it also includes research is perhaps not quite clear in all cases, but it is very clear that such proposals extend over the entire range of nuclear weapons systems. It should be noted that this is a much more radical proposal than the freeze proposal because the case of a war is also included and because it is an elimination (or no-build-up proposal), not only a freeze proposal. On the other hand, whereas the freeze proposal is in principle universal, the zone proposals are in principle regional as steps towards universal results.

The *no-first-use of nuclear weapons* approach apparently focuses only on the action aspect, but in practice extends way back through the preparation process chain, if it is taken seriously and not merely seen as a declaration and a piece of paper. If nuclear weapons are not to be used first, then it is their deterrence role rather than their fighting role that is to be emphasised. But this means that the fighting capacity has to be taken care of with conventional means. Looked at in terms of the preparation process, it means withdrawal of nuclear arms, strategic and tactical, from the theatres of war, including training/manoeuvres with them, and their return to the homelands from which they came, the superpowers themselves. But it also means, concurrently with this, the build-up of conventional forces including training/manoeuvres and deployment of conventional weapons. Formulated this way it simply means a substitution from nuclear forces to conventional *combat* forces, keeping the nuclear deterrent in reserve in case the other side should break the promise not to be the first. If both of them keep the promise, this is tantamount to saying that any war in the future would be a conventional war. Formulated this way, however, it leaves untouched the problem of whether the conventional build-up should include offensive or only defensive capabilities, a point to be developed later. The basic point here is only that the no-first-use of nuclear weapons approach is the only one of the four mentioned that goes all the way back to military doctrine and for that reason can be seen as far from modest; it may in fact be the most comprehensive one of them all. But this does not mean that the four proposals in any sense should be seen as alternatives to each other. They complement each other rather well as approaches around which the peace movements could focus their politics.

2. Why disarmament negotiations fail

The most remarkable fact about disarmament negotiations, as they have been known from 1932 onwards with the 50th anniversary in 1982, is that they fail. By that is meant the following: they do not contribute to the reduction of the total level of destructive power possessed by participating states. The data immediately confirm this statement: there is an accumulation of disarmament conferences and disarmament resolutions, but also an accumulation in the participating states (and in the states associated with them) of destructive power. Of course, the correlation between these two trends does not prove that disarmament conferences might not have had some limiting effect, quantitatively as well as qualitatively, on the armament process. But that is not the same as disarmament. In fact, it might be argued that disarmament conferences through that process have served to legitimise armament, or at least to conceal or mystify it as a process. From that there is a long step, however, to the hypothesis that disarmament negotiations actually may serve to stimulate armament, and even are deliberately used for this purpose.

The interesting question is what concretely there is about disarmament negotiations that might have such negative consequences, or at least not have positive consequences. It does not help to say that there is an "absence of political will": if there had been "political will" there might have been no need for negotiations at all, matters would have been settled more automatically. Nor is it a question of blaming the goal of the conferences. "Disarmament" is not at all an impossible goal. It does not mean "disarmament down to zero level": one might have much more modest partial goals. Neither, indeed, is it a question of generalised scepticism about conferences or negotiations: not only so-called modern societies, but any human social formation would be impossible without them. No, in the centre of a critical analysis would be some particular *aspects* of disarmament negotiations as they are known today. And the argument will be made that the hard nucleus in the mass of phenomena that makes disarmament negotiations so unsuccessful is the basic rules, even axioms, under which the take place: that any disarmament process

will have to be *balanced, mutual* and *controlled.* To many these principles
sound so obvious, so beyond doubt that only he who doubts them is to be
doubted.

What follows is an effort to show how unlikely it is that negotiations
undertaken with these principles as constraints could ever succeed. More
precisely, three reasons will be given why the principle of balance stands in
the way, three reasons why the principle of mutuality stands in the way and
one reason for the control principle — and in addition to that two further
reasons making nine altogether. One might perhaps say that this is to over-
explain the issue, but failure as a fact, in this case, seems so solid that a
correspondingly solid theoretical basis for its explanation is called for.

(1) Balance is practically impossible to define. If there were only two
parties and only one weapon system, one might perhaps arrive at an
agreement as to what interval/ratio constitutes balance, given that it is a
somewhat looser concept than exact equality. But if the parties are (loose)
alliances there is already the question of to what extent some of the parties
should be counted — as an example might serve the counting philosophies
for France and for China during the last 30 years. Then, power is obviously
multi-dimensional since the parties have more than one weapon system.
How to compare one weapon system and its destructive power with that of
another system? The destructive power, in turn, may be analysed in terms
of factors such as explosive yield and precision of delivery, and again the
problem of how much of one should compensate for how much of the others
might arise.

There are two possible ways out of this quagmire, both of them
problematic, to say the least. The first would be to simplify the situation by
trying to define it as being as close to the "two parties, one system" model
as possible, e.g. "middle range, land-based rockets, possessed by
superpowers, in Europe". Within that model an agreement about what
constitutes balance would not seem impossible; what seems difficult is to
regard the model as an adequate model of reality. Hence the second
approach, making the model more realistic, bringing in more parties, more
systems so as to come closer to the real world. When this is done, however,
it becomes almost impossible to arrive at an agreement about what
constitutes balance. Thus, as long as the injunction to operate under a
condition of balance remains, the choice seems to be between an unrealistic
world image where the concept can become operational, and a realistic
world image where the concept remains non-operational. Efforts to solve
this problem by fragmentation into types of weapon systems, "strategic",
"theatre", "conventional", may *postpone* some basic comparisons that are
problematic. but that is not a solution.

*(2) In the concept of balance the notion of degree of invulnerability does not
enter.* It can be argued that this notion is as important as that of
destructive power — after all, nobody would bet on who would win of two
knights fighting a duel and only knowing about their lances and not their
armour. Invulnerability also has many dimensions, such as psychological,
cultural, social, political, economic, and ecological ones. By and large the
more modern or "developed" a society, the more vulnerable it also seems
to be, and it looks as if the more vulnerable a society, the more it tries to

compensate by adding to its offensive, destructive power. This means that one country might reason as follows: "You on the other side of the table are much more invulnerable than we are, your population is more sturdy, more used to material deprivations; hence we are entitled to some compensation for this in the form of a higher level of destructive power". Needless to say such matters are not only difficult to measure, but even more difficult to make explicit during negotiations. It would actually mean using vulnerability as an argument for higher levels of armament; obviously unacceptable.

There is another approach: the country could also be admonished to reduce its vulnerability. But that would obviously be "interference in internal affairs" as the dimensions of vulnerability cut so deeply into internal politics. In this there is something tragic: very important aspects of the whole balance of power equation cannot be mentioned for the simple reason that they are seen as belonging to the intra-national not the international domain. Moreover, they are also seen as belonging to the nationally private rather than the nationally public, if such a distinction can be made. For an ambassador from a superpower to say that "recent blackouts in my country have shown how vulnerable the population is, how easily panic strikes when electricity disappears, how theft and even vandalism takes on epidemic, even endemic dimensions — hence we simply cannot afford to have such calamities happen", would be very difficult indeed. And yet that type of unspoken argument may be under the table and above the table, only not on the table, for the many reasons indicated. However, to disregard vulnerability level would make the negotiations border on the absurd in their lack of realism. In this, however, they are supported by the leading yearbooks in the field: neither the International Institute for Strategic Studies in London, nor the Stockholm International Peace Research Institute give any information about this aspect, nor is there any indication that they are conceptually aware of it. And the unit of counting is weapons, rather than their destructive power.

(3) The principle of balance presupposes that both parties pursue balance. Granted that "balance" means approximate equality or "parity", there is a blurred line beyond or below which "superiority" or "inferiority" is located. Assuming that we are dealing with the mind of parties that are not pursuing inferiority, they can be seen as pursuing either parity or superiority. If both pursue parity, no problem. But what if they don't? They could still participate in disarmament negotiations under the principle of balance, only trying to define the concept in such a way that were it ever to be institutionalised it would nevertheless be compatible with their pursuit of superiority. Whether this is done by focusing on one weapon system, gaining or retaining superiority through a highly limited parity obtained at the expense of neglecting all other weapon systems, or by a much more multi-dimensional approach, where the realities of power become hidden in the complexities of the comparisons, is of less importance. The point here, incidentally, is not that parties to negotiations may cheat, pretending to work for disarmament whereas they actually pursue the opposite; that is nothing new in human history. The point is that the principle of balance itself makes it so easy to do this. It almost encourages deceit because of the

impossibility of defining in any mutually acceptable way the key concept of balance.

(4) Mutuality means a de-emphasis on what governments can do on their own. Mutuality means doing it together. In principle this sounds fine, but not when it is interpreted as "doing only that which both parties can do as a result of co-operative negotiations, and in a parallel manner". The United Nations is the ideal setting for institutionalising this kind of approach, with its emphasis not only on internationalism and governmentalism but also on negotiations, co-operation and parallelism — the latter as a consequence of the universalism implicit in the whole UN approach to world politics. Rules should be for all member states, otherwise they are not rules, just political behaviour. The purpose of the UN machinery is to produce rules, and to produce the kind of circumstances under which they are adhered to. As a result of this the principle of mutuality may serve as an excuse never to engage in any unilateral action, however minute, gradual and stepwise. Why should one, if multilateral action may be just over the horizon? On the other hand, that multilateral action will not come about unless through one's own consent. This means that what might be called "the Geneva process" (also found in Vienna, in the MFR — mutual force reductions — negotiations) not only blocks unilateral processes, such as US troop withdrawal under the Mansfield resolution, but also has built into it efficient mechanisms to block multilateral processes. It may be objected that this also applies to many other multilateral negotiations, which is true. But in other negotiations, e.g. in the field of health, own gains through co-operative negotiations on multilateral agreements may be more immediate, more clear, and advantages from blocking multilateral agreements negligible or totally absent. In disarmament negotiations much more is at stake.

(5) Mutuality invites comparison of power profiles, and comparisons invite armament. Weapon systems profiles, giving for each qualitatively different system the quantity possessed by the parties to a disarmament conference, are hardly ever identical, nor do they run parallel to each other. They will tend to intersect. On some systems one party is superior, on the other system the same party is inferior. There are "gaps", defined as excesses or deficits, depending on the vantage point. Such comparisons are indispensable and indeed the necessary outcome of any negotiation process under the heading "mutual and balanced". If there is no consensus about how to simplify the situation through some kind of power index, a unidimensional concept of power, one can only obtain balance proceeding system by system in two ways: reducing gaps by eliminating excesses, and by eliminating deficits — the latter usually called "catching-up". The former would lead to disarmament, the latter, obviously, to further armament and even more so if the parties agree to meet at a point above their present level of destructive power as in Salt 1 and II. And they would tend to eliminate deficits rather than excesses not only because they prefer production of arms to their destruction, but also because they in general pursue the upper rather than the lower ranges of parity — this is where the theory of arms race dynamics from 3.3 enters.

The net result of all this is a *quantitative arms race*, further stimulated through the disarmament negotiation process itself, if not necessarily by it. It is difficult to understand how it could be otherwise: the daily confrontation with minute and considerable destructive power discrepancies would necessarily lead to a desire to catch up given the tendency to focus on own deficits rather than on own excesses. Moreover, it would lead to long-term thinking: what will happen if these gaps are reduced, if in fact parities are obtained? Would that not mean that my power is cancelled, neutralised? How can I justify working for the paralysis of my own power, thereby reducing my own political space? Would I not have at the same time to consider the expansion of the power spectrum through the introduction of one or more so-far-unthought-of new weapons systems, so as at least to be ready where research is concerned *if* negotiations under the heading of "mutual and balanced" should lead to nearly identical power profiles? And with that simple line of reasoning *qualitiative arms races* are also stimulated through participation in disarmament negotiation processes, if not necessarily caused by them. Conclusion: the whole weapons system moves towards higher and more "modern" levels — the older systems being sent to the Third World. Some of this will even happen under the heading of "bargaining chips" for "disarmament negotiations".

(6) *Mutuality proceeds on the basis of what governments agree on, and that may block discussions of crucial factors in disarmament/armament processes.* Security concepts based on reliance on armament, even on offensive arms, and even on weapons of mass destruction at that, are deeply rooted in the structures of modern societies — particularly the web of bureaucratic-corporate-intelligentsia interaction often referred to as "technology". These are the concrete structures that not only produce weapons, but also the conditions under which weapons are seen as the answer. Under the negotiations technocracies are represented by governments, and they are likely to see themselves as part of the solution rather than as part of the problem. Without taking a stand on the issue, positions to the effect that "disarmament will be served through less centralised patterns of government rather than more government", "building down MBCI complexes", will not easily emerge in a setting of governmentalism. Hence, such negotiations will tend to leave intact the structures that produce the conditions that are so much lamented, and it may perhaps even be argued that this very point is a major function of the entire exercise.

However, not only governmentalism, but also inter-governmentalism will be built into the untouchable kernal of the mass of negotiation material. In the current world system, as it is reflected in the United Nations, this means superpower ascendancy. Whether it takes the expression of having the superpowers as co-presidents of disarmament negotiations, or having them negotiate all alone "on behalf of" the others, it not only reflects but also reinforces the *status quo*. Again, one might argue that this leaves intact a basic structure producing the conditions that are lamented, and precisely as an outcome of the mutuality assumption. It becomes very much like having the major drug dealers as co-presidents of a conference to curtail the traffic in drugs; the prognosis as to outcome being the same.

(7) In the dialectic between efforts to control and efforts to cheat, the latter are likely to be more successful. Even surveillance satellites have not made the earth transparent. Hence they must have stimulated a tremendous amount of underground research, development and testing, production and stockpiling, even training and manoeuvres and certainly deployment. Spy networks are certainly also operating, possibly less densely than before. At the same time there is a clear move in the direction of weapons that not only have very high yield and precision, but are also easily hidden, like the cruise missile "Tomahawk", about 6.5 metres long and 70cm in diameter. Tougher control conditions or measures will stimulate more imaginative cheating measures and a possible new generation of mini-weapons (something for Japan to make!) Control measures are likely to be more effective as stimuli than as impediments. The asymmetry between those who hide and those who seek will be even more pronounced, and it is not obvious that those who seek shall find.

(8) In spite of all of these factors disarmament negotiations have a demobilising effect on the peace movement. There is considerable faith in the world population in negotiations. They are seen not only as instruments of agreements that may lead to progress in the field, but also as symbols of emerging peace processes: at the negotiation table peace *begins*. Such attitudes, however, are merely the result of confusion of this particular negotiation table with armistice talks or talks about, say, economic co-operation. Even talks about "development" have the advantage that there is at least one definition of "development", in terms of economic growth, that is precise, operational. There are conditions surrounding all negotiations, but it is not a general feature of conditions that they make impossible that which they are supposed to promote. The same applies to the outcomes. They are to be suspected, but the peace movement will tend to embrace them in frustrated search of a "victory". Example: in the partial test ban treaty of August 1963 — actually not even an environment treaty worth the name because of seepage — the lithosphere was not included, nor the use of underground tests for the preparation of even worse arms. Given this demobilisation, much of the outside pressure to produce results will subside before the work even starts, making it even easier to produce non-results. And in the meantime new weapons appear.

(9) The conditions stimulate the growth of a national and international disarmament bureaucracy with vested survival interests. Efforts to break the armament problem into small, neat and quantifiable sub-problems give rise to a hierarchic bureaucracy isomorphic with the problems. There will be a need for weapons-counters, for system-counters, for counters of parties to conflicts, and for synthesizers. With the flow of time these groups, national and international, centred in Geneva and New York, will grow. Each meeting will be an opportunity to design the agenda for the next: each conference an opportunity to design the instruments for the next. The system becomes self-perpetuating, having considerably more than its *per diems* to lose. If a solution should ever come up it would pass unnoticed, not only because it is not in the interest of the system but also because they would not know how to recognise it as a solution, being too cynical.

In short, the prospects are bleak indeed. This does not mean that the conferences will not occasionally arrive at some kind of agreements, only that the agreements will be seriously flawed. There has to be production of agreements, there has to be some justification for the conferences, there has to be some feed-back, if not so much to the governments at least to peace hungry and peace loving populations everywhere. The following is a short list of how major, recent arms control agreements have been seriously flawed:

1925 Geneva Chemical Weapons Protocol: the efforts to control chemical warfare are incompatible with binary gases because they only become deadly when combined over the enemy (where else should they become deadly?)

1963 Limited Test Ban Treaty: it was limited to atmosphere and hydrosphere and outer space, also to underground tests releasing radioactivity beyond state borders. However, the underground tests (in the lithosphere) after the treaty were more numerous than the total number of tests before the treaty, possibly partly because there was less population reaction due to decrease in health hazards from radioactive fallout. In addition France and China were not parties to the treaty.

1967 Outer Space Treaty: The treaty outlaws nuclear weapons in orbit and their stationing in outer space. However, it does not outlaw weapons not of mass destruction, and it does not apply to other links in the preparation process, such as research.

1967 Latin American Nuclear-Free Zone Treaty: the "Tlatelolco Treaty" bans testing, possession and deployment of nuclear weapons in Latin America. However, the major problem of the Western hemisphere from other points of view is the hegemony of the United States, and the treaty freezes the nuclear dimension of that hegemony. In addition the two most likely nuclear weapons states, Argentine and Brazil, were not parties to the treaty.

1968 Non-Proliferation Treaty: the treaty bans transfer of weapons or weapons technology to non-nuclear weapons states. However, a major problem in the world in general is the hegemonic influence of the countries that are also nuclear powers; the treaty freezes this dominance structure. In addition there have been no steps to meet the Article VI and preamble goals of disarmament and the end of all testing; parties can withdraw from the treaty with three months notice if "supreme interests" are in jeopardy; and the most likely countries to become nuclear powers in this century, Argentine and Brazil in South America, India and Pakistan in Asia and the two beleaguered countries Israel and South Africa are not parties to the treaty.

1971 Seabed Treaty: the treaty bans emplacement of nuclear weapons on the seabed beyond the 12-mile coastal zone; it allows emplacement of weapons of non-mass destruction on the seabed; allows weapons of mass-destruction on the seabed that are capable of "creeping" (e.g. in submarines with belts): it allows weapons of mass destruction that are moving in submarines and ships, and allows all weapons within coastal waters of states. Again, it does not address itself to the other links in the preparation process.

1972 Anti-Ballistic Missile Treaty: the treaty limits ABM-systems to two deployment areas in the superpowers and 200 interceptors in each country (later, through the 1974 ABM protocol, this was reduced to one deployment area and to 100 interceptors in each country). The treaty does not address itself to other links in the preparation process.

1972 SALT I Interim Agreement: the agreement freezes the number of strategic ballistic missile launchers deployed and permits an increase up to an agreed level for the two superpowers. The agreement does not address itself to other links in the preparation process.

1974 Threshold Test Ban Treaty and Peaceful Nuclear Explosions Treaty: the treaties ban underground tests with the yield above 150 kilotons and bans "group explosions with aggregate yield of over 1.6Mt and requires on-site observance of group explosions over 150Kt". The treaties have not been ratified by the US Congress.

1979 SALT II Offensive Arms Treaty: the treaty limits the number of strategic nuclear weapons in several categories but allows their deployment within these limits. The treaty has not been ratified by the US Congress.

With this record, are the treaties/agreements better or worse than nothing? We shall of course never know the answer to that since we cannot re-run history. They can be said to be better than nothing because they put some limitations on some quantitative, and in some cases also qualitative, destruction-level increases. They can be said to be worse than nothing because they serve as a substitute not only for less flawed treaties/agreements and stand effectively in their way, but also because they have a demobilising impact on the peace forces that might otherwise have been or be more effective, driving more consistently in the direction towards disarmament, and possibly transarmament. The latter is actually important: the single-minded focus on disarmament also stands in the way of a focus on transarmament, having as its premise a thorough look at military doctrines. Finally, it may be said that precisely because the treaties/agreements put limitations on the arms race they also legitimise the arms race; in other words that the only argument in their favour in fact becomes an argument in their disfavour.

However the conclusion to this more theoretical dispute might be in the future, the conclusion today seems very clear: disarmament negotiations fail, the evidence is overwhelming, the theoretical basis is more than sufficient to explain why they have failed. With that in mind let us look at some new approaches in the field; one negative example, and one more promising.

3. Some proposals examined

The Palme commission

With the exception of the proposal for a 300kms battlefield nuclear weapon free zone, starting with Central Europe and extending ultimately from the northern to the southern flanks of the alliances, the Palme Commission report has passed by remarkably unnoticed. There has been almost no debate. In the following I shall try to show why: *it is not a good report*; not up to the level one should demand from such knowledgeable people in our desperately critical situation.

I shall limit my remarks to the 44 concrete proposals in chapter 6. The general rhetoric of the report is of no particular interest — what is good in it is not new and what is new is not particularly good. But the commission has among its 17 members four present and former prime ministers and five present and former foreign ministers, so these are not people, like people in the peace movement, often accused of lacking in political insight. In addition the commission (like the Pugwash Conferences) is three-cornered, with West and East and South represented, meaning that they had to — no doubt often a very difficult task — *negotiate*: not merely function as a think tank. So, what did they come up with? A brief summary is needed. (See table 4.2).

Of the 44 proposals in the Action Programme, 36 deal with arms limitation and disarmament, divided into 20 short-term measures for "the next two years" (presumably from spring 1982 when the report was made public) and 16 "medium term measures", to be achieved over the next five years. A very positive aspect of the Action Programme should be underlined here: the programme is a *process*, there is a calendar for the various parts of the arms limitation and disarmament complex. First the SALT II treaty has to be clarified and adjusted; then substantitive reductions in strategic offensive forces; at the same time the anti-ballistic missile treaty of 1972 is to be "preserved" (meaning confirmed). For conventional forces in Central Europe a first phase should be concluded, defining the problem, then to be followed up by agreements on ceilings and reduced level. Talks on the battlefield nuclear weapons free zone are to start right away, resulting in the zone mentioned and in substantial reduction in general; mininukes and ERW (neutron bombs) to be ruled out by mutual agreement, also right away. Then there is to be agreement that the parties have rough parity in medium range nuclear capabilities so that NATO can forego the 572 missiles; after that come talks with a view to more reductions, including dually capable aircraft. To prevent short range nuclear systems from taking over by simply being forward based, they are to be banned. So are chemical weapons in Europe, and all over the world, ending with a disarmament treaty.

The comprehensive nuclear test ban is also to be agreed upon in the first phase; anti-satellite weapons are to disappear through agreements banning tests and deployment, and the non-proliferation treaty is to obtain "broader adherence" in the first phase and "universal adherence" in the medium term — together with an agreement on internationalisation of the nuclear fuel cycle. A new conference on confidence and security building measures will be convened in the first phase and conclude with agreement on a second generation of such measures in the second phase. There will be talks and guidelines agreement for conventional arms transfer. Biological warfare and experiments in molecular biology with possible military applications have not escaped the attention of the commission. Moreover,

Table 4.2   The Independent Commission on Disarmament and Security Issues (The Palme Commission): Action Programme

	Short-term (next two years)	_Medium-term_ (next five years)
1979 SALT II Treaty	1. _Agreement_ on clarifications or adjustments →	1. SU-US _agreement_, substantative quantitative and qualitative reduction in strategic offensive forces.
Anti-Ballistic Missiles 1972 Treaty	2. _Preservation_	
Mutual Force Reduction, Central Europe	3. _Agreement_, First Phase, Foreign Ministers' Meeting	2. _Agreement_, on equal ceilings at reduced level, conventional forces Central Europe.
Battlefield nuclear weapons free zone, Central Europe	4. _Opening_ of talks	3. _Establishment_ of free zone, first Central Europe, then to the flanks.
Mini-nukes and enhanced radiation weapons, Europe	5. (Agreement) on non-deployment	4. Agreement, substantial reduction in Europe.
Intermediate range nuclear forces	6. SU-US _agreement_ on rough parity so that NATO foregoes "modernisation"	5. Opening _negotiations_ on reduction of remaining nuclear weapons; including dual capable aircraft.
Short range nuclear forces forward based	7. SU-US _agreement_ on banning deployment.	
Chemical Weapons	8. _Agreement_ on estabishment of CW free zone in Europe.	

Confidence and Security Building Measures and Disarmament

9. Agreement to convene a *conference* in Europe →→ 6. Agreement on a second generation of confidence and security measures.

Comprehensive nuclear test ban

10. *Agreement.* →→ 7. Opening of *negotiations* for disarmament in all of Europe.

Anti-satellite weapons: tests and existing systems

11. Agreement on ban on tests and dismantling existing systems →→ 8. Agreement on a total ban.

Anti-satellite weapons; deployment

12. Opening of *negotiations* →→

Chemical Weapons Disarmament treaty

13. SU-US resumption of *talks* →→ 9. Conclusion of chemical weapons disarmament *treaty*.

Geneva Chemical Weapons Protocol (1925); Biological Warfare Convention (1975)

14. Agreement on consultative procedures for the resolution of problems →→ 10. International *convention* prohibiting secret work on military applications of molecular biology.

Non-proliferation treaty

15. Broader *adherence* →→ 11. Universal *adherence*.
12. Agreement on nuclear fuel cycle.

Conventional arms transfers

16. Opening of *talks* →→ 13. Agreement on guidelines.
14. Universal *compliance* UN general Assembly resolutions.

Reporting military expenditures

17. Broad *compliance* UNGA res. →→

Economic security, military expenditure

18. Regional *conferences*

Public awareness of dangers

19. Launch major *campaign* →→ 15. Substantial savings transferred.
16. Military R&D converted.

Defence savings for development assistance

20. Devise specific national plans.

countries shall pay more attention to the UN resolution requesting them to
report military expenditure; this is to increase from "broad compliance" in
the first phase to "universal compliance" in the second phase. In the first
phase there will also be regional conferences around the world focusing on
economic security and reduction of military spending. At the same time
countries will make national plans about how to convert savings when
disarmament starts (and general and complete disarmament is the goal of
this commission); in the second phase there will be conversion for national
needs and development assistance. And to top it all: "a major campaign to
increase pubic awareness of the dangers of military competition, including
dangers for economic security".

What could be wrong with such an impressive list?

First, the programme shows an almost unbelievable faith in
negotiations/agreements as the carriers of arms limitation and
disarmament processes. Of the 36 proposals in this field, 19 are
agreements, treaties, and conventions to be arrived at; two are efforts to
give more life to old approaches (ABM and chemical weapons
disarmament); four are aimed at obtaining broader (and then universal)
adherence to existing agreements; and seven are proposals to open new
talks — altogether 32 or 89 per cent. The remaining four are the national
plans, the substantial savings and conversion of military research and
development, and the public awareness campaign — these are not put
forward in negotiation/agreement language. Is it a social-democratic bias
to believe that much in the negotiation approach?

Second, the *structure* of these negotiations/agreements is very
conventional. Four of the 32 are between the superpowers, from 24 that
are clearly East-West conflict oriented. Of the remaining eight there are
six that deal with what might be called North-South problems — the other
two are more general (reporting military expenditures). Perhaps this is a
correct proportion, as the most serious problems by far come out of the
Northern part of the world. But there is something paternalistic in those
six: how to limit to zero the access of the South to nuclear arms with no
guarantee that the North will have nuclear disarmament; how to
internationalise the fuel cycle. And the guidelines for conventional arms
"transfer" will, of course, stimulate greatly Third World arms production
since they are not linked to conventional disarmament in East and West
either. Thus, the total package is not only conventional, it is also biased in
the traditional way. Where are conferences of the non-aligned; of the
neutrals in Europe; of all countries but with the superpowers only as
observers; of non-governmental organisations? Has this kind of top-
heaviness ever proved effective in this field?

Third, the *content* is utterly conventional. It reads like so many
Committee of Disarmament agendas from Geneva, with the one exception
of the battlefield nuclear weapon free zone mentioned above. From the list
of consultants and papers one reason for this becomes clear: there has been
no direct contact with the peace movement. Even such relatively
conventional peace movement proposals as nuclear free zones (starting in
the North and the South of Europe, then involving the central parts) and
the nuclear freeze (that was so well accepted by the US public in the votes

of autumn 1982) have not found their way into the list of proposals. Groups capable of mobilising over two million people in demonstrations all over Europe in autumn 1981 should not be a factor to be neglected by politicians who see themselves as democratically inclined. And the literature of the peace movement is full of ideas that are more forward looking, particularly in the field of alternative defence. But the commission makes no distinction at all between offensive and defensive forms of military systems (except for some passing references), but accepts the totally unrealistic "general and complete disarmament" as their goal. Very many in the peace movement are more realistic when they see a world with *defensive* systems as a goal, not these "commissioners" (their own term) repeating an over-used UN formula (see 4.4).

Fourth, the proposals do not cut deeply enough into the preparation process. Most of them focus on the last links in that chain; none of them on the first — the military doctrine and the MBCI complexes. There is also insufficient attention to research and to testing/development. Above all there is that inner, one might even say organic dynamism of military preparation as a process which is inadequately reflected. Of all of this the inattention to military doctrine is the most serious omission.

For any one of the proposals on the list there is no difficulty seeing how it can be circumvented. Thus, any 150km zone on either side will greatly stimulate the production of "short" range systems with 300 + km range; any nuclear limitation will encourage non-nuclear offensive arms, including "modern" conventional arms (already tested in Lebanon); any nuclear test ban will encourage component testing and even more over-production to compensate for increased uncertainty about the "quality" of the product; any universal non-profileration treaty will greatly stimulate Third World nuclear autonomy and not only for civilian purposes; reporting of military expenditures will in times of economic crises be one more reason why military production has to become even more research-intensive (to save money per unit of destructive power); banning anti-satellite weapons will stimulate a race to colonise the moon as a platform or, if not, a rebirth of the now slightly outmoded and discredited profession of spying, on the ground. And defence savings for development, the great carrot to get the Third World to press for disarmament, is also rather problematic: the problems of the Third World elites may be such that they can be solved with money (e.g. more Western technology) but hardly the problem of the people. Moreover, if that money were really made available it would come with too many strings attached from the major consumers of those funds today, the NATO/WTO powers in general and US/SU in particular. They are not known as unconditionally generous.

But this presupposes that agreements are arrived at. In addition to being ineffective they are also hard to arrive at. If balance really is to be pursued or maintained then it implies comparisons so complex that the talks become endless, or obviously objectionable if a too simple formula is used; as witnessed in the talks in Geneva about land-based, middle range systems. But worse than that: the multilateralism in the approach *releases the parties from any obligation to do anything themselves,* even the smallest little unilateral step — total unilateralism being hardly believed in by anybody. They have, as mentioned in 4.2, "to wait for the outcome of the negotiations" — in the meantime they can continue increasing their own level of destructive power. Seen in that perspective the Palme Commission approach, not drafted by naive people, becomes almost sinister. They have some kind of process. The document is logical, as if written by a student for his thesis on "Current issues in arms limitation and disarmament". *But it lacks the political starter,* the thing that could set it in motion, in spite of the fact that these people are professional politicians; they are the ones who should come up with it. If each one of them had only had *one* proposal for his/her *own* country, something to start working on right away! But multilateralism protects them from any unilateral approach, from any real start.

But not even the idea of a no-first-use policy is included in the list of proposals — it had been around for a long time by the time they concluded their report in April 1982. The Russians had talked about this for many years before they made their unilateral pledge at the UN Special Session in June 1982; there was also the US "gang of four" and their *Foreign Affairs* article in Spring 1982. Of course, the Russians could cheat in a war; of course, a pledge is a scrap of paper. But that is missing the point. NATO in general and the US in particular made the unforgiveable mistake of not taking up the challenge. They could have said: *Yes,* but only if you withdraw X per cent of your tanks, and give us a little time to develop further our conventional, non-offensive defence systems (such as short range anti-tank weapons). Nothing of this kind is included in the programme. Was it too new? Were the Americans against, and was that good enough reason for not including it? In whose model did it not fit?

Leaving all the negotiations/agreements envisaged aside — is there anything else of interest? There is the *campaign,* a major one, to increase public awareness. But this almost sounds like a joke, or maybe those politicians have not discovered that such a campaign is going on all the time, that this is what the peace movement to a large extent is about, and that public debates painfully clearly show, in all kinds of countries, how much better informed large segments of the public are than their leaders? And I might add: often the social democrats are the most poorly informed. The conservatives usually have so many military people and politicians who believe in the military machine that they also have knowledge. Social democrats all over Europe have tended to accept some kind of division of labour: leave the military to the conservatives in all parties, on the condition that they let the others build the social welfare state, and on the condition that the military systems do not cost so much that the welfare state and employment are in danger. If this can only be done by means of nuclear systems, so be it — and social democracy has tended not to question that assumption. Today, however, both welfare state and employment are threatened and social democrats are looking at the equation again. They will have much to learn from the peace movement information campaign, and it would be fine if they would finance some of it. Unfortunately, they are now out of power in most places. Will they use the resting period to study peace and disarmament issues?

Then there are the eight points to promote international security. Three of them have to do with UN peace-keeping forces and are very old, but not for that reason bad. It is only strange that the commission did not come up with the obvious proposal of stationing some of these forces in the 300km belt they want — have soldiers from the South try to keep East and West from getting at each other's throat. And as to the report by the UN Secretary General to the Security Council "at the Foreign Minister" level, his "state of the international community": this would have been more interesting if the Secretary General could only be elected for one period. If he has a re-election motive those reports would hardly be very good reading.

Proposal No.38, that "the Security Council should meet from time to time outside the UN Headquarters" sounds interesting: that is where very creative demonstrations sometimes are held. But I am afraid something else is meant — and not something very important.

Finally, there are some general words about regional conferences, zones of peace and nuclear weapons free zones with no maps and borders indicated. However, the report does not stop there. Right after this tame ending, obviously not worked through by the drafters, comes the only part really worth looking at, but then not a proposal from the commission as such: the *Comment by Egon Bahr.* He suggests the withdrawal of all nuclear weapons from European states which do not themselves possess nuclear weapons including the US weapons in Britain — leaving weapons in the five (six?) nuclear states, three of them in Europe. Then he wants approximate balance in the field of conventional forces and the alliances left untouched.

This is interesting and it is to be hoped that Bahr will continue along this line, particularly in his own country. The proposal has the virtue of simplicity. It can be understood. It does not ask for balance, assuming that at the present level of overkill there is enough balance already. It is coupled to balance in conventional forces (and here Bahr — in other contexts — emphasises very much the significance of defensive weapons, that tanks can be balanced by anti-tank weapons rather than by other tanks). *And this is real politics,* as he says: "Even the intention of negotiating such an agreement would provide the world with new hope". It is, incidentally, not identical with the slogan of the peace movement, a nuclear weapon free Europe from Portugal to Poland, but lies in that direction. It can also be combined with the no-first-use pledge mentioned above as a first step, and with the non-nuclear pledge process advocated by Nobel Prize winner Alva Myrdal. It could even be started by the West as a first step.

But the Palme Commission as such does not point in such directions. It is 99 per cent a rehash of old, overused ideas, probably written by people themselves prisoners of a logic that threatens to kill us all. I am afraid they are prisoners of, rather than liberators from, the system. Maybe it merely deserves the oblivion into which it has sunk, and may serve to remove some more illusions about some politicians.

The Union of Concerned Scientists

This report, dated 29 December 1982 from Cambridge, Massachusetts, USA can be seen as a follow-up to the famous article in *Foreign Affairs* of

spring 1982 on non-first use of nuclear weapons. That article had four
authors: McGeorge Bundy, George F. Kennan, Robert S. MacNamara and
Gerard S. Smith, whereas the report has 16 signatures, among them the
German generals Krause and Løser, the British Lords Flowers, Gladwyn
and Zuckerman, and Admiral Gayler who together with Kennan has
suggested a 50 per cent general cut of all nuclear weapons systems. In
short, an important assembly of military and political expertise.

What is so impressive about this report should be mentioned
immediately: it is the only one that has come from quarters outside the
peace movement that can be said to address itself to the core issue: the
military doctrine itself. Hence the report is far broader than the titles
should suggest. It is not only concerned with no first use in case of war,
characterised in 4.1 above as a moderate and modest proposal. It goes far
beyond a no-first-use *pledge* to a no-first-use *policy*, with implications for all
aspects of the preparation process.

The premises for their thinking can be summarised in the following seven
points:

— in several actual and potential situations, from Dien bien Phu to the
  Persian/Arab Gulf where conventional forces did not seem to be
  sufficient, the USA has contemplated using atomic weapons. Nuclear
  warfare is in fact built into the assumptions, plans, organisations,
  attitudes, doctrines and programme for both the USA and NATO — in
  the final instance United States strategy is a nuclear strategy.
— the only rational function nuclear weapons can have is deterrence,
  preventing others from using nuclear weapons. To make use of nuclear
  arms for any other purpose will in the long run be catastrophic: "either
  bluff or a suicide pact".
— the present first use strategy for nuclear weapons will in all probability
  lead to a catastrophic nuclear war; it is both intellectually and morally
  unacceptable, and it has a divisive impact among the nations in the
  NATO alliance.
— there is considerable doubt as to whether the United States really will
  make use of nuclear arms against a conventional attack from the
  Warsaw Treaty Organisation countries, if the certain consequences
  would be the destruction of the United States.
— a no-first-use pledge would liberate the United States and NATO from
  the absurdity of defending themselves with a threat of suicide, and from
  the inhumanity of causing millions of deaths of innocent human beings.
— a no-first-use strategy should have a revolutionary impact on the tasks
  of the conventional forces; from top to bottom they would understand
  that the responsibility is now theirs, that there are no longer nuclear
  weapons available in order to cover insufficiencies, incompetence,
  defeat.
— tactical atomic weapons could be moved to less provocative locations
  and thereby reduce the pressure to make use of them before they are
  lost, and also remove them as major targets for enemy pre-emptive
  attacks.

The authors address themselves to the various freeze proposals, geographical (zoning), or functional ("freeze", as usually interpreted) and find the purposes of such proposals excellent, but also that they fall short of something rather important. They do *not* reject the use of nuclear weapons. They do *not* change nuclear weapons strategy, the first operational expectations, the planning. Even if the entire list of such arms control and disarmament proposals were to be implemented — these authors maintain — in the sense that they were negotiated, were ratified and put into practice, the operational and conceptual linkage to nuclear warfare would nevertheless remain the same as today. A non-first-use policy or strategy even, on the other hand, would imply that a major part or even most of the arsenals of nuclear arms would be removed from legitimate tactical and strategic planning and expectation. And this is, according to the authors, the point where the change has to be set.

In other words, it concerns military doctrine itself. They then go on attacking the idea of nuclear weapons as a reserve to be coupled to ongoing warfare even with a certain automaticity when conventional defence is insufficient. However, their proposal does not stop at this point, which is rather well-known. They also go on to elaborate an alternative with new military dispositions, affecting the MBCI complex in terms of its composition, its planning, its production planning in particular, its research, testing and development, production, manoeuvres and deployment. The whole preparation chain is involved, down to the minutiae of the instruction booklets written for the lowest levels.

Concretely their alternative is as follows:

1. make much more use of light, very mobile infantry units equipped with modern anti-tank weapons (particularly proposed by General Løser and Field Marshal Carver).
2. territorial impediments, fortifications — certainly no Maginot line — but very many small and hardened installations that can be camouflaged and randomly distributed in the territory — also with appropriate decoys. Tubes can be buried underground and be filled with explosive liquids before an attack, and then explode and function as an anti-tank barrier which would require special equipment in order to be passed.
3. bigger reserves for the army, conventionally equipped, better stocks.
4. "deep interdiction", the possibility of incapacitating troops and supplies behind the front, in Poland, Czechoslovakia and DDR.
5. more advanced technology: It is particularly a question of precision guided munitions, "smart" rockets, bombs, grenades; with reference to the wars in the Falklands/Malvinas and Lebanon in 1982.
6. defence behind the front, hardening the most important military assets, and airplanes in particular, in silos etc.

They criticise in very harsh terms present NATO planning, alleging that the flaws to a large extent derive from the circumstance that the doctrine is based on first use of nuclear arms. That doctrine itself functions as a cover-all, a carpet under which the weaknesses should not be visible.

The authors then go one step further: they calculate the costs. Least expensive are those involving construction work, which also is rather labour intensive and hence would be a contribution to solving unemployment problems. Impediments and fortification would not cost more than one billion dollars for Central Europe, and silos and airports only about 3 billion dollars. Increased stocks and reserves are calculated as high as 40 billion dollars, extra equipment for American Forces 7 billion dollars, for reserve divisions 43 billion dollars. All together this is less than 100 billion dollars over a period of six years, corresponding to a 2 per cent annual increase of NATO's budget per year, in other words less than the 3 per sent NATO decided on in 1978 and much less than the 4 per cent per year 1983 to 1988 that General Rogers, NATO's commander in Europe, wants (his alternative would cost 200 billion dollars).

In other words, this kind of proposal should bring in its wake not only much less risk of nuclear war and a considerably better conventional defence, but also be less expensive and more job creating. And, according to these authors, fully realistic: for them Soviet conventional superiority is regarded as an article of faith, a myth which they nevertheless very effectively argue against. The Soviet Union has superiority in certain dimensions, but insufficient to win a war.

Of course there are things that can be criticised also in this proposal. In the list above, for instance, point (4) is rather doubtful. Such forces (mainly aeroplanes) can also be made use of offensively, and will be seen as provocative in spite of the assurances that they are only offensive counter*force* weapons, and thus fuel a conventional arms race. The authors are actually basing their entire analysis on the distinction between nuclear arms and conventional arms, not between offensive and defensive, even if in practice they come very far in that direction. One may also miss other types of defensive defence such as guerilla and non-military defence, not to mention a stronger society in general.

In addition to this, like so many others they have no idea what can possibly be done about France — a very difficult problem in any future scenario in Europe. And the use of East Germany, Czechoslovakia and Poland (not the Soviet Union) for interdiction means treating Eastern Europe as a buffer. Will Western Europe accept being treated as a buffer for the United States in case of a Soviet attack? Nuclear strategy is a suicide pact, but for that reason also more egalitarian.

Nevertheless, this type of thinking should be welcomed as major progress. First it addresses itself to the whole preparation process. Second, it comes up with an alternative. Third, it comes from people who are themselves, or have been, in the very centre of the Western military/political planning. Of course, many or most of them are now in opposition — one does not know fully what they would do if they come into office again. But their ideas can also be carried on by others, not only by themselves. And perhaps that is their major contribution: precisely that they have ideas, they have shown military, political and social *imagination*, in times of crisis. A scarce commodity.

4. Is disarmament at all possible?

From all that has been said in the preceding sections it does not look like the prospects for disarmament are bright, and that is certainly part of the conclusion with which this section starts. The point is simply this: if disarmament has as its precondition that it should be "mutual and balanced" then that precondition itself would seem to turn any attempt towards a negative arms race into a positive arms race, in the way described in 4.2 above. If in addition the negative arms race has to be "controlled", and this even involves on-site inspection, then the contradiction between military secrecy and disarmament inspection would become a major obstacle not only in the Soviet Union but also in the United States. In short, the point of departure would be that the conditions that have been stipulated for a disarmament process are such as to make that process if not impossible at least highly unlikely.

However, this is not necessarily a reason for despair. There may be other ways out, and it may also be that the whole disarmament concept is based on some misunderstandings. Just as there is vulgar liberalism, vulgar Marxism and vulgar Christianity there is also a vulgar balance of power idea (see 3.1) and there is a vulgar disarmament idea (see 4.1).

The vulgar approach to disarmament actually comes in two versions, multilateral and unilateral, as follows (the sign means "tending towards or equal to")

(1) $\qquad$ $D_1 \rightleftharpoons 0 \ and \ D_2 \rightleftharpoons 0$ $\qquad\qquad$ $D_1 \rightleftharpoons 0 \ or \ D_2 \rightleftharpoons 0$

$\qquad\qquad\quad$ *multilateral* $\qquad\qquad\qquad\qquad$ *unilateral*
$\qquad\qquad\quad$ *version* $\qquad\qquad\qquad\qquad\quad$ *version*

The multilateral version presupposes that both are abolishing their arms together and completely, and the unilateral version takes the abolition by one of the parties as the point of departure. It has been pointed out above that it does not work this way. But what could be wrong about this, understood as a goal, or in other words: what is vulgar about it? Would it not be ideal to get rid of all the armaments in the world, and no longer have to think in terms of opportunity costs (meaning the opportunities that are lost because of all the money that goes into armament, more than 1 million dollars per minute)? Why should this not be the goal?

The argument against would be that this approach is *neither necessary, nor sufficient,* to bring about the goal that is superior to the goal of disarmament: that of *peace,* at the very least in the sense of prevention of war. That it is *not sufficient* is easily seen: *there is no built-in stability.* Armament levels may become very low on either side, but what is to prevent them from shooting up again? The obvious answer would be a detection and control machinery, that international level institution corresponding to the state in national society, having monopoly on ultimate power, or "power over power", as one might also say. Such an institution might be able to disarm everybody else and maintain them in that state of affairs, as by and large is being done inside most nation states, even the big federations such as the United States, or the Soviet Union, or India. In all three the wars of some states or republics against other states or republics would seem highly unlikely today. Thus, if India is seen as an international system with 22 states, the size of a continent, with a highly complex racial and ethnic situation, then it is remarkable how disarmed India is. The point is not that violence does not take place, but that it does not take place on the basis of one alliance of states against another. India may be a failure seen as a nation state since it proves so unable to satisfy basic needs for the most needy, yet be seen a success as an international system — far superior to Europe, for instance, which is of comparable size.

The trouble obviously, however, is that no such institution exists today at the world level and as argued above: if one of the superpowers tries to arrogate to itself that position the other superpower would certainly not agree, but only see it as one more move in the arms race. And the two together seem to be incapable of organising any disarmament. Hence, even if disarmament should take place, rearmament would be a very real possibility. And it may then be argued that it would overshoot because it is so much easier to rearm than just to arm: it is like driving on roads already known and going faster since some of the problems can better be foreseen, and some skills have already been acquired.

More significant, however, is the argument that a total abolition of all means of destruction is not even necessary. One argument might be based on equation (1) above, the idea being that invulnerability levels have to be taken into account. It may be argued that it is enough to disarm down to the point where the level of invulnerability of the other side would balance one's own destructive power so that we would get:

$$(2) \qquad D_1 - I_2 = 0 \ and \ D_2 - I_1 = 0 \qquad D_1 - I_2 = 0 \ or \ D_2 - I_1 = 0$$
$$\textit{multilateral} \qquad\qquad\qquad \textit{unilateral}$$
$$\textit{version} \qquad\qquad\qquad\qquad \textit{version}$$

The difficulty is that this type of thinking already presupposes the possibility of a war, that weapons have in fact been tested against concealment, hardening, dispersion and additional capabilities of the other side and found unable to destroy much. Of course, we do not even want that war. In a medieval tournament this would make more sense: the lances should not be able to pierce the armour lest the game becomes lethal, and if military powers require playing fields to carry out some corresponding exercise, that might also be in order. The populations in general would rather not see this kind of experiment carried out at their expense, however.

But the reason why total disarmament is *not necessary* lies not in the relation to invulnerability but in the distinction between offensive and defensive means of destruction. This has been explored in 3.4 above and will not be repeated here. The point is only that once that distinction between arms with limited range and impact area on the one hand and those with long range and/or impact area on the other, then the whole discussion changes. Defensive arms are no longer provocative, can no longer be used for attack (except against the country's own citizens, a rather important exception) meaning that much of the rationale behind disarmament as an instrument for peace at the world level disappears. Both thinking and action in this field have been indiscriminate, not sufficiently geared to the quality of the arms, only to their quantity — as reflected in equations (1) and (2) above for vulgar disarmament theory. It is unnecessary to repeat the arguments here, suffice it only to say that from a world system point of view disarmament down to the level of zero is not necessary: down to the level of abolishing offensive arms would be sufficient.

However, this position is also problematic, as witnessed by the typical United Nations stance in the UN formulation of the goal of the disarmament process:

> "General and complete disarmament under strict and effective international control shall permit States to have at their disposal only those non-nuclear forces, armaments, facilities and establishments that are agreed to be necessary to maintain internal order and to protect the personal security of citizens in order that States shall support and provide agreed manpower for the United Nations Peace Force". (art. 111, SSDI, UN 1978).

It is interesting to see that this formulation of the desirable state of affairs does not make use of the offensive/defensive distinction, but of the distinction between external and internal security. Of course, the formulaltion has been accepted by governments and they would (1) be concerned with their monopoly of force inside their own country — internal security — and (2) not accept formulations that would put severe limitations on offensive capability. Given the formulation quoted, any government can say that it needs such and such ("non-nuclear") armaments to maintain internal order, including armament with offensive capability, and thus be able to convert real or imagined internal threats into offensive capability. The worse the country internally, the worse *may* it become externally. And, a majority of such countries under the second part of the formula, involving United Nations Peace Forces, might be able to constitute such forces (since they would have more to offer having been permitted more) for purposes of their own. Thus, the formula actually puts a premium on totalitarian and authoritarian regimes, assuming that they are the ones with the most severe internal contradictions.

But this formulation comes out of a long tradition in Western peace thinking. From the late Middle Ages and onwards a number of proposals have been put forward which share, roughly speaking, the same two characteristics. *First*, there is the idea of a division of the world into two parts, the good and the bad, the former being white and European and Christian, the latter, pagan, Muslim, Turk and also Russian. Needless to say, out of such material a distinction between the liberal/capitalist good "free world" and the Marxist/socialist bad "communist world" will fall on fertile soil and be acted out as explored in 2.3.

And then, *second,* there is the idea of a world government for the nations of good part, partly to integrate and unite them, partly to defend them against the bad part, partly to integrate, "civilise" the bad part. To do this, normative and remunerative power may not be enough, coercive power may also be needed. Hence the idea of a world government with *force* at its disposal — the formulation quoted above being a pale shadow of that idea. Of course, the tradition just quoted finds a more perfect expression in NATO with communists/Russians being the latter-day successors of Muslims/Turks; than with WTO as the response to NATO. But the United Nations also has such characteristics. Originally an organisation for the

Allies against the Axis powers, later on an organisation dominated by the First World, now considerably more universal and consequently no longer thinking in terms of anything in the direction of a world government with police forces. Whoever see themselves as good are not entirely in command, and whoever are in command (such as the permanent members of the security council) are neither that united, nor in agreement as to what it means to be good.

Thus, we arrive at the conclusion that the goal of general and complete disarmament, all over the world and for all weapons, is neither necessary, nor sufficient, and may also be the product of a tradition of thinking in the Western world, probably stemming from the Roman Empire as a model, that may be not only irrelevant and meaningless, but also dangerous. So much for the *goal,* what about the *process* of disarmament?

Let us first take up one point which is closely related to the Western world government tradition for "eternal peace" mentioned above. It has been assumed, and it is still assumed, that the process towards disarmament will essentially have to be a legal one. There has to be norm-production, in the form of draft treaties, based on conferences and negotations. After that the drafts have to be ratified by the appropriate national bodies. When that is done a set of standards will have been brought into existence to classify international behaviour as "comforming", "indifferent" or "not conforming" to these standards — for instance about testing, production, and deployment of weapons.

So far, so good — this is about as far as one has come. The problem appears the moment some country has engaged in behaviour that can only be classified as "not conforming" to the standards. In that case adjudication is required, first to *verify* whether the observation was correct, second to *convict,* either not guilty or guilty. That may work with small powers, but already to pronounce such a statement about a big power in the world of today is either problematic or inconsequential. And that applies even more to the logical next step: *sentence,* and then administration of sanctions, whatever they may be. This may not even work against small powers: the experience is that economic sanctions by and large seem to lead to exactly the opposite of the consequence that was intended. And it does not help when the process has been validated by an appropriate competence group, in this case probably the United Nations General Assembly, certifying that everything has been done correctly. Structures are stronger than norms.

What is missing is, of course, a world central authority with appropriate power, including coercive power. The model taken from municipal law presupposes that at the world level there is something corresponding to the government at the national level, as has been pointed out very many times. What has not been pointed out so many times is that this missing link, if it ever were to come into existence, might be even more dangerous than the disease which it is supposed to cure. Imagine that somebody, an individual, a group/class, a country meets with the wrath of the majority deciding the sanctions of a world central authority: then there is nowhere to go, nowhere to seek asylum, nowhere to hide, barring inter-planetary and inter-stellar travel.

What is left, then, is exactly the first steps: disarmament conferences as a machinery for the production of norms in the field of armament/disarmament. Nobody would dispute that this is important, but one could only hope that since they are not backed up by any sanctions anyway, they might just as well form much better models of what the normative system should look like, eliminating all those holes and other shortages pointed out for some of the more important treaties/conventions in section 4.2 above. As it stands today the process itself is almost meaningless, not only the goal, as not even the paper formulations are alternatives.

An alternative would be a process that is more structuralist, less legalist. By this is simply meant a switch from the production of legal norms to the production of descriptions, of better understanding of how the system works. Of course, there is no scarcity of international relations research in general and armament/disarmament research in particular, much of it also found within the United Nations system. However, it could be raised to a much higher level of prominence, and used to shed even more light on the real process. What happens in the world today is that even the descriptive task is heavily resisted by the superpowers and the major military powers in either block or outside: they do not want the searchlight of empirical research to penetrate too deeply into what they are doing, and the results to shine too prominently from the highest levels of the United Nations. One exception to this might be some of the remarkably honest studies about the effects of nuclear war carried out by the UN in New York and by several other members of the United Nations family. This approach consists in drafting hypotheses, and having them confirmed or not by appropriate empirical evidence, looking at the data of the time to see whether the hypotheses are "true", "unverifiable" or "false". In other words, it would go beyond merely establishing an inventory of facts. It would also go into theory formation, thereby accumulating knowledge and the basis for adjusting the theories when something comes up that is contrary to expectations. This is known as scientific behaviour, just as what was described above is known as legalistic behaviour, and it can be used to reveal the structures and the processes of the system. Of particular interest would be a structuralist approach to study the legalist approach, in order to clarify the strengths and the limitations of that approach. It may look as if the present author thinks there are no strengths at all: this is not true. As an approach to normative production, and thereby to a model, more or less explicit, of what a better world would look like, it is not only indispensable but also most clarifying. And sometime, some places, it probably helps.

However, a transition towards a better mix between legalist and structuralist approaches, with less prominence to lawyers and natural scientists and more to social scientists, would certainly not be enough. It would only be marginally different from what the situation already is today. Much more important would be to look into the basic axioms that have been governing the disarmament process so far, "mutual and balanced". If mutual and balanced does not work, what about "mutual and unbalanced"? Here one should distinguish between two cases: that the point of departure is unbalanced, with one of the parties superior, but the process is balanced; versus the case where the process is also unbalanced. In the first case there is a simple enough formula to use: "let us both cut equally the destructive power of some kind". But what is meant by "equally"? Imagine the two sides have actual destructiveness levels of 100 units and 150 units respectively. Balanced disarmament in the *absolute* sense of destroying, say, 50 units each would mean that the other side suddenly is twice as strong instead of only 1.5 times stronger: clearly unacceptable from a balance point of view. But balance in the *relative* sense of cutting 50 per cent so that the relation becomes 50-75 might also be problematic if the stronger of the two has an invulnerability level high enough to withstand an attack with 50 units (but not with 100 units). So again we are back to the same point: the moment offensive power is to be discussed and even decreased, nothing meaningful can be said or done unless invulnerability levels are also taken into consideration. However, the percentage approach is better as a balanced way of reducing the level of destruction, even when the point of departure is unbalanced. And unbalanced multilateralism as a process can be disregarded. It is the kind of result no multilateral conference could ever go in for — it would be against the whole ethos of such conferences. They are based on *quid pro quo, do ut des,* and can only be concluded if both parties concur that what has been agreed upon is some kind of balance. There has to be balance *somewhere.*

However, whether the balance is there to start with or only in the process, multilateralism does not seem to work. From this conclusion, however, it does not follow that unilateralism would work either, if "unilateralism" is taken in the sense of one side disarming completely: no weapons, defensive or offensive, low level of invulnerability. This course seems dangerous and will in all probability lead to a quick rearmament and overshoot in times of crisis. But if we permit and even support the components of invulnerability and defensive weapon systems, one might still ask the question whether a unilateral, one-sided transition *to* that position, for instance *from* that of being a vulnerable country with offensive weapons, would not be possible? What would happen if a country, today rather than tomorrow given the precariousness of the curent situation, simply said as follows: *"enough is enough,* this situation of mutually assured destruction is MAD, we have to get away from it. Somebody has to be the first and we are willing to do it, not only by decreasing our offensive weapons systems, but also by increasing the defensive ones, and our level of invulnerability!"

It should be noted that the position associated with the British Labour Party, which is today in opposition, so far only covers the first point: that of nuclear unilateral disarmament. There is no agreed alternative. And it is usually this kind of unilateralism people have in mind, unilateral disarmament rather than unilateral transarmament. But *unilateral transarmament* would be a much stronger position, certainly easier to defend intellectually, and also — it seems — to carry out in practice. Above all, a much more secure position than the nakesness of unilateral disarmament.

So, imagine that one country or a group of countries announces this as their intention and takes significant steps in that direction. Would it be naive to hope that some country on the other side could then follow this up, and also undergo a process of unilateral transarmament? If this should happen, one could talk about *multilateral unilateralism,* which would be a third approach, distinct from both multilateralism, and unilateralism, and with a *prima facie* plausibility considerably higher than either. It should be noted that it brings in a different paradigm for defence as well as for disarmament, instead of ritualistic rocket counting and conferences to establish "rough equivalence" in search of the plateau from which joint descent, in a balanced and controlled manner, should take place. There is now *a process that can be initiated by a country alone,* without any prior and cumbersome conference process, with uncertain outcomes. A nuclear weapon free zone based on the idea that no nuclear weapons will be sent out of the zone in return for a pledge that no nuclear weapons will be sent into it either, would be one example of unilateral nuclear disarmament, which may or may not be combined with a transarmament process. But this "may or may not" is rather important, and may actually be the crux of the matter. If zoning is combined with transarmament, it may be so attractive from the point of view of security that others will imitate it as soon as it is initiated by some country, including imitation by those on the other side. Only in that case would it become a "multilateral unilateralism" *process,* not merely the original approach chosen by one audacious actor alone.

And this is what now has to be discussed, and not only by the military establishment, but also by the anti-military anti-establishment. From the fact, now well established, that the multilateralism of the former does *not* work, it does not follow that the unilateralism of the latter *does* work. There is a third position, based on *transarmament rather than disarmament* and *mutual unilateralism rather than simplistic multilateralism or unilateralism,* which is the approach proposed here.

What would then happen to the weapons? Generally speaking, what happens to weapons once they have been produced and stockpiled? Let us try to trace the possibilities systematically as one more way of gaining some insight into the process of disarmament/transarmament. By and large there seem to be five possibilities: they can go to war, be converted, be destroyed, be taken out of stock, or remain in stock. For each point there are a number of possibilities.

First, if the weapons go to war they may be destroyed in action; or they may survive the war, "good as new". In that case they may be destroyed after the war as unnecessary: one of the circumstances under which weapons are known to be deliberately destroyed. Or, they may go back into stock again.

Second, if the weapons are in stock they may still be destroyed. They may simply be the victims of attrition, rusting away one way or the other. Or they may become obsolescent, in which case some of them may be destroyed, others may be given away or sold to allies, non-aligned countries or even the other side, to make money. Finally, there is the possibility that new weapons are deliberately destroyed without having been in a war, and that would be the possibility corresponding to disarmament. Some comments on that possibility are made below.

Third, there is the possibillity of conversion. In this case there is no physical destruction but conversion from swords to ploughshares for civilian purposes, possibly conversion into smaller swords for defensive purposes, or even into bigger swords for more offensive purposes. The term "conversion" in itself says nothing; it is not enough that there is a conversion *from*, there also has to be conversion *to*. Obviously it is conversion for defensive purposes that would be compatible with transarmament, whereas conversion for civilian purposes would point more in the direction of disarmament. One does not exclude the other.

Fourth, there is the possibility of de-stocking, of deliberately taking arms out of the stockpile, but neither for destruction nor for conversion, nor for war. One possibility would be deployment, which is not the one compatible with disarmament or transarmament (if the weapons are offensive). Another possibility would be de-stocking for proliferation, giving/selling them to the three possible customers mentioned above.

And fifthly there is the possibility of the weapons simply remaining in the stockpile, probably the most frequent outcome. But we actually do not know. A matrix of transition probabilities from all the five states to all of the five states would be most important in the analysis of what happens to the world arsenal of destructive power.

Let us then return to the possibility of wilfully destroying weapons that are perfectly good, yet have not seen a war. How likely is this in a puritan civilisation, disinclined to destroy capital of any kind, where children are always taught to be careful about things, where there is no ritual sacrifice of material goods of any kind as one can still observe in "traditional" and "primitive" societies? How likely is that in a merchant oriented society, where goods that can fetch a market value, and even a high value at that, are seen as essential to the entire running of an economy? The future of society is seen as depending on the ability of markets to accept goods, not the ability of gods to be pleased with goods sacrificed. Of course, the probabilities are very low, except on one condition: that the wilful destruction of arms would guarantee that new orders will be forthcoming for new arms, of different qualities and preferably higher quantities so that the machinery can run in the customary direction, meaning the direction of re-armament. Again, that is precisely the type of process we do not want.

So we are up against the same thing: the more one looks at the disarmament process, the more absurd does it appear, probably because very few people ever care to think it through in its ultimate consequences. This being the case, conversion looks so much more realistic because there would not be that much destruction of capital involved. However, that conversion should of course not be for even more offensive, or equally offensive, weapons. It would have to be for defensive weapons, which is probably the easier course, or for civilian purposes. As to the latter, one note of warning should be struck against the facile idea that conversion to civilian purposes will also serve to alleviate major problems of development in the Third World. First, development problems in the Third World seem to depend more on structural change than on massive transfers of capital, for instance such as would be available by liberating funds from armament. Second, such massive transfers might even stifle development since it would permit highly unjust and exploitative structures still to continue for some time and would strengthen the top-heaviness of these structures since military funds would come with supply structures that could only be met with a demand for highly capital-intensive, research-intensive and administration-intensive modes of development. In addition to that it should also be mentioned that on top of these funds would come the two superpowers, not known for giving away funds without ties, usually specifying very clear conditions. If there is anything the Third World countries would not need today, it is exactly that type of internal top-heaviness, combined with superpower dominance.

There is still a very important aspect of the disarmament/transarmament process that has to be taken into account: who are the participants in the process? In the figure below some possibilities are indicated (two pyramids taken from 3.2 above) reflecting the conflict organisations with the first confrontations from the early part of Cold War I. As is very well known, most disarmament negotiations are between the superpowers, imposing their mental framework on the rest; then there are conferences with their clients from client countries, and then the protest countries, and then some non-aligned/neutral countries. Actually the most "sensitive" negotiations are not between the two superpowers but between one person from either — two very small people relative to the magnitude of the problems; accountable to very few — except for humanity and history.

So, what have I done in figure 4.3 is to put in another pyramid, upside down, between the other two — a naive pyramid, but so terribly important. On top of this pyramid are *people* everywhere. They have grievances, they may or may not be in line with their governments, far from perfect, sometimes insightful, sometimes bigoted. But they have one thing in common: they are afraid of nuclear war, of the threat of war, and they do not think that the problem of contemporary society is that the level of armament is not high enough (see 1.3, conclusion). But people as such can never be actors in a disarmament/transarmament process: they have to be organised. Governments (G) have a charming term for those organisations, for all political parties, religious movements, trade unions, consumers organisations, women and youth organisations, or what not: *non-governmental organisations* (NGOs). To compensate for the negation "non" in this designation a parallel one has been indicated to the right: people's organisations (PO), which makes us see governments as non-people's organisations (NPO); more or less — it varies with the country. People who can even contemplate mass extermination as "politics by other means" are certainly more non-people than people.

Under people, then, come the governments and their organisations, including the UN; and they are listed here as they appear in the book, in accordance with the theories of peace forces and security. On top are the governments of the neutral countries, then the non-aligned, then the protest countries, then the client countries, and then, at the bottom, the superpowers. And here comes what so many US citizens have difficulties understanding: it is perfectly possible for a European (leaving alone one from the Third World) to place the United States below the Soviet Union, for the many reasons pointed out in connection with the exploration of the

Figure 4.3   Who are the disarmament/transarmament actors?

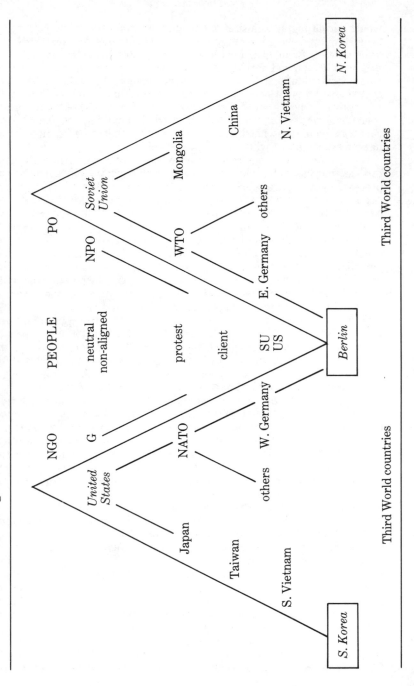

East-West conflict (2.1, 2.3), and the factors behind the arms race (3.2). It is perfectly possible to see the world this way and yet not be "communist" or "Marxist" or "anti-American" — simply out of a cool analysis of what is happening in the world. They way things are shaping up in connection with nuclear war it is not people against governments; but people *with* some governments, and *against* some other governments. The US is today (1983) worst, then comes the Soviet Union, then the client countries since they are followers, not initiators. Peace forces against war forces, but with changing borderlines and conversion possibilities all the time; a quite dynamic situation.

Obviously the point would now be to explore those forms of conferences and processes in general that could play down the role of the conflict organisation pyramids, and play up the role of that other, "naive", "upside-down" pyramid. Such conferences are today going on all over the world, inside and outside the peace movement. There are countless meetings of all kinds of NGO groups, from the most expert to the most anti-expert. The distance in terms of content of the resolutions coming from the people level and from the government level is often considerable. But that is not so important as the fact that there are so few ways in which the two are coupled together, in spite of the many excellent efforts made in the UN system to have NGO fora accompany all major UN conferences. It might be interesting to experiment with bicameral disarmament sessions, one more representative of G/NPOs and one of PO/NGOs; one of governments and one of people, to use more common terms. When resolutions differ they would have to work out a compromise between the two chambers, or make a second try. The ultimate judges are humanity and history; they cannot do worse than the present system.

But that is still for the future. More realistic would be conferences that still are governmental but with the roles turned upside down. The (co-)presidents would come from neutral and non-aligned countries that would also play major roles in the preparation of the conference. Bloc members that have evinced their ability to play a relatively independent role would also be given prominent places; for client countries the role would have to be more modest. In Europe this would call for conferences of the neutral/non-aligned, with countries like Romania and Greece. The superpowers would find their place as observers, in the corners. They will be informed of how others see the problems, and of what others intends to do, whether they agree or not. To ask them to comply or to take real action initiatives is obviously unrealistic, past records giving sufficient testimony in that regard. To those who object that this would not be "realistic" the answer is clear: it cannot possibly be less realistic than what has been attempted so far. Moreover, it does not exclude the traditional form as long as it is no longer seen as the only one. Thus, governments could learn to become more modest, handing over some of their unsolved problems to non-governmental organisations, studying what proposals they come up with, in the hope of getting unstuck.

*   *   *

Let us then try to summarise what has been said in this section. What would be the *indicator* of something positive happening? The first indicator would be a serious concentration on the offensive/defensive distinction, declaring the latter legitimate, the former not. In other words, the ultimate goal of disarmament would be less than total abolition of arms, but more than the abolition of weapons of mass destruction. The focus of the conference would be *increased security through transarmament,* this would include disarmament of offensive capability but also, when needed, armament for defensive capability and lower levels of vulnerability — among other reasons to deal with the problems of defence in a disarming world. "Arms control" in the sense of "let us at least try not to increase the arms level, or at the very least, let us try not to increase the rate of growth of the arms level", in other words controlled and thereby legitimised armament should be denounced clearly; "arms control" in the sense of diminishing "the chance of unintended war and destructiveness" possibly not (although it has a legitimising aspect). The basic point is to try to have this happen in a co-operative spirit, seeing offensive capability as a common enemy, as something to be "sought and destroyed", and defensive capability at a modest level as a common good, as something governments and people can help each other build. As mentioned in 3.4 offensive capability should be approached in the spirit of a smallpox joint eradication campaign; defensive capability in the spirit of a joint nutrition/inoculation campaign. It must become a co-operative game, security must be not only *seen* as common, but *acted out* as something common. More particularly, the very negative practice of justifying a continued arms race because some pieces of armour are needed as "bargaining chips" is to be clearly denounced.

With these as goals the *process* then has to be changed. There has to be much more involvement of an empirical as opposed to legal perspective, but not to the exclusion of the latter. International law has a very important role to fill, particularly when relations are good, and as a way of propagating norms. But it should also be remembered that international law was used to justify colonialism, to justify abuse of one's own people, and to justify offensive capability, in other words threatening neighbours in the name of "defence". Moreover, it leads to too much weapons-counting, so dear to disarmament bureaucrats, and to moralism, not to understanding. Correspondingly, there has to be much more involvement of people's organisations as opposed to governments, and among governments of those ones less responsible for the arms race as opposed to the more responsible — but not to the exclusion of the latter. *And then:* there has to be a clear view of what to do with the offensive capability and the whole MBCI-complex backing it, exploring at full speed the possibilities of conversion to civilian, defensive and (but with care) United Nations Peace Forces purposes. But a view is not enough: action is indispensable, some countries have to take the first steps towards transarmament. Others will follow, there is enough commonsense in it. In short, *mutual unilateralism* as the third option.

To conclude: it is all a question of underlying military doctrine. Only when that is fully understood can there be any progress at all in this field. Only then can the problem be attacked at the very roots of the preparation process with consequences for all weapons systems and links in the preparation chain. Only then can it be clearly understood that it is offensive capability that is dangerous, not the defensive one; that the goal is security, not total abolition of arms, and that security has to become common security. Only then can something serious be done about the basic internal driving forces, the MBCI complexes, stopping the never-ending urge to come up with new offensive arms (such as laser beams and particle beams), but not by eliminating these complexes (they are too strong for that), but by redirecting them, in a defensive direction. Hence, as the first step, to do what the peace movement is doing: to question, to analyse, to criticise the doctrine itself, including coming up with a constructive alternative — all over the world.

5

Alternative Security Policies

1. Overview: A peace researcher's guide to security in Europe

The goal of defence is security, and the idea behind security is to keep one's society as intact as possible, even if a war should come, and even if a war should be fought on one's own territory. This is a stiff bill to meet: it means the survival of (almost) everybody in the country, the preservation of society the way people like to have it, the preservation of human made things, the preservation of the environment — and preferably also the preservation of the defence organisation itself. In short, the ideal would be that the war does not touch one's own country, or if it does, only very slightly. Seen in this way which country in Europe would appear to be most secure? And which ones would be least secure?

Basically, this is a question of how likely it is that a country will be exposed to nuclear attack, and if it is, a question of its capacity to survive intact, with the capacity for relatively quick recovery.

Let us try to be systematic about this, building on the ideas of the preceding chapters to see how far, and where, they carry us. Essentially, what has been said is that security is based on an appropriate mixture of purely defensive means of defence and invulnerability. Offensive weapons are dangerous (1) because they are perceived as a threat regardless of how peaceful the motivations may be, just because of the potential capability for destruction and (2) because they invite pre-emptive strikes and retaliation. Unfortunately, however, it is not enough not to have offensive weapons on one's own territory. If one is linked in an alliance to a superpower (or another power for that matter) that has offensive weapons and might make use of one's own territory, in times of war, as a launching platform — using airports for long-range bombers; using sea ports for surface ships and submarines that may be used for launching missiles from within or without the territorial limits; using navigational devices, etc to guide and warn either of them — then one is objectively a part of the offensive system, regardless of whatever protestations are made during the times of peace. It is all a question of the *degrees of coupling* to the superpower in question: if one's territory is going to be used, then it is going to be used, whether it is by consent and according to a plan already agreed upon in peace, or according to rapid, panicky, even enforced decision-making in times of war.

Hence, the first component in the formula for security would be the extent to which the country can be said to be *low on offensive weapons and high on defensive ones.* Obviously these are two different dimensions, even independent of each other: a country may be high on both, low on both, high on one, low on the other. Only one combination offers protection and is not threatening: high on defensive weapons and nothing offensive. But moves in that direction may also lead to higher levels of security; in other words *transarmament,* even if not carried out completely.

Decoupling from the two superpowers would be the second key component of security. It is not obvious that in addition it has to take the form of neutrality, in other words absolute impartiality, not even taking a stand in any underlying conflict, for instance. In the nuclear age it might be argued that the status of "neutral", so important traditionally in international law, pales in significance relative to the status of "non-aligned" since the latter already implies that there will be no bases, no strategic assistance given to one block or the other, no nuclear involvement. A country might in fact even have a nuclear capability of its own: the question still remains whether it is coupled to one of the superpowers with a reasonably high probability that it will be used in times of war, in an aligned manner.

Then there is the question of invulnerability. In preceding chapters we have actually made an implicit distinction between two types of invulnerability: *invulnerability deriving from inner strength,* or absence of inner weakness (such as a vulnerable ecology, dependence on trade for the essentials, too high level of centralisation, too sophisticated technology, too deep rifts and fissions in the social structure, too low morale), and *invulnerability derived from outer usefulness.* In any war there are certain things the adversary does not want to see destroyed in the country he is attacking: at least *some* human beings, memorials, pieces of art in general, some types of administrative and productive capacity, and so on. A country densely packed with such things might be less vulnerable. Best would be the case where the country itself, as such, is useful: Switzerland being an obvious case, so interwoven with banking services, humanitarian services and conference facilities that would be useful in peace, when war threatens, when there is a war, as well as in the reconstruction period afterwards.

There is also that more intangible element of moral status, of being invulnerable because one has somehow become untouchable. To attain that status the country probably has to acquire a reputation for good deeds over a longer period of time, particularly if the deeds are *direct,* relative to the adversary rather than to a third party. Concretely, to believe that one acquires invulnerability in the East-West conflict because one has been generous with technical assistance in the so-called North-South conflict (interpreted very differently by the two sides in the East-West conflict) is naive. However, there may be a certain *indirect* effect: he who attacks a country that has been helpful to third countries — by giving technical assistance during the phase of liberation (arms to guerrillas, for instance) or during the phase of reconstruction (building infrastructure, for instance) — may see third parties turning against the attacker. But much more useful would be the *direct* effect of being known as a kind country. Thus, one of the best forms of defence Norway has against the Soviet Union is probably still the aid given to Soviet Armenia in the earlier stage of its formation, when hunger and starvation were rampant — administered by the famous Nansen, assisted by a young Norwegian officer, the infamous Quisling.

Below, then, is an effort to synthesise this type of thinking in a table giving countries points on a scale 0, 1, 2 according to how they may be said to rate on these four dimensions (see table 5.1).

The table (also see 1.1) should be seen as indicative of a way of reasoning, and not be taken too seriously where the numbers are concerned. The only country receiving a full score, being the most secure country in Europe according to this type of thinking, in other words Switzerland, can be seen as the prototype for the five *inner core* non-aligned countries in Europe. Switzerland is not only non-aligned, but bolsters the non-alignment with a relatively consistent policy of neutrality (although there is no doubt that the Swiss in general are very "Western", even in some sense to the west of the West). Swiss military strategy rules out long-range offensive weapons and consequently also retaliation against the civilian population on the other side, and is based on a highly defensive concept of Switzerland as a fortress. The ecology is relatively stable. There is a well-thought-through plan for self-sufficiency in foodstuffs, health inputs, energy and weaponry in times of war. Switzerland is already decentralised in the cantons, with a federal capital playing, relatively speaking, much less of a role than the capitals in other European countries. A certain Swiss conservatism might also make the country less technologically dependent. And the Swiss have centuries of experience in patching up rifts along class and ethnic (religious and linguistic) borders — all of this yielding a population with a rather high morale. The outer usefulness of Switzerland is legendary, already referred to above. Switzerland has something unique to offer, a considerable comparative advantage.

The other non-aligned countries come close to this, but fall short in some dimensions. Thus, it does not look as if Finland, Austria and Yugoslavia have such consistent plans for self-sufficiency in times of war. Both Finland and Austria might more easily become clients because of certain dependencies; Yugoslavia perhaps not. But then Yugoslavia has the famous ethnic rifts inside the country, the importance of which certainly has been exaggerated in the past. For a long time, the major NATO scenario of how the Third World War would start always had as its point of departure Tito's death, struggle between Croats and Serbs, Soviet intervention, and so on. But Tito died and nothing remotely in that direction followed. The outer usefulness of all these countries is high, however — although again not quite as high as Switzerland's or not of as long standing. In this connection Albania must also be mentioned: low in outer usefulness, but very high, or so it seems, in inner strength. Neutrality in the sense of being against almost everybody does not make many friends, however.

In the case of Sweden and Malta there might be some doubt about the non-alignment, and whether the weaponry does not also have offensive components. Sweden seems to have a certain coupling between its own secret services and the CIA; known to train some of her officers in NATO countries but not in the countries of WTO; known to buy important military

Table 5.1 A guide to security in Europe

	defensive vs. offensive	decoupling from superpowers	inner strength	outer usefulness	SUM	security class	No. of countries
Switzerland	2	2	2	2	8	****	1
Yugoslavia	2	2	1	1	6	***	2
Albania	2	2	2	0	6		
Austria	2	2,1	1	1	6,5	**	4
Finland	2	2,1	1	1	6,5		
Sweden, Malta	1	1	1	1	4		
Romania, Greece	1	1	1,0	1	4,3	*	7
France	0	1	1	1	3		
Cyprus, Spain, Ireland, Iceland	0,1	1	0,1	0,1	1,3		
NATO, WTO client countries	0	0	0,1	0,1	0,2	0	10 5
							29

equipment from Western suppliers — hence Sweden is not entirely non-aligned. Some of the aircraft also have a range well into the Soviet Union, for interdiction purposes, with radar guidance supplied from Swedish territory. On the other hand, and this applies to all the countries mentioned: one of the most important ways of being non-offensive is of course simply by being small, objectively incapable of launching any attack alone. There is some virtue to smallness, although it should also be admitted that even the mini-states of Europe, equipped with one cruise missile with nuclear warhead would possess considerable offensive capability in spite of their smallness. But a condition for smallness to be virtuous is, of course, that one is not a client-state of some highly non-virtuous superpower, or ruled by some terrorist group.

Next in line come the half-allies, Romania and Greece in the first line, then France. Obviously, France cannot be said not to have offensive weaponry with its *force de frappe*. But it is half-way non-aligned like the other two by virtue of not being part of the integrated military system of the aligned. On the other hand, the potential usefulness of France for both belligerent blocks — in case she manages to stay outside — is rather important after a war, because France is a big country. France could play a role in reconstruction. This also applies to the other three ambiguous countries, Cyprus, Spain and Ireland to which one might add Iceland.

For the other countries in Europe the security level is put very low. They are by definition aligned — 10 of them in NATO (excluding Iceland, with a big base) and five in WTO — and are parts of strategic concepts, both as potential senders and potential receivers of nuclear arms. That the weapon systems are offensive is beyond doubt. Here again it should be pointed out that military thinking has to be so-called worst case thinking: one has to assume that an offensive capability can be used offensively, while at the same time, of course, studying the shifting motivation patterns on the other side. When it comes to level of invulnerability, these countries differ very much. But since they are all client-countries of superpowers, all of them will have the assumption that the superpower ultimately will come to their rescue, not only militarily, but also in terms of other supplies. That makes the level of self-sufficiency lower, at the same time as the country no longer has an aura of untouchability. These are not small, "virgin", countries fending for themselves.

Hence, our conclusion would be that, if there should be a war in Europe, the safest place to live in Europe would be Switzerland, followed by the other non-aligned countries, with some doubts as to Sweden and Malta. The fourth category would be the semi-allies, the protest countries on either side, together with the "outer" non-aligned. The most insecure would be the bottom category, the client-countries, because they would be destroyed most in the effort to destroy their destructive capacity. Of course, the security of about 1 per cent of the 500 million non-superpower Europeans living in Switzerland would be threatened by the amount of secondary radiation (fall-out) caused by nuclear warfare; and the same applies to the other countries not directly hit because there is nothing worth hitting. The life expectancy will be lower, especially for the young since cancer takes time to develop. But survival it is, nonetheless, even if it is in a much less attractive world.

In general, it should of course be mentioned that there is the possibility of nuclear wars so cataclysmic that everything explored in the table becomes not only invalid, but simply irrelevant. Holocaust could be holocaust for everybody, regardless of what kind of weapon system the country has, whether the country is non-aligned or not, independent of what kind of subtle or non-subtle inner or outer invulnerability it might possess. This is true, yet it is the type of truth that is not useful as a basis for analysis. It is like saying that because certain types of cancer today are incurable it makes no sense to try to cure the others, or to find a cure for the common cold, for that matter. The worst, not only the best, should not kill the search for the good!

Besides, my own intuition would be that the global holocaust scenario is unrealistic and essentially functions so as to simplify the cognitive picture of the future. Extremists on one side can say: "it makes no difference whether you have nukes or not, so you might just as well have them!" Extremists on the other side can say: "nothing a country can do is of any use anyhow unless we get rid of all nuclear weapons everywhere". There are three serious difficulties with this type of reasoning: (1) we are not going to get rid of all of them in the foreseeable future, (2) the easiest way of getting rid of them may not be by destroying them, which seems never to happen, but pushing them back geographically and preparation-wise, by detargeting them, storing them away, stopping the whole preparation process, waiting for rust and rot to do their job, slowly forgetting them and (3) the best way of obtaining this is probably by developing alternative ways of defence, by acting *as if* the weapons did not exist. Then time *may* come to get completely rid of them.

On the other hand, scenarios about a limited war, conventional but then with a few and mainly tactical nuclear exchanges, also seem unlikely: if the war has come that far either side would probably use more of what they have with the hope of achieving a more devastating blow. Both of them may, however, also come to the conclusion that "unacceptable damage" has been obtained and agree to stop. In short, something between the highly limited and the highly unlimited is probably the most likely. But about this we are all agnostics: we have neither the empirical experience nor the theoretical guidance to tell much in advance. All we can say is that if the war is not unlimited then the bombs are more likely to explode some places than other places. Where *is* important? It is not random but contingent upon factors such as the four given above, and as a consequence it would be utter irrationality not to take this into account. And that is precisely what the countries at the top of the list have done, more or less deliberately, and what the European peace movement, highly outspoken and explicit in the West, more implicit in the East, is also steering towards: a new basis for security.

Looking now at Table 5.1 the question is how to explain this pattern. There are 29 countries in Europe, not counting the mini-states (Gibraltar, Faroe, Andorra, Monaco, Liechtenstein, San Marino, the Vatican, Åland) and the maxi-states the Soviet Union and Greenland. Very rarely does one see a list with Switzerland, Yugoslavia and Albania at the top. They seem

Table 5.2 Second World War and Cold War status compared, I

	defensive/non-aligned ***	**	*	offensive/aligned 0	SUM
neutral	Switzerland	Sweden	Ireland, Spain	Portugal, Turkey	6
major contribution to the war	Yugoslavia, Albania	Malta	France, Greece, Iceland, Cyprus	UK, Poland	9
occupied, not major contribution		Finland		Norway, Denmark, Netherlands, Belgium, Luxemburg, Czechoslovakia	7
axis countries		Austria	Romania	FGR, GDR, Italy, Hungary, Bulgaria	7
SUM	3	4	7	15	29

so different. In political terms (see 2.4) Switzerland is (capitalist) *blue,* even dark blue with considerable faith in the free market system at the national and transnational levels. And Albania is (socialist) *red,* even dark red, with considerable faith in state planning at the national, if not the transnational level, being a member of no economic bloc. Then Yugoslavia, which is profoundly inbetween, combining self-management *(samo upravljenje)* with state planning and national market competition, and a high level of integration in the world capitalist market — it is red, and blue. So, what do they have in common in addition to their position in this particular classification?

Maybe that they all have an element of the *green,* a faith in the local level; the canton and municipality in Switzerland, the *local* self-management in Yugoslavia, the commune (in the Chinese sense) in Albania. And maybe that derives from the circumstance that they are profoundly *peasant* societies. *Ecrasez le suisse (la suissesse) et voilà, le paysan (la paysanne)!* They are societies with traditions in fighting, successfully, feudal and foreign domination on their own soil. Far-reaching territorial, geo-political architectonics have not been their style. This is not the place to develop that theme but it might be interesting to explore a typology with autonomous, careful, highly defensive, *peasant* societies; then ambitious, geo-politically oriented, offensive, *aristocratic* societies; and finally the followers, or servants of the latter, the *serf* societies. Societies are then seen as cast in these roles by historical circumstances that may leave a long-lasting imprint. Elites internalise and assume these roles and "modernise" them in accordance with new weapons technologies, geo-political concepts and political ideologies. The peasant societies become defensive and try to stay outside the struggle among the big; the aristocratic societies become offensive and the serf societies — more or less willingly — accept the status of "allies", i.e. protection with rights and duties as in feudal societies. They become client countries.

Let us now try to combine this perspective with the perspective developed in 2.2, the legacies of the Second World War, and the perspective of this section on the security classes. We may then distinguish between only four classes of countries according to their role in the Second World War. There are the neutral countries, and the countries really in the Axis; the Pact-of-Steel countries, (with Austria, but not with Albania) and the Three-Power-Pact countries. Among the rest there are on the one hand the fighters, some free, some used as bases, some occupied but with major sacrifices towards their own liberation; and then on the other hand countries that we occupied but without major sacrifices for their own liberation (the borderline is not a very sharp one). The result is as in table 5.2, when for simplicity we also combine the top two security classes. But the table becomes more clear if we simplify the dimensions even further, as in table 5.3.

The correlation (Q = 0.82) is convincing even if the classification may be controversial in some cases. *The axis countries with their "serfs", and the occupied countries unable or unwilling to undertake major sacrifices in the last war, are the client countries of the present cold war — grosso modo.* As always, the exceptions are interesting and shed more light on the European

Table 5.3   Second World War and Cold War status compared, II

		towards defensive/ non-aligned	offensive/ aligned	SUM
Yule Q = 0.82	neutral; anti-axis, fighters	11	4	15
	occupied; axis countries	3	11	14
	SUM	14	15	29

scene. Thus, the United Kingdom, for a long time almost a solitary fighter (ostensibly to honour her obligations to Poland), the aristocrat country *par excellence*, knew perfectly well that the Soviet Union bore the major burden and that the US was indispensable on the Western side. She becomes a cold war client country, assuming the forward base, unsinkable hangarship function, even that major upgrading of the nuclear target worthiness, the Cruise/Pershing II launchers, together with the major axis powers (Western Germany and Italy) and two non-fighters, Netherlands and Belgium.

Portugal and Turkey became client countries without having to — one of them even very far from any possible Soviet threat — but the military caste probably wanted it. Poland became a client country, certainly without the consent of the strongly autonomous people — at least in recent years — but the ruling elites wanted it. And Finland and Austria, deeply involved with the axis, had to assume a non-aligned status, probably with the consent of the people — at least in recent years. And then there is that maverick country, Romania, which should have been an obedient client but somehow refuses. Maybe she never was obedient?

Looking at Table 5.3 again, one might say that down to the right there are the beaten, pretending aristrocrats of the Second World War (the Germanies, Italy), their serfs and some other countries looking around for protection. Up to the left are the peasant countries to which we may also add the three islands (Iceland, Malta, Cyprus), Ireland, and Greece and two former aristocrats, Spain and France. Spain has given up most pretensions in that direction, but still has elites wanting to join NATO. France, in all likelihood, has not given up, and probably has ambitions of her own. But she obtains some security and non-client status by pursuing her interests more independently of the superpowers. In that she certainly differs from Italy where — not quite like Spain — the pattern of clientship inside the country is reflected in clientship without, if not by being on top, then by being submissive. But then neither Italy, nor Spain, can be said to harbour Napoléonic aspirations. They hardly see themselves, not even to some extent, as chosen nations — like France does. Is this an explanation for the relatively weak peace movements in these countries?

Some additional remarks about the Nordic countries may be in order; the thinking may also apply to others. To use Hakan Wiberg's felicitous expression: the Nordic countries were playing lottery before the war with Norway and Denmark having a low military profile and being neutral, Finland and Sweden having a high military profile. Finland combined this with confrontation with a neighbour, Sweden with neutrality. The war came, one country won in the lottery, Sweden — the other three did not, although the war was rather soft on both Norway and Denmark compared to what happened in Finland and many other European countries. Wiberg's point is simply this: the country that won in the lottery of course drew the conclusion that the policy had been a wise one and continued with that policy: Sweden — a high military profile combined with neutrality. And the countries that came out of it hit and hurt drew the conclusion that their policy had been the wrong one, and changed that policy. Finland adopted a low military profile and a treaty of friendship with the Soviet Union, Norway and Denmark a high military profile and alignment, with NATO membership. There were conditions though: no nuclear weapons on their territory, no permanently stationed foreign, particularly US, troops in peace time (in addition Norway has a restriction against manoeuvres with foreign troops close to the Soviet border). In a sense this made Norway and Denmark, if not half allies, three-quarter allies. The argument was and is that this was in order not to provoke the mighty neighbour to the East. In reality, it means a limitation in the sharing of risks in the alliance, if not in the sharing of costs. A pre-emptive attack would be less likely against Norway and Denmark as long as the two self-imposed conditions are operational (as long as that is only "in peace time" it does not mean much).

So there are historical factors conditioning the surprising variation in political-military profiles in Europe; the distribution is certainly far from random. There are short-term factors back to the Second World War; there are long-term factors, more difficult to catch, that extend considerably further back in time. But correlation is not the same as causation, and certainly not the same as determination. The presence of exceptions already testifies to the possibility of breaking out of any kind of predetermined role, by an act of will, of ruling elites, people or both.

The basic point is that present amongst us in Europe are countries with an approach to security policy totally different from that pursued by the alliances, and even if one does not share the present author's conviction that they (particularly the top three) are *more* secure, there seems to be a general consensus that they are at least *not less* secure. And they pursue highly concrete policies that are meaningful *today;* they do not represent paper-solutions — in a sense they are concrete, really existing utopias. Moreover, those three societies are very different in their socio-economic formation, so different that this type of policy evidently does not presuppose a very definite position on the continuum from dark blue to dark red societies. This is important, it make us more free in the pursuit of security. So, let us look more closely at the four dimensions to see what countries can do. For all these factors that condition foreign policy are not determining factors in the sense that a country is condemned to a certain policy. There are policy choices, decisions to be made — otherwise foreign policy would not be so dynamic. But insight into one's own geo-history is always useful; necessary if not sufficient.

2. Transarmament: from offensive to defensive defence

The world-pair "offensive/defensive" is problematic, but also crucial. In an effort to have a fresh look at the whole problem of security, the following figure, giving a spectrum of reactions to an attack on a country, may be useful:

Table 5.4   A spectrum of reactions to attack

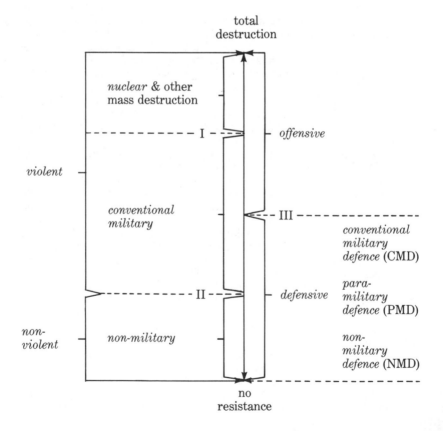

The spectrum is one-dimensional which means that it is simplistic, possibly too simplistic — but it may nevertheless be useful.

At the bottom end is no resistance at all in case of an attack; at the top end total destruction, meaning of oneself as well as of the attacker. In between are all other forms of reaction — the spectrum includes all "wavelengths", so to speak.

A basic thesis of this book can now be formulated: almost all the current debate concerning which reactions to make use of is focused on two major cuts along this dimension, *between nuclear and conventional arms* on the one hand, and *between violent and non-violent reactions* on the other. The latter is the distinction around which not only pacifism but also large sections of the peace movement is organised: the rejection not only of nuclear arms and other weapons of mass destruction, but also of violence in general, meaning all kinds of conventional military systems. Although most people might agree that there is such a distinction, only relatively few would share the optimism of pacifists — when they point to such examples as Gandhian actions in India against the British Empire — with regard to the efficacy of non-military reactions *everywhere, alone.* Hence, as is very well known, it is the distinction between nuclear and conventional weapons that dominates the political debate and action completely, and not only in the military and political establishments (including the war establishments), but also in the peace movement. The thesis, then, is that *this is most unfortunate,* that it means cutting the dimension at points that certainly are important but have the distinct disadvantage that one of them is located too high on the scale of destruction, and the other one too low.

Hence, the argumentations here is in favour of a third cut, that *between offensive and defensive reactions* to attack. In trying to define this cut, which like the other two by no means is a sharp one, it should first all be emphasised that it refers to the objective capability of of the reactions "systems" (the weapons being a part of that concept), not to the subjective motivations that may be attached to them. In other words, it is not a question of whether a reaction system is intended to be used for an attack; the whole issue is whether it is capable of being used for an attack. Hence, the best judge as to whether a weapon system is defensive or offensive is a possible target of the system, the adversary, not the subjective mind behind it. Thoughts and words come and go, actions depend on what is objectively possible, given by the constraints of natural laws only. The adversary is the best judge; just as we, in our self-defence, are the best judge of the adversary.

Hence, I would locate the definition of the offensive/defensive distinction in geographical space: *can the weapon system be effectively used abroad, or can it only be used at home?* If it can be used abroad then it is offensive, particularly if the "abroad" includes countries with which one is in conflict. If it can only be used at home then the system is defensive, being operational only when an attack has taken place.

Locating the definition in space makes it possible to formulate the problem in terms of two variables: the range (of the weapons carriers) and the impact area (of the weapon itself, whether it is a classical impact weapon, an incendiary weapon, a high explosive or weapon of mass destruction — chemical/toxic, biological, radiological, nuclear or geophysical). If we now divide "range" into immobile/short/long and "impact area" into local/limited/extended then we arrive at the nine combinations in figure 5.5, four of them defensive according to the approach taken above, five of them offensive:

Figure 5.5   Offensive vs. defensive systems

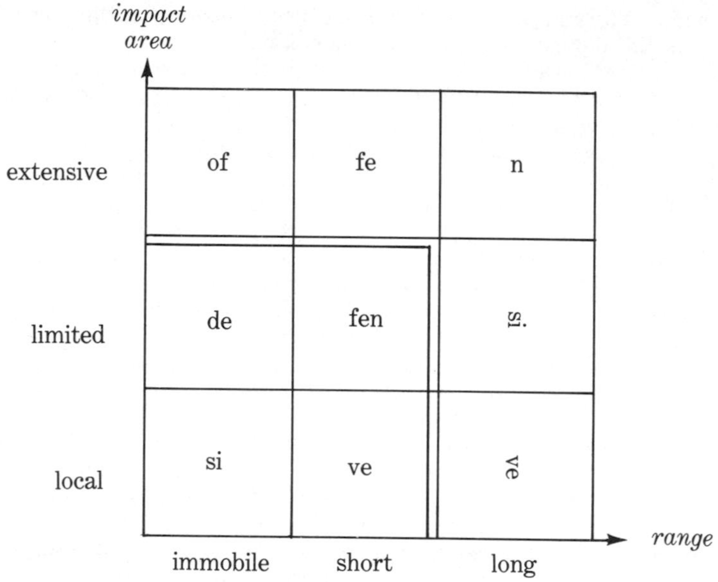

Of course, it all depends on where the borderline between "short" and "long" on the one hand, and between "limited" and "extensive" on the other, is located. An indication is already given above: the effects of the reaction to an attack should be within one's own country. Of course, there may be countries so small that almost any weapons system would reach outside and/or have an impact area that would also include adversary territory. In general this would call for research into other types of weapon systems, for the use of highly immobile systems with only local impact along the borders (border fortifications are a classical answer in this connection), leaving the "short"/"limited" combination to the core area of the country. But even if some of this should reach into some minor parts of adversary territory this does not in any major way affect the type of reasoning we are trying to develop here.

In order to discuss this more fully let us contrast the extremes in figure 5.5. On the one hand, in the upper right hand corner, are very long range weapon systems with extensive impact areas: inter-continental ballistic missiles, long range bombers and submarines, all of them with dual capacity, also for weapons of mass destruction. They would certainly be classified as offensive by anybody.

On the other hand, in the bottom left hand corner would be such weapons systems as land, sea or air mines with local impact only, or a pipeline buried underground that can easily be filled with an explosive, ignited and make hundreds of kilometres impassable for tanks. As mentioned, fortifications also belong in this category, but some of them would have guns with an impact area that would no longer be "local", but "limited". Real long range guns would be alien to the logic of purely defensive defence, however.

Then there are all the inbetween categories, and they are numerous. However, they are not that difficult to handle from the point of view of the present analysis. Long range weapons systems with local impact would clearly be offensive: a Pershing II is still an offensive weapon when equipped with a conventional war-head with a highly local impact; a very long range gun with a nuclear war-head would be an offensive weapon even if stationed "at home". More interesting is the exploration of the "short"/"limited" combination since that would bring us to the borderline between offensive and defensive.

"Short range" means mobile, but mobility should not be useful for offensive purposes. One would be thinking in terms of jeeps and similar vehicles on land, motor-torpedo boats on water, small submarines, and small aircraft using roads as airstrips, possibly with vertical take-off and landing, possibly helicopters. There would be nothing against these means of transportation being very quick: the problem is not speed, but range. In speed there is protection, and the possibility of coming quickly to the rescue where defence against aggression is needed. Speed is certainly also important in aggression, but only useful when combined with sufficient range to reach outside one's country.

Hence, one would be thinking in terms of *highly mobile, small* units with *limited range,* on land, in the water, in the air. In order to compensate for the limited range they would have to be well dispersed all over the national territory, but because of the limited range essentially with only local or district (sub-national) functions. If the range from one end of a country to the other is so long as to also reach possible adversary territory, then one should renounce weapon systems with ranges of that type, letting the non-offensive charcter of the system take priority over the wish to use all systems all over the national territory (which would probably be impossible anyhow). However, if they are to operate in a dispersed and essentially *local* manner, they also have to be relatively *autonomous.* This does not mean that they are not under national command, only that they are capable of operating even if that command should be seriously impaired through adversary attack.

Having now estabished that they should have *short range* but possibly *become mobile very quickly, be well dispersed, small, local* and *autonomous,* we can turn to the impact of the weapons. It should be "limited" for the very simple reason that it is limited how much one wants to destroy of one's own territory, even if a more extensive impact area would be more destructive to adversary forces. This, then, would point in the direction of *very efficient, precision-guided weapons* with considerable destructive power but limited impact area; an example being "smart rockets". They certainly exist today and are generally seen as very effective against tanks in the form of anti-tank weapons; against ships, but perhaps less so against aircraft particularly when they make use of the old trick of interposing themselves between defensive forces and the sun. However, there would be ways of dealing also with this problem. Let it only be added that such forces, in addition, would have weapons with a highly local impact such as ordinary guns, thereby completing the four cells in the defensive area of figure 5.5.

Of course there is a grey one in between. There is the famous case of the anti-aircraft guns that are defensive when pointing upwards, yet can be used as highly offensive weapons when mounted at a different angle on a carrier for targets on the ground (a ship, for instance), with a long range. This, however, is no argument at all against the distinction made. What has happened in this and similar cases is that a new weapon system has been created, from something immobile with limited or even local impact area to something long range with limited area. That one major physical component in two weapons systems could be the same, or the same with a minor modification, is trivial. A country that wants to base its security on defensive forms of defence would simply not undertake that type of transformation of the weapons systems, and try to make them so that they cannot be suspected of it either. At the same time, however, this serves as a warning not to be naive in believing that any component of a weapon system is *inherently* defensive or offensive; it depends on the total system. It should not, however, depend on motivation. As motivations change so may the objective character of the weapons system — hence it is an engineering problem to make systems that are highly resistant, "robust", to such changes, retaining the defensive character over a vast range of transformation of the components.

Going back to figure 5.4, there are still a number of clarifications to be made. More particularly, if we make use of all three cuts that have been made on this dimension, cutting the dimension in four regions, some comments about each of the four regions might be in order to bring out the issues.

First, there are the weapons of mass destruction, with most of the public debate and action concentrated on nuclear arms. They are classified here as offensive, and that is not entirely unproblematic. The reasoning was indicated above: weapons of mass destruction are so destructive that nobody in his right mind would only use them at home, at most against an adversary, and even then only against a much-hated adversary. One reason for this is that the weapons are not only destructive of the homosphere (human beings and their settlements) but also of the biosphere, lithosphere and the hydrosphere — in other words of the whole environment (the atmosphere too for that matter, but that effect will be dispersed relatively quickly). In other words, nuclear weapons (and other weapons of mass destruction for that matter) are simply not credible as defensive weapons which, of course, is a major reason why they are usually conceived of and discussed in connection with long range weapons carriers like those found in the US/NATO triad. A country may have short range carriers (such as 155mm howitzers mounted on trucks or trains) with dual capacity (e.g. for ERW, "neutron grenades") — the question still remains whether they are credible for use on one's own territory. Admittedly the answer is not a very clear-cut one indicating that the dimension in figure 5.4 is not entirely one-dimensional — but the basic thesis still remains: that weapons of mass destruction are essentially offensive weapons in the sense used here. In fact, they are so aggressive that they are for destruction rather than for conquest of enemy territory. It is not strange that some are now being withdrawn.

Then there is the *second* category which is a very important one: conventional, offensive weapon systems. When the basic distinction is made only in terms of nuclear versus conventional then it is easily forgotten how extremely *offensive* conventional weapons can be. The Second World War was an example of that, so were the Korean and Indochina wars and all or most of the other local wars after 1945 for that matter, such as Lebanon or Afghanistan. Of course, a major war today would not be fought with exactly the same arms, but, for instance, with the missiles, bombers and submarines now at the disposal of the super-powers, but "only" with conventional warheads. They are so destructive, and also so offensive that although reduction or elimination of nuclear arms would be advantageous, most of what has been said about the danger of war still remains valid, with conventional offensive weapon systems doing the job. And it is precisely because the third cut along the dimension in figure 5.4 has not been made that it becomes possible for certain political and military establishments to smuggle in conventional offensive armament as a "compensation" for a possible nuclear disarmament — riding on the fear of nuclear arms.

Then there is the *third* category: conventional military defence. It has been described in some detail above, so let us here only look at one more point. If the units carrying the burden of conventional military defence (CMD) are short-range, mobile, small, local, quick, dispersed and autonomous then they are very much like guerrilla forces. The only difference between CMD and para-military defence (PMD) would be that the latter would tend to be even more local, more embedded in the local human and natural environment, and operate less in the open, although they would probably wear some kind of uniform in conformity with the regulations of the laws of war. The often used term "militia" also enters the picture here, including some of its policing functions. In this connection it should be pointed out that PMD probably has proven, after 1945, to be the most effective form of reaction to an attack, whether that attack takes the form of direct violence of military forces or the structural violence of excessive exploitation within and/or between countries.

Then there is the *fourth* category of non-military defence (NMD). Most models of that type of defence would also operate on the assumption of small units, local and autonomous, dispersed — in other words the same structure that has already been argued for CMD and PMD. One might say that there are two reasons underlying this: never to offer the adversary any targets with such a high concentration of defence potential that it would be worthy of a nuclear attack, and at the same time being able to resist an attack in all corners of the country. (Of course, he may destroy the whole country, but that he may do anyhow). For the case of non-military defence this obviously means not only *territorial* defence in the sense of resistance in geographically well defined units, but also *social* defence in the sense of all organisation and associations in a country finding their own ways of resisting attack by not producing goods or services for the adversary etc. Clearly this is defensive as it is only meaningful in one's own society. This becomes even more clear when one looks at the following short-list of 12 fundamental strategies for NMD, organised in three groups with four strategies in each:

I. *Antagonist-oriented defence strategies*
A. "Attack should not pay"
    1. Self-inflicted sabotage on objects of value to adversary;
    2. Non-co-operation and civil disobedience, "emptying" social structure.

B. "Incapacitating the antagonist"
    3. Creating empathy
       a. Positive interaction before attack; helpfulness, assistance;
       b. Co-operation with the person; non-cooperation with the status
          — friendliness at the personal level;
    4. Creating sympathy through suffering inflicted by adversary.

II. *Defence strategies aimed at protecting oneself*
    5. Efficient communication inside one's own group;
    6. Effectively hiding selected people and objects;
    7. Decreased vulnerability of the population through alternative structure;
    8. Communication and enactment of one's own values.

III. *Defence strategies aimed at deterring the antagonist*
    9. Organisation of NMD prepared in peace time;
    10. Communication of preparedness through manoeuvres;
    11. Communication of commitment to NMD;
    12. High level of satisfaction in one's own group.

Of course, it may be argued that NMD speciaists can penetrate international frontiers and organise the population elsewhere in attempts to overturn their regimes, as can PMD volunteers. This is true, but in that case it is a question of transfer of know-how; the real fighting will have to be done by the local population against its own leaders. It is more like sending a book across the border, or a teacher, less like sending a nuclear-tipped missile.

Looking at the total dimension, again, the case has now been made that on the one hand there are offensive reactions to an attack, with weapons of mass destruction (including nuclear weapons) and with conventional offensive weapons. On the other hand there are defensive reactions, and they are of *three* types: *conventional military defence, paramilitary defence* and *non-military defence*. Just as an offensive reaction today is conceived of as including both nuclear and conventional weapons (in Soviet/WTO strategy the nuclear weapons are not for first use, in US/NATO strategy nuclear weapons also, possibly, for first use), a defensive reaction could include all three types, combining CMD, PMD and NMD. The problem of whether they are combinable is an important one, just as it is for offensive strategies. That problem, however, will be taken up below.

The basic point to be discussed here is not so much the structure of offensive vs. defensive systems, as their function. The key difference is that offensive systems can be used for *attack*. They are potentially aggressive, and hence provocative. Whether they will be used for attack is another matter, the important point is that any possible adversary may have reasons to suspect that they could be used for attack simply because what is possible may also become reality. What is impossible may not, this is the whole point underlying an objectively defensive posture.

At this point some comments about the ambiguities of the two important words "defence" and "deterrence" may be in order.

The word *defence* obviously has two meanings: *any* reaction to an attack, in other words the use of any weapon system from any point on the dimension of figure 5.4 (including the bottom point which may also be some kind of defence, perhaps in the longer run); and then the other meaning of a limited part of the spectrum only, what is here somewhat clumsily referred to as 'defensive defence'. And this spills over into the double meaning given to the word "deterrence": deterring an attack through the threat of effective retaliation (German: *Vergeltung*), or deterring attack through the promise of effective resistance (German: *Verteidigung* not including "Vergeltung"). One may say that there is a broad use of the terms defence/deterrence covering all points on the spectrum, and the narrow use limiting it to the (purely) defensive systems only.

It is probably not possible to change the semantics since word usages are so deeply ingrained at this juncture. But it is absolutely impermissible when people participating in the debate do not clarify what they mean. At any point where the words "defence" and "deterrence" are used it should be made clear whether the terms are limited to (purely) defensive systems, or also to systems operating on the territory of the adversary.

Offensive defence is offensive, in both senses of that term: it *can* be used to start an offensive in the sense of *aggression,* and it is offensive in the sense of *provoking* the other side. It is not the manpower, capital, research and organisation work that goes into a military system in general that provokes; it is the offensive component of all this. Thus, to analyse arms races in terms of the magnitude and rate of growth of all the factors that have been put into the organisation, or − better − the destructive capability of the organisation (the "bads" and "disservices" that can be rendered) is misleading: *only the offensive components should be counted.* On the other hand, it is quite clear from what has been said above that the borderline is not a very sharp one (although sharper, it is argued here, than most people believe) − hence the easy solution is to count all military assets totally disregarding the offensive/defensive distinction. The distinction that *is* made use of: army, navy and the air force, has approximately the same level of intellectual depth as the corresponding division for the animal kingdom: animals on land, in the water and in the air. Zoology made a great step forward when the distinction between vertebrates and invertebrates was made systematic use of; it is high time that similar distinctions — actually very old in the field of military science — became much more prominent in the debate.

*   *   *

Let us now have a look at this type of defence; a triad consisting of conventional, paramilitary and non-military defence. The major arguments in favour are obvious: a defence of this kind is not provocative since it cannot be used for an attack, hence should not lead to any arms race. Within this type of defence doctrine it would be entirely possible for both parties both to have a *high* level of security and a relatively *equal* level of security. In addition it is possible for them to *co-operate:* it would be in the interest of either party to make the other party feel secure, which would mean that there could even be an exchange between adversaries of techniques of defensive defence (not necessarily of their exact location, however). *This means that a setting is given for common security* as outlined in 3.4 above, and that is already something.

With this approach there would still be arms and even armament, but with the distinct possibility that a stable plateau can be achieved, in other words not only common security but a stable and common security. Of course, in world history this has probably been the normal state of affairs for most pairs of neighbouring countries; the accumulation of offensive arms, and offensive arms races being an exception. But in addition to this a strong defensive defence should have a high deterrent value, "deterrence" then taken not in the sense of retaliation, but in the sense of being able to stave off an attack. Nevertheless, should the attack come, and that would be the third line or argument, then the level of destruction would be lower since there would be no incentive (except for pure terrorism) to use nuclear arms and the other weapons of mass destruction. Not only the defence system but also the social system itself (see 5.4 below) would be organised in such a way that no immediate target would present itself as being worthy of a nuclear attack.

This, however, does not mean that the type of defence advocated here is unproblematic. The following is a short list of some basic and critical considerations, for a debate that now should take place not only within the peace movement but in our societies in general.

First, defensive defence presupposes a high level of national self-reliance in defence matters. If weapon systems are not supposed to be quick, long range, mobile, then they cannot be transported from one country to another in order to help that other country (rather than attacking it) either. Under a doctrine of defensive defence military alliances based on high levels of mobility are severely curtailed. This, of course, does not mean that there cannot be all kinds of diplomatic, otherwise political, and economic support in case of an attack. World public opinion would still function, and even more so than before because a country with purely defensive defence cannot possibly be accused of having provoked an attacker. This may look like a severe reduction of defensive capability, but could also be seen in exactly the opposite manner. Clearly, a country which is used to relying on allies, and particularly on a superpower ally, will not mobilise all its defence resources. This is true in times of peace and even more so in times of war. Military forces in a client country in an alliance, given the idea that "I have to fight for 24 hours till help comes from the superpower, possibly even with superweapons", will certainly not exercise their defence potential to the maximum. Rather, the strategy would be to put up a decent show but trying to do so in such a way that national and personal honours are preserved, yet one manages to survive till the major burden of the battle is taken over by the superpower. A policy of national self-reliance would rule this out. If one really means what one says, that freedom is worth a fight, then that fight has to be made by nobody else than oneself. The triad advocated above (CMD, PMD and NMD) is so diverse, and on the other hand so dispersed throughout the country that it should serve exactly as a network capable of mobilising all kinds of defence potentials.

Second, a policy of defensive defence presupposes a high level of local defence self-reliance. If the units are to be small, dispersed and locally supported, very often also locally based, the conclusion can only be that there has to be a high level of local capacity to keep a fight going even if the national centre has been rendered incapable of doing so. Again the same reasoning applies: in a highly hierarchical national defence system, itself possibly a replication of highly hierarchical international defence systems, the local units might tend to wait for support from the centre and thus yield much less resistance than they otherwise could do. If no such support is forthcoming they might give up, capitulate. But if everything has been prepared in advance they might not only continue the struggle, but also, knowing that they have only themselves to rely upon, do more than otherwise could have been expected of them. Hence, it is obvious that a policy of defensive defence presupposes not only a higher level of national self-reliance, but also of local self-reliance. This type of military doctrine, therefore, is structurally compatible with a social structure much more based on national and local self-reliance in general, just like the vertical alliance pattern with hierarchical organisation inside a country is compatible with the social structure one finds, for instance, in transnational organisations. Obviously the economic structure does not completely determine the military structure but there is a relation between the two. A complete change in defence structure would presuppose at least some change in economic, political and social structure in general. It may be argued that this is to ask for too much. It may also be argued that this type of change probably will have to take place anyhow as a reaction to the general world crisis, and that the change is not that fundamental.

Third, a defensive defence is vulnerable to an enemy who attacks the system with offensive arms from his own community. As a matter of fact, all the adversary would have to do would be to set up a long range gun on his own territory, capable of hitting targets in a systematic manner, and destroy them from one end of the country to the other. Aircraft would have to operate over the territory; a long range gun (or battery of missiles) would not. Hence, it stands to reason that a defensive defence would have to be supplemented by some element of *interdiction capability*. These are counterforce weapons, for instance aircraft capable of hitting the gun just mentioned. And then we are, of course, back to the problem: any interdiction capability would also be an offensive capability, and hence possibly be provocative. Consequently it is a question of having as little as possible, making them very counterforce and not countervalue, building them into the military doctrine, to the letter of the instruction manuals, at all levels of the military organisation, as interdiction weapons only. How much is necessary and how much is sufficient would be difficult to say; military experts close to the peace movements would be the ideal persons to advise on this. Clearly, very soon it becomes too much, too provocative.

Fourth, a policy of defensive defence is not offensive towards an outside adversary, but could be highly offensive towards an inside adversary. The types of weapons that are described above as being defensive are defensive because they cannot reach outside national borders in any significant manner. But they can certainly hit inside those borders, otherwise they would not have any capability at all. And they would not necessarily distinguish between external and internal foes of the regime. As a matter of fact, they are exactly the type of weapons that a repressive government might use against insurgent forces, whether their claims are justifiable or not. They are more adequate than offensive weapons: the case of the Iranian revolution showed rather convincingly how helpless the Shah was with his "modern" weaponry designed for long range operations against a *levée en masse* of the population. Clearly this is an important problem, and a typical example of how a policy designed to solve one problem may not only not solve another one but also aggravate it. The only solution I can imagine would be insisting on the points made under 5.4 below, reducing or even eliminating major contradictions within the country, and as a consequence distributing the control over these means of destruction, the weapons, in a more equitable manner amongst the population, not regarding it as a total monopoly of the government. This does not necessarily mean going so far as one does in Switzerland in the sense of people having arms at home. That would be too similar to the US situation where a countrywide dispersion of firearms has increased the level of *insecurity* considerably. In-between formulas would have to be found.

Fifth, a defensive policy presupposes a higher level of readiness for defence in the population. It clearly supposes a higher level of mobilisation; self-reliance at the national and local levels, and consensus. But this does not necessarily mean militarisation. I do not think that it can be said that a highly mobilised Norwegian population against nazi and quisling rule was militarised because it wanted to defend itself. Militarisation has much more to do with excessive MBCI-complexes, over-armament, offensive armament and such things. Nor is it necessarily the case that this type of defence presupposes a constant hostile image or *Feindbild*. In times of peace a policy of non-alignment and even neutrality would serve to build down such *Feindbild*. In times of war it would come about anyhow, only the non-military component of defence would try to see to it that it would be directed against the enemy as a soldier and not the enemy as a person. But what is absolutely clear is that a defensive policy, because it relies much more on popular participation, would presuppose a high level of consensus. That, of course, has the major advantage that mobilisation of the military potential cannot happen against the popular will, as when forces are used offensively in total disregard and contempt of what a population might feel, relying on professional soldiery and a general decoupling of military society from civilian society. International adventurism would be impossible.

Sixth, a defensive defence with three different components presupposes that the three components do not work at cross-purposes. This is the famous problem of the mix between military and non-military types of defence. Suffice it here only to say that the problem may be more important in theory than in practice. In practice there are several possibilities. There is the mix in *space:* conventional defence along the borders and in thinly populated areas; PMD and NMD elsewhere. There is the mix in *time:* conventional defence first, then PMD and NMD as fall-back possibilities. There is the mix in what one might call *functional* space: conventional defence for geographic and precise targets, PMD and NMD for more diffused and dispersed targets such as the population as a whole, society as a whole, nature; then CMD and PMD for more offensive purposes inside one's own territory, NMD for more defensive purposes. There is the mix of all these mixes — the question of course being whether it becomes mixed up? Wartime experience seems to indicate that it does not, that the population is able to entertain different types of defence at the same time, and that the adversary also makes a distinction between the three, perhaps behaving in the most aggressive way against PMD, less so against CMD and much less so against NMD. Perhaps; it could also be the other way round under certain circumstances. In any case, the task remains that of making the country indigestible.

That, however, is a discussion that would lead far beyond the scope of this book. Suffice it here only to say that the strength of this type of defence is precisely its versatility, and that the enemy of it would be those whose thinking has become so one-dimensional that they can only think in terms of one foot of the tripod, not in terms of all three. In fact, the argument against it is probably not so much that it is ineffective as a deterrent and as a defence. The argument might rather be the opposite: it is so effective that it could also be successfully turned against the countries' own governments. In other words, the opposite of the argument above where the emphasis was on conventional military defence as an instrument which in the hands of the government could be used to crush a rebellion. Paramilitary defence and non-military defence, meaningless unless they are in the hands of the population itself, could also be used to topple a government. One might say that this already constitutes a balance of power, that one type of defensive defence may be the answer to the other in internal power struggles. But the much better answer, of course, would be to say that a condition for a purely defensive form of defence is that the country has come so far in ridding itself of basic internal contradictions that neither a government, nor the population, would use force in order to provoke some basic discontinuity in the history of the country.

In conclusion let us put this aspect of alternative security policies in perspective. Evidently, it is filled with contradictions, reflecting the fact that we live in a perilous world, partly of our own making. Some of these contradictions can only be softened, possibly overcome, if other aspects of alternative security policies are also enacted, very often referred to as "political" — in the present book in terms of "non-alignment", inner strength" and "outer usefulness", to be dealt with in the following three sections.

What should be emphasised here is only one point: *the focus here is on transarmament, not on disarmament.* It has been argued in 3.4 above that disarmament of offensive forces is absolutely indispensable, and it has been argued in chapter 4 that the route via disarmament negotiations as practised so far is a blind alley. The policy advocated here is a combination of disarmament and transarmament, not the obviously fallacious policy of trying to obtain disarmament in offensive weapons through armament in offensive weapons, but an effort to obtain disarmament in offensive weapons through transarmament to defensive weapons. Some of the latter are still highly violent, there is no doubt about that. But within the defensive defence concept argued here there are three different types of defence: conventional, para-military and non-military. Over time this might develop, if one should dare some optimism in these troubled years, towards non-military defence which is more or less the way in which we handle conflicts in civilised societies, with strikes, some civil disobedience, non-violent conflict resolution mechanisms and so on. Many would feel impatient, why not go straight to non-military defence, why not general and complete disarmament and not this approach via conventional military defence? And my answer would be along two lines: first, because the overwhelming majority of the population does not believe in non-military defence, only a part of those who are conscientious objectors, or pacifists in some other way, do. We need a consensus in defence matters, hence three kinds of defence in order to have a choice. Second, because a glance at world history in general and European history in particular should convince anybody that we live in a dangerous world. Security does not come automatically, there is a need for some kind of defence. But that presupposes political approaches, to which we now turn.

3. Non-alignment: gradual decoupling from the superpowers

From the world of defence we are now in the world of international politics, or more precisely inter-governmental politics. The general problem to be discussed is how a country understands itself relative to its international environment, in terms of rights and obligations in connection with the exercise of force and destructive power. More particularly, the basic question to be explored is how a country relates to the two major alliances in the world today, the North Atlantic Treaty Organisation and the Warsaw Treaty Organisation. An alliance constitutes a set of rights and obligations; the question is which set will best serve the interests of a given country. I think the discussion of that question depends very much on whether the alliance has in its midst a superpower or not, particularly a superpower that sees itself as a carrier of a major historical mission, and/or has major national interests with a global reach to secure or defend. An alliance of more equal and more modest powers will be very different from the two alliances we have in the world today, both dominated by a superpower. But this is the world in which we live, hence the only realistic point of departure.

No doubt this all relates to the *attitude* of any person living in these countries, any group, any government, any country as a whole (whatever that might mean) to the superpowers in question. Their records are bad, as witnessed by the exploration in 2.3 above, or any similar exploration of contemporary history. But that record may be overshadowed by all kinds of allegiances. The generation of people who were personally fighting the scourge of nazism and fascism with the help of either superpower, perhaps even operating on or from its territory, might feel a particularly strong allegiance, but that generation is rapidly dying out now. The second generation, those reaching adulthood during the first phases of the East-West conflict have grown up in a period of strong allegiance to "their" superpower: learning the language, studying there or having relatives and friends who did so, to a large extent accepting their images of the world. But not so the third generation that reached adulthood during the later phases of the East-West conflict: the détente phase, the phase of heavy intra-bloc conflict or crisis within the alliances. For that generation the proportion of people who see their own superpower rather than the other superpower as the major danger and threat to peace in general is probably considerably higher than for the preceding two generations. This may no longer be the case with a fourth generation now reaching adulthood, however. But it is still too early to say and they have not yet attained political maturity even though they vote, and in the West seem generally to vote conservative, which may mean having a more positive view of their own superpower (which would be compatible with the Cold War II atmosphere in which we now live).

If we now see it from the point of view of the superpower, an alliance is tantamount to an extension of superpower territory for military purposes. Whether for attack or defence a country member of an alliance puts its territory wholly or partly at the disposal of the superpower for military positioning. That makes it possible to think in terms of a range from being totally available to being totally unavailable. In a world with two superpowers that gives us four possibilities: available to neither, to one or the other, to both. Normally the last possibility is disregarded although it may not be so unreasonable as it sounds. And the first possibility, available to neither superpower (or their allies), is what is usually referred to as a "neutral" country; neither in times of peace, nor in times of war in any way being militarily useful to either side. Closely related to this is the status of "non-aligned" which means exactly that, not to be a member of any alliance with the militarily relevant rights and duties this implies of a relatively automatic nature, by superpower dictat, or by alliance consensus, or majority vote. A non-aligned country may still exchange military services with the superpower, or an alliance, but probably more on an *ad hoc* basis and according to its own inclination. If this is done in an asymmetric manner, being more available to one superpower than the other, the neutrality may of course become less credible. The Swedish formula of "non-alignment in peace; tending towards neutrality in war" is an effort — or so it seems — to obtain both. How successful is another matter.

In 5.1 above we have implicitly defined a country that is maximally available, within the given rules of an alliance, as a "client country" to the superpower. That is the bottom rung of the ladder so to speak. The image would then be that of a country climbing upwards, restricting the availability as it climbs, by announcing constraints. These are likely to be on duties rather than on rights, which means that they are open to the important question of whether a country can put some limits on its obligations inside an alliance and still benefit from the advantages the membership might offer. It should be remembered, however, that the focus here is on obligations of a particular kind: availability to the superpower.

In the following this availability will be discussed under three headings for the members of an alliance: the presence of superpower (conventional) bases in the country, the willingness to accept nuclear tasks to be performed in and from the country, and subordination under superpower command. It goes without saying that any one of these three would be incompatible with a status as non-aligned, not to mention neutral: whatever kind of military availability might be compatible with the status as non-aligned would be at a level below the three just mentioned.

Table 5.6 outlines some of the possibilities.

The table is a compromise between the empirical situation of today, reflecting to some extent the debate in the year 1983, and the logical possibilities that are more numerous than the eight appearing in the table.

On the first rung of the ladder would be Denmark and Norway with their "self-imposed restraints", accepting the integrated NATO command system which in practice means superpower command, but with the provisos that there will be no nuclear weapons stationed in Norway in times of peace (meaning when there is no war or threat of war), nor US bases. There has been very much debate in the two countries about what this means in precise terms, particularly if everything on Danish or Norwegian soil is prepared to receive nuclear arms and US troops (including their beds and food) and US troops are only a short flying distance away, for instance in England or on ships in international waters off the coast.

Then comes the next step on the ladder where a no-first-use doctrine is introduced. There are three possibilities: it could be for the alliance as a whole, it could mean that a country would leave the alliance if any other country in the alliance uses nuclear arms first, or it could be for that country alone (meaning no-first-use on or from the territory of the country). And the same distinction applies to the next step where de-nuclearisation has set in: it could mean for the member countries in general, as a condition for a particular country to remain, or for that country or countries alone. And it applies to the next step, step 4: here there has been a change in military doctrine, in the direction of conventional defence and a high level of national self-reliance.

Obviously, if the whole alliance decides to move up the ladder, then the

Table 5.6 Decoupling from superpowers as a range of possibilities

Step	Alliance membership	Military availability	Superpower command	Nuclear tasks	Superpower bases
7	no	none in peace, none in war	no	no	no
6	no	some in peace, none in war	no	no	no
5	yes	some in peace, some in war	no	no	no
4	yes	change in military doctrine, pure defence only	yes, but	no, defensive only	no, national only
3	yes	nuclear arms free zone	yes, but	not even in wartime	not in peacetime
2	yes	no-first-use	yes, but	not as first use	not in peacetime
1	yes	"self-imposed restraints"	yes, but	not in peacetime	not in peacetime
0	yes	unlimited	yes	yes	yes

character of the alliance as a whole has been changed. If one country sets this as a condition for continued membership then it will have either an effective veto on organisational policy or have to leave the alliance. If a country introduces a no-first-use doctrine, or a no-use-at-all doctrine meaning for all practical purposes a nuclear arms free zone, not to mention that it starts changing military doctrine in a non-provocative defensive direction, then the problem arises of whether it fulfils its obligations inside the alliance if all or some of this is done unilaterally. Norway and Denmark have been able to get up to step one: the question of whether countries can take further steps, singly if not combined, may be on the future political agenda.

However that may turn out, one thing is certain: any step up the ladder reduces superpower influence. Any step up the ladder makes the country somewhat less integrated into the superpower scheme of things because it becomes less available. The ultimate consequence of that would be to withdraw from superpower command, including for nuclear tasks commanded by the superpower and for superpower bases: in other words, French policy after 1965/66. Again, history shows that it was possible for France to stay within the alliance even if it was no longer part of the militarily integrated system. As a matter of fact, it was also clear that France could have imagined staying on as a full military member of the alliance, but in that case the system of command would have had to be different (the famous three-power "directorate"). France at the same time developed an independent nuclear force: whether that was a positive factor or not in keeping alliance membership is probably difficult to say. What matters here is only that both at step one and step five actual European countries have found formulas compatible with membership in the alliance. Which means that the alliance can change.

It is only at the level of the next two steps that the alliance is left behind in favour of non-membership. The two steps indicated correspond roughly to what above has been referred to as "non-aligned" and "neutral" countries respectively.

In order to explore these concepts a little bit further let us use Sweden and Finland as examples. The thesis would be, of course, that Sweden might be "neutral" in war in the sense of being non-available to belligerent powers (although the transit of German troops through Sweden up to Northern Norway in spring 1940 did not in general convince Norwegians that this was a fruitful interpretation of "neutrality"). And Sweden may be non-aligned in peace, in the sense of not being a bloc member. But that does not mean that Sweden is unavailable to the two blocs or, more importantly, that it is symmetrically available. The acquisition pattern for Swedish arms is probably relatively parallel to the acquisition pattern in the Swedish economy in general, meaning that very high technology items are acquired in the West, particularly from the US; Swedish officers attend training courses in NATO countries and not in WTO countries; there has been a famous case in Sweden alleging co-operation between Swedish military intelligence and the CIA, whereas an equally famous case of a person high up in the Swedish intelligence co-operating with the KGB was denounced as espionage; there is the problem of whether Swedish radar installations are linked up in any way, directly or indirectly, with corresponding NATO installations; and there is the very cordial reception that was accorded to the US defence minister in the autumn of 1981 (Norwegians might also add that the transit of US heavy material through Sweden from Gothenburg to central Norway in 1982 for the prepositioned US bases is certainly a way of being available, not least by giving an air of legitimacy to a programme undertaken by the Norwegian government, supported by the Norwegian Parliament but hardly by the Norwegian population). These points are given here not so much as a critique of Swedish foreign policy than as examples of dimensions to watch out for if one wants to take non-alignment as a policy really seriously. It is one thing not to be a member of a bloc, another thing to be non-available to the two blocs, and a third thing to be asymmetrically available, however much that may be an expression of the asymmetry any country will have in terms of ideology — social, political — not to mention economic structure and interaction patterns abroad, and so on. Sweden does badly in the third aspect.

The case of Finland is defined by the famous treaty of friendship, co-operation and mutual assistance of 1948. The key part of it is Article 1, according to which Finland has to use all its armed forces in order to defend its territory, on land, on sea, and in the air in case Finland or the Soviet Union is exposed to an armed attack from Germany or a country allied with Germany, through Finland. In a sense this defines Finland as an ally of the Soviet Union, in another sense not. Finland is an ally in the sense that Finland has to do something in case the Soviet Union is attacked by Germany or an ally of Germany (the focus on Germany was of course more understandable in 1948 than 35 years later); on the other hand the Finnish action is limited to Finnish territory, and to attacks on or through Finland. The article goes beyond the usual obligation of neutral states to make their neutrality, meaning here their military non-availability, credible through defence: the Soviet Union will come to her assistance in a way agreed upon between the two parties. But then, again "on the other hand": the treaty article imposes upon Finland the duty to defend herself not against any attack, it is focused only on an attack from Germany and an ally of Germany. So, evidently this makes Finland militarily available in case of war to the superpower in the East, if only under the condition of mutual agreement. In times of peace Finland can steer a fairly neutral course, not only being "non-aligned"; the acquisition of weapons over time (with a Western bias to start with, now with a Soviet bias) is an example of that. So is the voting pattern in the United Nations.

This is not the place to go further into these matters; suffice it only to say that all these concepts are as complex as the history of the countries in the post-war period.

Instead of developing this scheme further, let us turn our attention to the steps of the ladder or, more correctly, to the ladder as a whole. The metaphor raises two problems: is it a ladder worth climbing on to for all the countries of Europe, and if it is, how could that process come about?

The first question is central to the whole book: gradual decoupling from the superpowers is seen as one way of increasing security, not only for the decoupling, or decoupled, country, but for the system as a whole. The emphasis in saying this is not only on the word "decoupling", but also on the word "gradual": this is not a question of member or not of the alliances, but what kind of member, inside what kind of alliance. Thus, if all countries attained steps 4 and 5 combined, with no over-arching superpower command, at the same time as a process of transarmament is taking place with change of military doctrine, the nature of Europe would change even if the alliances are maintained. It is also clearly seen that the simplest way in which this could happen would not necessarily be with countries withdrawing or threatening to withdraw, but with the *superpower* gradually or totally withdrawing from the alliance, with their bases and nuclear capabilities. A Warsaw Treaty Organisation of that kind would not even have to be renamed; NATO would probably have to be renamed and the most appropriate corresponding name right now would be the Brussels Treaty Organisation (BTO). This would bring to mind such organisations as the Western European Union (WEU) which for that matter could be expanded to include all present European NATO members who would like to join, possibly also Canada. Names do not matter, the concept matters: alliances with superpowers playing a much more modest role or no role at all, with the understanding that the superpower will always tend to demand forward basing of conventional and nuclear capabilities as well as being on top of the command structure within the alliance. Change those three and the superpower role also changes.

In short, the point is made that much more important than membership or non-membership is the military posture and the degree of coupling to the superpowers. I would also go so far as to see many positive aspects in maintaining, in the West, a Western defence alliance. First, it constitutes a multilateral setting for discussion of all these problems, not only for forward basing, but also for withdrawal. Second, inasmuch as security is a legitimate concern for any country, defence is also a legitimate concern. A multilateral forum of relatively like-minded countries to discuss these concerns, and enter into patterns of co-operation, comes naturally. Third, even with transarmament, building down offensive capability and building up of defensive capabilities, alliances do not become quite meaningless. The nature of the weapon systems would by and large preclude quickly mobilised, long range systems (except for some interdiction capability), but that does not necessarily stand in the way of some countries having some purely defensive conventional forces from other countries stationed on their territory in peacetime. If this serves to demobilise one's own defence potential it may be harmful, but there are also certain geographical and demographic asymmetries, etc that could call for an arrangement of that type. At any rate, it would be so much more desirable than the present provocative and unstable state of affairs, that arguments against it from a more purist point of view are insignificant in comparison. After all there is a collective aspect to security; there is legitimacy to the idea of solidarity. The problem is only that collective security as presently practised by the alliances in general, and the Western alliance in particular, is not only provocative and unstable, but also much too easily combined with planning for attack. Hence not all countries would necessarily have to practice the self-imposed constraints of countries like Finland and Romania to the extent that their troops cannot be used abroad, including manoeuvres, except as United Nations Peace Forces.

However, there is a quite different dark cloud hanging over the upper steps of the ladder, from step 4 onwards. It is actually related to step 5 and the case of France which became militarily autonomous within the alliance, but did not adopt an inoffensive defence posture but the *force de frappe* instead. What this indicates is actually that the steps on the ladder themselves are ladders, and to some extent independent of each other. Thus, it is quite possible to imagine today all forward foreign bases in general and nuclear capabilities in particular withdrawn to the countries of origin, not only in Europe but also in Asia. Remaining on European soil, if the Soviet Union is counted as a continent in its own right, would be only the French and British nuclear forces, and on the European continent only the French. The question, of course, is whether the neighbouring countries in general and the Federal Republic of Germany in particular would be satisfied with this state of affairs or would demand parity. If they do, that could be obtained unilaterally, bilaterally or multilaterally: by the FRG having its own nuclear capability, sharing it with France in a more or less symmetric manner, or developing a (Western) European Defence Committee (EDC) where the French nuclear forces would play an important role. None of these solutions would be satisfactory to the Soviet Union or to some of the other Eastern European countries for that matter, possibly with the unilateral option for the FRG as the least satisfactory given Russian/Soviet experiences with Germany and Germans. The question of French nuclear disarmament then arises, and that opens up two clearly negative aspects of the French "going it alone" policies. First, a policy of independent nuclear forces makes France less subject to any multilateral transarmament decision that NATO might go in for. Second, precisely because of all these policies the French population seems to be less concerned with such matters than the populations of client countries in the two alliances, hence there is much less pressure from any independent peace movement for disarmament/transarmament as the presence in the French population at large of an active sentiment in favour of independent nuclear forces as something compatible with the status that France should be accorded in the international system. France seems to be governed by a general, Napoleonic party.

Does this mean that no country should go it alone inside an alliance, that they should all wait for the slowest country to catch up so that by consensus the system as a whole could move up the ladder if that is deemed desirable? Certainly not. It is probably only through the interplay between unilateral and multilateral decisions within an alliance that some progress can be made. Right now (autumn 1983) the clouds are dark; the chances are slim indeed. But that may change; another administration in Washington and social-democratic regimes all over Northern Europe might even change it very quickly if one does not assume that the military complexes of these countries are so firmly entrenched that efforts to change the political *status quo* will only make the state of latent military *coups d'état* in these countries more manifest. Time will tell; the argument here is in favour of both unilateralism and multilateralism. It is also in favour of co-ordinated unilateralism, as when countries in Northern Europe might go in for a nuclear weapons free zone concept, whether it is for countries bordering on each other so as to constitute a geographically contiguous area or for scattered countries (a "club"), and whether it happens with countries opting for nuclear free status simultaneously or with one country starting and others joining over time (as one would expect in a club with open membership).

Again, time will tell. Considerable statesmanship is needed and this is a scarce commodity. Some relaxation of tension is probably also needed as tension tends to lead to stereotyped action and conservative non-action. And that leads to the problem of possible first steps, to be discussed in 5.6 below.

4. Inner strength: towards less vulnerable societies

From the world of defence we moved to the world of international politics, and we are now proceeding to the world of domestic politics, the society as seen from the inside. Unfortunately, modern societies have accepted a division of labour whereby international affairs are to some extent seen as something independent of the way society is organised, as witnessed by the fact that very different societies often tend to have the same type of foreign policy establishment and almost identical military establishments. The basic position of this section is that there is a strong continuity between the way the inside of a society is organised and the way it behaves in external relations. This is a rather trivial statement; what we shall attempt to do is to explore some of these relations in a more precise way. More particularly, the problem to be explored is how a society can be built so as to enhance total security of a country, in other words the probability that it can survive in peace and freedom.

We hardly need a definition of invulnerability in order to start this exploration. It is the ability to withstand force and threats of force from the outside, by being strong on the inside. The medical parallel is obvious: this is the capacity of the human body to withstand any assault, from micro-organisms or from other sources, so that they do not have any "bite". The healthy body adequately nourished, clad, protected from the hazards of nature, (particularly in terms of excessive cold or heat, or excessive moisture) is one important precondition. Another is that the capacity of the body itself to fight off any intruder through the defence mechanisms of the cells of the human body, a capacity well related to the one just mentioned. And beyond that, should the other two fail it is the capacity of the body to engage in a more lasting cure, to undertake its own repair work. Hence, what we are looking for would be the mechanisms by means of which the social body could do the same, all the time drawing on its own resources, not being dependent on an outside that might be partly or wholly hostile. Another word for this, of course, is *self-reliance* as the general key to the problem of generating strength through one's own resources. From the very beginning it should be emphasised that this in no sense means cutting oneself off from the rest of the world. It only means, for any problem that the society feels has to be solved, that primary reliance is on one's own resources, with a view to building up a sufficient capacity to be self-sufficient *in times of crisis*. But in normal periods self-sufficiency is no goal. It does not give strength: as will be elaborated in the next section invulnerability is also derived from interaction with other countries, from having trade relations, for instance. But under the heading of self-reliance one would *first* try to become independent by using one's own resources, *second*, try to become inter-dependent by solving the problems that cannot normally be solved nationally or locally through exchange but then in an equitable manner. What is to be avoided is *dependency*. Independent and inter-dependent, but not dependent on others (nor making others dependent on oneself); that is the key to self-reliance.

To explore this further the usual distinctions between economic, ecological, political, social, cultural and military aspects may be useful, however unsophisticated it is theoretically.

Economic strength. The key has been given: using one's own resources as far as possible, meaning one's own natural resources, labour, skilled and unskilled, own capital, own ingenuity and research, own administrative capacity. But one does not have to practise this in all fields. Fortunately there is a theory as to which fields are more important than others, the theory of basic human needs. In this connection we only have to bother about the more material aspects of human needs: food, clothing, shelter, health, education, energy, transportation/communication *and* weapons for self-defence. The list can be made longer, but hardly shorter. The basic point is to have an economic practice tending towards self-sufficiency, in times of crises, in all these fields. More particularly, that means working towards self-sufficiency in food without necessarily practicing it in times of peace but with a definite plan as to how self-sufficiency can be obtained in times of war. Clothing and shelter may be less problematic since they do not have to be supplied on a continuous basis. The same may also apply to health and education although there is the need for supply of medicine, and this, then, turns into an important argument why every country should have its own capacity to produce the fundamental drugs, which are hardly more than a few hundreds in number. Energy self-reliance calls for heavy reduction of the dependency on foreign sources of energy, particularly oil-less countries, and training of the population in becoming better acquainted with new resources of energy. Needless to say this cannot be atomic power plants unless they are extremely well protected (for instance inside mountains): they only increase the vulnerability of a country by having catastrophic fall-out consequences if hit. And then this kind of programme calls for all kinds of emergency measures to maintain transportation (the Vietnamese were rather expert in this in the way they coupled bicycles together so as to make it possible to engage in even heavy transportation on rather primitive tracks) and communication (two-way miniaturised radio systems, and so on). A population with no alternatives to cars that, in turn, have no alternatives to petrol, and no other communication system than one-way radio/television and a highly vulnerable telephone system is certainly not a strong population.

One basic point here would be that exactly the same reasoning also applies to the local level. The purpose in making the national level self-reliant is to make it independent of other countries so that it can neither be blackmailed by countries on which it is dependent nor be tempted into aggressive excursions with rapid deployment forces to secure supplies. The same reasoning applies to the local level because the national level (in practice meaning the capital) may either be destroyed or be captured by an aggressor capable of forcing the rest of the country into capitulation. Continuation of resistance from the local level is only credible if a basis exists which is at least very close to economic self-sufficiency, in times of crisis. It should be noted that this means in practice a mobilisation of production capacity not only in the nation but also at the local level, above what is generally done under the assumption of "comparative advantages" governing world trade, meaning that a country does not necessarily produce what it needs but gets it in exchange for that which it thinks it has in excess, for instance some raw material or cheap labour.

Ecological self-reliance. This expression is only another way of calling for what is more technically known as "stable eco-systems". A stable eco-system has two major characteristics that are of significance here: the resources are not depleted, and waste products are adequately absorbed by the system so that pollution, including toxic pollution, does not become a problem, possibly even leading to efforts to export the pollution. Thus, a stable eco-system serves as a guarantee against dependency on natural resources from the outside, and general degradation of the natural environment through pollution, including the inhabitants.

Again, the point is not to argue in favour of only using one's own natural resources, never importing raw materials. The argument is in favour of maintaining ecological balance at a very high level, making use of nature's capacity to reproduce itself by relying as much as possible on renewable natural resources. More particularly, the point would be to organise the economy in such a way that in times of crisis the eco-system has not already been so degraded that it breaks down completely (eco-catastrophe) because of the pressures that will be put on it from a population possibly cut off from the outside. And the basic point here is to integrate ecological thinking with security thinking, seeing the two not as two separate aspects of human activity and politics, but as continuous with each other. In fact, there are so many strong interconnections between environment and security. Wars, for instance, are often over resources, meaning over the environment. Military activity is almost always destructive of the environment, and if these two points are combined it is clear that the destruction of the environment may lead to even more wars over resources. Concretely, water is a human necessity; the more that water is polluted and contaminated, for instance from a war where ABC-weapons have been used, the more likely is continued warfare in order to capture more water. It is a vicious circle we can ill afford to enter.

All that has been said so far applies to the local level, exactly for the same reason as the economic policy. Not only the national eco-system but also the local eco-system should, ideally speaking, be stable. Guerrilla movements know exactly what this means: being able to reap from nature a sufficient basis for biological sustenance, without leaving traces, is almost a necessary condition for guerrilla warfare. Without in any way saying that this is the ideal model of a human society it can nevertheless be said that some thinking and some preparation in this direction would greatly enhance the level of invulnerability of a country.

Political self-reliance. What this means is political independence, also known as autonomy, the capacity to derive one's own goals, and one's own strategies to pursue them. This goes beyond having national institutions capable of formulating means and ends of politics. The conclusion from what has been said above is also that there has to be a high level of autonomy, including institutions for adequate decision making. The general formula if one wants to combine national and local autonomy is a federal system, with the local political units being as much as possible the same as the locally self-reliant economic units. Such a country is strong not only because loss of autonomy in the political centre does not immediately imply the loss of autonomy everywhere, but also because a system of this kind has a great capacity for mobilising the local defences. Switzerland can be seen as an example here: Berne is less important relative to the rest of policy-making made in Switzerland than would be the case for the capitals of most other countries. On the other hand it is also clear that many of the cantons in the Swiss confederation are very far from small enough to mobilise really local resources of any kind. And it is also clear that some strong national decision making capacity is needed, for instance to direct a change in the politics of peace and security. To take only one example derived from above: a country striving for vulnerability cannot afford to depend only on electronic technology as it is so vulnerable to the electro-magnetic pulse (EMP) emanating from atomic explosions high up. It has at least to have a fall-back technology, for instance electro-mechanical or simply mechanical or — for some of its short distance rockets — it might probably need a glass fibre technology, seen as invulnerable to EMP. But this requires a lot of co-ordination and decision-making at the national level.

Social self-reliance. I would define this as the capacity of the country to handle its own conflicts in such a way that it is not weakened by the internal contradictions that any country will have. Groups, defined by age, gender, nation (whether defined linguistically or religiously), race, class, geographical variables inside a country, or political/ideological variables inside a country are related in contradictions, meaning conflicts in latent form. Sometimes they erupt, and that takes the form of destructive attitudes and destructive behaviour. This may cause considerable vulnerability not only because one of the conflicting parties may prefer to appeal to outside forces for help, but also because a country split by conflicts in latent and manifest forms will be less capable of mobilising any adequate defence against an intruder. If this situation is long-lasting then it may simply be because the country does not deserve to continue as a country. But a more constructive approach would, of course, be to see how the contradictions could be overcome.

More concretely this usually means either to settle them, or at least to have a conflict solution machinery capable of arriving at settlements as the conflict manifestations become too deep and too many. That is what sociology and politics are about, and this is not the place to go into any

details. Suffice it only to be said that efforts to solve the problems of class
by state ownership have proved highly unsuccessful, because they generate
a new upper class. It looks as if that problem can only be solved by having
enterprises must, and should be relatively small in size. And the problems
and some measure of direct democracy. In practice this means that
enterprises must, and should, be relatively small in size. And the problems
of age, gender, nation and race, all of them being attributes of the
individual with social implications, are either solved through some kind of
proportionate representation, or through separatism geographically
speaking, inside a country, usually calling for a federal structure, or outside
a country, meaning that a new country has been born. Whichever course is
taken matters less than that accumulation of such contradictions will
weaken the country considerably, making it more vulnerable and hence
more tempted to prefer offensive military systems to defensive ones. This
certainly applies to political/ideological differences and here, with all its
shortcomings, it looks as if it is hard to beat parliamentary democracy with
constitutionally guaranteed division of power in legislative, executive and
judiciary branches as a conflict resolution mechanism. The only problem is
when a majority decides for a minority and the decision affects the
fundamental, basic human needs of the minority — at this point
parliamentary democracy has its limitations. The offended or exploited
minority will and should continue to fight, possibly with separatism and
parallel institutions as the outcome.

One reason why the Soviet Union appears so threatening may have
something to do with this. Unable to overcome the contradictions in the
security belt surrounding the Soviet Union (and in the Soviet Union itself,
for that matter) it must be tempting for the Soviet leadership, like the
Israeli leadership, to want a security belt outside the security belt. A stable
GDR with most contradictions overcome might serve as a security belt for
Poland, herself a protection for the inner security belt; and so on. Any
thinking in this direction would lead to an expansionism which then would
be socially motivated rather than politically and/or economically. And there
is also an obvious defensive aspect to it: precisely because the Eastern
European countries look so riven by contradictions the Soviet Union might
be tempted to use offensive weaponry in order to have the fighting on West
European soil, and then not only to avoid material destruction. In order to
counteract this, and for a number of other reasons besides, introduction of
parliamentary democracy in Eastern Europe would probably be a major
contribution to peace and security in Europe. That it is possible in a way
compatible with at least a number of interests of the Soviet Union is
already proven in the case of Finland: "Finlandisation" pointing to a
political/social course that hopefully will be much more utilised in the
future. Finlandisation of Eastern Europe would be a tremendous step
towards peace and security in that region, combining that type of freedom
for the Eastern European peoples with increased security for all.

Cultural self-reliance. This is the capacity of the system to generate its
own values and norms, making it clear to the inhabitants what is the end to
be defended, and what are the means to do so. These goals must be created
continuously; old formulas may be quickly out-dated. It calls for a creative

process of national self-determination. Of course this is not the only factor contributing to what is usually called a "high morale"; that is probably the outcome of a qualitatively generally satisfactory way of life. What is pointed to here is that any way of life has a qualitative, cultural dimension; it is not only a question of supplying material goods and services. This is where such words as "freedom" and "identity" enter the game, and very much so, in a dialectical manner. Identity means having something to believe in, to live for. Freedom points to the possibility of changing one's identity, expanding it, contracting it, switching to other foci. One without the other can lead to a very empty life; together they would make for very strong people indeed. And again one has the feeling that a country which is not good at providing cultural identity will have to compensate with military weapons that are offensive in their nature. Of course, a major and still highly important type of identity is known as "nationalism", the willingness to fight, even die for one's own country. No doubt this type of identity can compensate for a high level of material deprivation or lack of identity in other respects.

Military self-reliance. The two preceding sections dealt with exactly this. It means non-reliance on assistance from the outside (unless it is already built into one's defence posture in times of peace, and then only at the level of inoffensive weapons). It is based on one's own capacity to produce inoffensive weapons, and to organise defensive defence in general. Invulnerability is also based on ability to make weapons invulnerable; in practice this means stationing aircraft, boats, vehicles in general in mountain caves or other places where they are not easily destroyed. It may also mean hiding them; at any rate it means dispersing them, as argued above in 5.2.

And, if weapons can be made or should be made invulnerable, the same applies to human beings. There is nothing in this argument against civil defence, for instance in order to protect a civilian population against fall-out from atomic explosions on the territory of neighbouring countries. What is to be strongly rejected, however, is any combination of a strong civil defence with offensive capability, not only because it makes the country appear even more threatening ("Are they thinking of a first strike since they are protecting the civilian population against a possible retaliation from our side?") but also because it is utterly unrealistic in the atomic age and hence builds up illusions in the population.

And then there is a third argument which belongs under this heading. It is a problematic and dialectical one, and very important. *There is invulnerability in vulnerability.* A country laying itself open to an all-out nuclear attack without any capacity for retaliation is in a sense doing the same as animals are known to do: if one turns out to be stronger, then the inferior in a struggle may signal its vulnerability through special noises, lying down on the ground; and by making it evident that the other side can kill it is able to avoid that killing. Human beings are not known to be as civilised as animals, they are not known to pay that much attention to such cues. But there are also some indications that this mechanism may work. And that may serve as an argument against too heavy civil defence. The better the population is protected the more the other side may think:

"Okay, it does not matter much what we do since they are protected anyhow".

In short: there are highly concrete steps to make in order to give a country more inner strength. But invulnerability also has an external or outer aspect to which we now turn.

5. Outer usefulness: a new departure for peaceful coexistence

It sounds like an eternity ago, but it is actually only 16 years: 1967. Major things had happened in the East-West conflict process. The French President, Charles de Gaulle, had disinvited NATO from France and with it a number of military installations, and taken France out of the integrated military command of the North Atlantic Treaty Organisation. At the same time there was clearly the beginning of something new called "co-operation". *Détenté* had started, although it took some time before there was general and shared awareness that such a thing was around, not only in plans and speeches, but in reality. NATO even produced a paper, over the name of the Belgian Foreign Minister Pierre Harmel, a document from which there is still quite a lot to learn.

In Strasbourg the Council of Europe was interested in exploring, in general terms, possible new patterns of East-West co-operation and asked the newly founded International Peace Research Association whether such a study could be made. The task fell on the present author and the document was produced the same year. In that document there are some elements of a theory of peace, or more precisely, a list of conditions under which co-operation is seen as conducive to peace. Five such conditions are singled out for special attention: there has to be *symmetry* or some degree of equality between the partners; there has to be *homology* or some degree of structural similarity between the partners; there has to be *symbiosis* in the sense that co-operation is really important for both partners; there has to be some element of *institution-building* at the supra-national level; and there has to be *entropy* meaning that the co-operation has to take place in all kinds of channels, well distributed, not only government to government and between the superpowers, for instance.

It is easily seen in retrospect that the critical condition among these five is the first one, the condition of symmetry. The partners are relatively homologous, after all they are all countries in the Northern hemisphere, modern and industrialised with bureaucratic and corporate institutions, with professions and urbanisation. They only differ as to whether capital should dominate over state, state over capital, or they should be in some kind of balance; and they differ with respect to political institutions, the extent to which rulers should be accountable to the population in elections. Moreover, there was no doubt that the co-operation was symbiotic and still is: East needs technology, West needs raw materials and energy so there is at least that basis to build on, as is very clearly illustrated today in the famous gas-pipeline from East to West. But it has been equally clear all the time that suspra-national instituton building has not been on the agenda beyond the very limited functions provided by the Economic Commission for Europe under the United Nations Economic and Social Council, located in Geneva; much as it has also been clear that the level of entropy has been low, co-operation has been governmental although certainly not only between the superpowers.

The crucial condition is that of symmetry, and here five more specific points were mentoned: the gains should be about equal, the inputs should be about equal, the level of dependency on the co-operation about equal, participation about equal, and the change caused by the co-operation about equal. The rationale underlying such conditions becomes very clear when one considers the situation when they do not obtain. Imagine that one party puts very much into it because it means so much, depends on it, participates with great eagerness and as a result exposes itself to the risk of change. It would also have to gain a lot in order to feel that the pattern of co-operation is reasonable. On the other hand, imagine a party that does not put very much into the co-operation, neither depends on it nor participates very much, changes nothing: in that case, if it does not gain very much it may not matter much. But if it gains a lot it has certainly made an advantageous deal. And since this is politics, not simply a question of trade, it is not sufficient that gains are seen as off-setting inputs. It is also important that the *net balance* should be relatively equal, that participation in joint enterprises of all kinds should be relatively equal and that changes should balance out. For if they do not, then one party can use, or has already used, the co-operation or co-existence as a lever in order to, for example, make the other party more "capitalist", that certainly is politics. Either party may feel that one or both *needs* change more than the other and that the other is justified in using the leverage it has. But such feelings are not very helpful in this connection. We are dealing with parties that are both tremendously self-righteous at least at the higher levels of power. Both see themselves as carriers of the message and the cause that will ultimately prevail, neither is willing to be subject to or submit to the other. And co-operation inevitably leads to change.

Hence, conditions such as these, or similar conditions, have to be taken seriously. The frequently quoted expression to the effect that co-operation should be to "mutual benefit" is a more general formulation in that same direction. It is also relatively easy, against the background of such conditions, to see what went wrong in East-West co-operation. Take the case of Poland as an example, extreme but also fairly typical. Trade relations are set up, basically exchanging raw materials, semi-manufactures and agricultural products, and some finished products from the earlier phases of the industrial revolution from the East, with much more advanced technology and products from later phases of industrialism from the West. In a sense this pattern is normal, this is what East-West trade has been about for centuries, as has also been the case for North-South trade, only even more so. And that makes the results quite predictable. More particularly, there are three basic changes that will take place in the Eastern country (or the Southern country): the people will get addicted to the type of consumer goods that become available under the deal; the elites will become addicted to the capital goods or resources in general that become available through them, since it will enhance their power, at least in their own eyes; and the deal will in general be decreasingly favourable to the East (South). This is so because of the tendency of the terms of trade between the processed and the unprocessed to develop to the disadvantage of the latter, with the notable exception of energy resources, since 1973. But this is not true for all types of energy resources: Poland did not benefit from improved or equal terms of trade over time for its export of coal; the Soviet Union did benefit because of the export of gas and oil. The same would generally apply to agricultural products: to pay for technology with agricultural produce will tend to become an uphill fight.

Hence, the options available to the Eastern (Southern) country in the deal become increasingly limited. One measure would be to compensate for deteriorating terms of trade through increasing output, by increasing the productivity and/or the input of work in number of workers, number of hours — the latter possibly disguised as "voluntary contributions". Another possibility is to fill the gap between the imports and exports with loans that then will have to be serviced. If one engages in both at the same time the net result will be a tendency to exploit workers more and more at the same time as the country sinks into debt that tends to consume closer and closer to 100 per cent of the income from exports, meaning that the policy is self-defeating. In this kind of situation the addiction of the people to the life-style of the West, combined with increasing exploitation of them in order to pay for it and for the considerably higher life-styles of their own elites, not to mention for the waste in the whole process, cannot but lead to revolts, even attempts at revolution. When an addicted system has managed to paint itself into the corner the room for manoeuvre for the governing elites is very limited. Whatever it grants to the population in general and the workers in particular, in terms of consumers goods or improved working conditions (including decreased hours of work) will have to be more than compensated for by increased productivity and it is not at all obvious that that would be so high on the agenda of those who want a system change. The rest of the story, given the case of Poland, is rather well known.

This is not to say that the system would have reacted differently had East-West trade been differently structured. There are certainly also over-riding political causes for the Polish débacle, some of them located inside Poland in the struggle between the Polish people and the power elite fighting for survival as a group; and outside Poland with the fear in the Soviet Union of losing a client country or even having it turn against the Soviet Union, and the interest of the US in seeing this happen. The non-symmetric way in which that trade pattern was structured certainly was one important factor in it all. Basic changes were being wrought inside the Polish social formation without any corresponding change taking place in the West as a result of the pattern of exchange. Dependency was very high, inputs equally so, the net gains more and more dubious. If the purpose was to promote security through co-operation, not only through the highly dangerous means of deterrence, even balance of terror, then the purpose was not obtained. It was simply a bad piece of social engineering at the international level. If the purpose was to wreak havoc inside Poland then the purpose was obtained, but in that case it does not belong under the heading of "active peaceful co-existence". Hence, and this is the net conclusion of this exploration so far: it has to be done in a different way if we are to attempt it again.

But before we try to say something about that it should once more be remembered how epoch-making the changes at the end of the 1960s were as a phase in East-West history. A new paradigm was being ushered in. There was to be less concern with the military, even with the military balance, and more concern with other types of relations between East and West; less concern with moralism and political conflicts in general, more concern with factors that could unite or at least serve as a basis of co-operation. After all, this was the type of politics that had been started in the 1950s and formalised in the Rome Treaty, eventually leading to the European Community whereby two arch-enemies, Germany and France, were to be brought under a common roof in a pattern of symmetric, homologous, symbiotic, supra-national, and highly entropic co-operation. Even though the situation was different could one not try to make what seemed to work in the case of the European Community also work at the East-West level?

Today, 15 years later, the question sounds totally misplaced. The United States has an administration bent on trying to bring the Soviet Union down on her knees, through military threats, political action and economic pressures, beyond what the US thinks the Soviet Union can stand. That policy will not succeed; the Soviet Union is not to be blackmailed into capitulation — this may be one of the few things that the elite and the people in that enormous country might agree on totally. But it certainly means that the atmosphere could not be much worse, short of a hot war. The five rules mentioned above are traffic rules in a gentler international climate, rules of behaviour for *associative* politics, building peace by coming closer to one another, yet not so close that the identity of the systems is threatened. They are rules that presuppose that both parties see their own security as somehow predicated upon the other party feeling secure, not insecure. Here it should again be remembered that if security is the probability of keeping one's own system intact so that possible changes are truly endogenous changes, then co-operation *may* threaten security. It *does* involve the risk of change, one reason why both parties will probably prefer to keep co-operation below certain limits for themselves. But then they must at the same time also understand that there are such limits for the other party; a good example here being television co-operation by beaming TV programmes from satellites even if this is not wanted by the ruling elites. An unnecessary provocation.

Singling out the present US administration for attention in no way means that there is not a constant under-layer of efforts by both camps to subvert the other. No doubt this is most pronounced in the superpowers; only that at present there is an explicitness, a directness and something viciously aggressive about US behaviour in this regard. But that administration is not going to last forever, for which reason it makes sense to ask the question: what would be some new departures if one should try again? In other words, if once more one should try to build security on co-operation rather than deterrence (and in addition to that build it on defence rather than retaliation), then precisely what should one do?

Assuming that there is something to the principles listed in the beginning, the first conclusion to be drawn may be what one should learn from the past 15 years: *Do not give to economic relations, whether in the form of trade or joint ventures, such a dominant position in the whole co-operation picture.* Of course there are exceptions to this rule: between countries at a relatively similar level of technical-economic development there should be no objection, relations between Bulgaria and Greece possibly being an example, and there are others. With the terms of trade developing the way they tend to do, and adding to this the very asymmetric spin-off effects, inegalitarian deals are doomed to be destabilising, not only inside Eastern countries, but also for the relationship as a whole.

The second major conclusion to be drawn would be something like this: *do not give to intergovernmental relations, whether in the field of economics, politics, military matters or whatever such a dominant position in the whole co-operation picture.* That good, even co-operative inter-governmental relations are a necessary condition for good international relations in the contemporary world goes without saying. But they are not sufficient as a condition. Much more has to be done at the non-governmental level, and it is possible to do so. I can give a small-scale testimony to this myself, having been 20 times to the Soviet Union during the 30 years from 1953 to 1982. On most occasions it was for meetings and conferences, usually in the context of some type of co-operation between an organisation in the Soviet Union and an organisation in the West. All the first 19 occasions were instructive, but visit number 20 in summer 1982 was by far the best one: a camping trip with the other members of the family, by car through the Western part of the Soviet Union from North to South, entering from Finland, exiting through Romania weeks later.

Very many people have done this, and the exchanges of information and opinion at night, at the camping sites, almost always tended in the same direction: once inside the Soviet Union the freedom to move around appears unrestricted (except that one should show up at night at the place where overnight facilities have been booked in advance) *and* that the Soviet people in general are as warm, charming and interested in talking and discussing with foreigners as is humanly possible. That there are material shortcomings relative to the affluence still prevailing in the West is well-known. That does not have to stand in the way of a most positive experience. And the one single headline that can be written on top of that experience, in fact on top of all 20 of them, would be: *the Soviet people want peace not war.* It sounds like a platitude, but if so it is a rather important platitude and it is one that, unfortunately, cannot be said of all peoples in the world.

Of course, travels of that type should be reciprocal. If our individual tourism cannot be fully engaged in when travelling in the Soviet Union it can to a considerable extent be so in Eastern Europe, and millions make use of this opportunity every year (if one includes Yugoslavia). Most travellers, however, would be surprised to find how much latitude there is for individual tourism also in the Soviet Union as long as one accepts that there has to be some planning in advance and as long as one is not limited by group travel: the groups have a tendency to be "processed" with political overtones, substituting for the economic overtones in the corresponding type of processing in the West. This is stupid propaganda in both places.

Whether the Soviet Union will give this opportunity for individual tourism to its own citizens in the near future remains to be seen; if not group travel is also a possibility and should be much more encouraged. But I will go further than that: given the state of extremely dangerous tensions between East and West, tourism as such becomes a luxury, and a political dimension should be added. Discussions, dialogues should be encouraged. Informed or uninformed, critical or constructive, or all four combined, does not matter so much. What matters is that as many people as possible try to explore together what the problems are that seem to divide our countries and groups of countries and what the possible solutions might be. If in the East this should lead to the introduction of officialdom, of discussions that are more controlled than people in the West are used to, then that should not be a major objection — at any rate it would be a part of contemporary reality. Imagine thousands of such encounters, not so spectacular as when Scandinavian women were marching to Minsk in summer 1982, but involving many many more people: does it not stand to reason that this could increase the level of mutual concern, the number of people who would start thinking constructively of how negative stereotypes could be counteracted, not merely by changing images of the other side but by doing something about our own side so that the other side has reasons for changing its images? Add then to this the dimension of people meeting within their professional or other concerns, physicians meeting physicians (as they have done, and very effectively so, in the area of warning against any faith in the health system being adequate to handle the consequences of a nuclear war), retired people meeting retired people, young people, students, women's organisations — whatever. I am thinking in terms of Europe as one great peace seminar, for people in general and for people that are somewhat similar one way or the other; if possible reporting their findings to the population at large so that it would give more people more material to consider. As is always the case it might very well be that the process is more important than the goal, that discussions of how to achieve peace may themselves lead to more peace than the proposals that come out of the discussions.

However, good feelings and understanding are important, not only at the governmental but also at the people level, but politics is also made of harder stuff. The basic idea behind this approach to peace and security is symbiosis; that *countries are mutually useful to each other*. The security of a country is a function not only of its usefulness to its own citizens, so that they remain relatively satisfied, but also of its usefulness to the outside. This can only come about through interaction. Much of this usefulness will have to be economic, but it can also be political, humanitarian, ecological and cultural to mention several. Switzerland has been mentioned above: using its banking services, its conference services and its Red Cross Organisations as examples of being useful to the world community along the first three of these dimensions. The invulnerability of France relative to any adversary may consist not only in excellent French technology that can be bought, but also in the everlasting significance of French culture. The security of Norway, on the other hand, may rest more on a humanitarian factor: the image of Norway as a country that comes to the rescue of others in distress, including Armenians after the First World War. In short, there are so many formulas; and each country may develop its own formula. But over all of them the following has to be written: they only contribute to security if it can be convincingly shown that they are better available when the country is free and intact than when it is conquered and destroyed.

And that points to an important analytical distinction. Whenever a country has something to offer to the world community in general, and adversary countries in particular, the latter might think: "This looks nice, I would like to possess it completely, forever — a war has its risks but it might be worth it if possession will be the outcome". The outer usefulness of a country, hence, depends on its ability to show that the usefulness is only available under conditions of peace and freedom; if not, those things will either be destroyed by warfare itself, or by self-inflicted sabotage. Any country with important raw materials is useful to others when these commodities are floated on the world market, and this may add to its security. But it may also add to its insecurity by tempting others into conquest. To counteract that, usefulness in peace should somehow be accompanied by uselessness in war — for instance by finding a process whereby raw materials, even ores, would be destroyed in the war process. To take an example: if it is really true that the ice-free harbours in Norway constitute a temptation to the Soviet Navy then some way of making these harbours useless in war, if not blocking them on a permanent basis by artificial ice, then by some other method, should be found and the results should be communicated.

However, all of this is a rather negative approach. The basic approach would have to be positive, and be based on national self-reliance. Concretely this would combine inner strength with outer usefulness in a carefully worked-out balance. On the one hand there would have to be sufficient mobilisation of economic factors inside a country to guarantee self-sufficiency in times of crisis, so that the country cannot be blackmailed into surrender because essential products are not produced within the borders of a country. Beyond that level, however, the country would reach out for partners all over the world, including, indeed, potential adversaries, in the search for symmetric (equitable) trade structures.

To concretise: the gas pipeline from the Soviet Union to Western Europe constitutes a link between East and West of a highly symbiotic nature. That linkage, however, should never constitute the only answer to the energy supply problem of the countries in Western Europe. It should come on top of a programme of energy self-sufficiency by means of the many methods that now are known in the field of energy conversion, including insulation and the fight against waste. Only that way can the needs of people and the interests of countries be turned into the raw material out of which peace and security can be constructed, partly through inner strength ("independence"), partly through outer usefulness ("inter-dependence").

It is on top of an infrastructure of national self-reliance, combining a maximum self-sufficiency with equitable trade at the international level that much deeper webs of human interrelations can be spun, ultimately based on thousands, indeed millions of person to person contacts.

And in that connection maybe one should conclude with one little point: Eastern Europeans are so much more competent in Western European languages than *vice versa*. As a very minimum the level of knowledge of that beautiful (although unnecessarily difficult) Russian language should increase: there were good attempts in the early years after the Second World War that should be taken up again. The suffering caused by the intricacies of Russian grammar are considerable, but more than compensated for by the beauties of the language and the culture to which the language is the key. And the Soviet Union could contribute greatly to this by organising summer schools in Russian as so many Western European countries do for their languages in their many resort areas, thereby also opening their country more to meaningful tourism.

6. What kind of Europe, what kind of world? — a dialogue

The time has now come to try to pull together the lines of thought that have been developed, and also to look at them critically. In order to do that I shall from time to time make use of the dialogue form between *Reader* and *Author*. This will certainly not exhaust the problems in the mind of any reader; there is nothing final about anything in this field, but it may perhaps inspire in some readers even more questions and more critical ones.

First, a short summary, the shortest possible. The basic idea of the book is simply that there are four approaches to the terrible danger in which we find ourselves, and one of them itself splits into four approaches. There is conflict resolution, balance of power, disarmament and alternative security policies; the latter dividing into transarmament, non-alignment, inner strength and outer usefulness. Some basic propositions in these seven fields have been put forward:

Conflict resolution: The conflict is an incredible tangle of ideological issues and interests, of competition for the best strategic positioning, of all the issues related to block formation in the two alliances and to the military-bureaucratic-corporate-intelligentsia complexes. Any solution of the underlying ideological issue as to what constitutes the correct approach to social development, the blue or the red options, will have to be for the future; let it only be noted that an injection into the theory and practice of development of more options (green, pink, yellow) will tend to depolarise the issue. The conflicts of interest cannot be settled in the short-run either, given the systemic need of capitalist countries for world encompassing economic cycles and the historical need of the Soviet Union for security along its border. But the other three issues could all be alleviated through alternative security policies that would lead to a pull-back of offensive forces and creation of defensive military postures, thereby eliminating the most provocative, threatening aspects of the current situation, to the softening of the two alliances, and to the transformation of the MBCI-complexes in a more self-reliant, less superpower dependent direction. In addition to this it has been pointed out repeatedly that even if the basic conflicts cannot be solved in the forseeable future, much can be done to soften them if each side were able to alleviate some of the basic fears of the other side. Concretely this would mean, in the Soviet Union, a consistent and successful fight against Stalinism in all its manifestations inside the country itself, and in its relations to her allies; in the United States it would mean an equally consistent and successful fight against the economic crisis of the system in the country itself, and amongst her allies. All of these are policies which one could start today if the political will were present; in addition there is some motivation to do so, from time to time, but perhaps not sufficient capability.

Balance of power: Here the basic point was simply that there is no such thing as balance of power in the sense of any reasonably stable point, or relationship, as long as weapons are offensive and provocative. On the other hand it was pointed out that there is a mutuality to security, and that the Palme Commission formula of "common security" could be made very meaningful if based on the understanding that security has to be as high as possible for both parties, as equal as possible and as co-operative as possible. More concretely this points in the direction of defensive weapons. In a world with only defensive weapons the problem of balance of power, in the sense of some type of matching with the other side, no longer arises. A number of co-operative tasks in establishing such a system have been pointed out: it would be in the interest of both parties to teach each other how they could best develop a credible, defensive military posture and use the UN for peace-keeping, satellite control, etc.

Disarmament: The basic point made was that there will not be such a thing as long as the conditions for the disarmament process are that it should be mutual, balanced and controlled. For that reason *transarmament* looks like a much more viable approach. But that does not liberate us from the disarmament problem: there is still the problem of getting rid of offensive weapons in general, offensive weapons of mass destruction in particular, and nuclear mass destruction weapons even more particularly. Technically they can be brought to a third country, one missile from each side or according to a more complex formula, inspected for their content, dismantled with the possibility that fissionable material is put at the disposal of atomic power plants after it has been diluted. A basic point of the whole book, however, is that no such thing is going to happen unless there has been a change in military doctrine and some transarmament process, in order to give a feeling of security in a dangerous world in general, including Europe, which has a very bad record of belligerence and repression. Moreover, it has been argued that for anything to happen a very different composition of disarmament commissions, conferences and negotiations fora has to be called for.

Transarmament: It has been pointed out that there is a triad of conventional military defence, paramilitary defence and non-military defence that could be developed, and is already developed in some neutral/non-aliged countries of high standing in Europe. It is not that new.

Non-alignment: It has been pointed out that there are a number of steps here, from being completely available, military speaking, to the superpower, to being completely unavailable. It is certainly not only a question of membership or not of a military block.

Inner strength: It has been pointed out that this is basically a question of a higher level of self-reliance economically, ecologically, politically and culturally and of building stronger societies, less full of contradictions through processes of decentralisation, local self-reliance, and efforts to handle successfully the conflicts inside the countries. Ultimately, inner strength becomes a question of creating a society worth living in for all its citizens.

Outer usefulness: It has been pointed out that this is partly a question of creating an associative structure between countries and blocks of countries, based on symbiosis and symmetry; less on economic co-operation than before and more on non-economic forms of co-operation; less on governmental co-operation than before and more on non-governmental co-operation. Then there is the second approach: to find out how a country can make it credible that it is very useful to other countries when permitted to live in peace and freedom, intact, undestroyed by any force or threat of force *and* that this usefulness will suffer a considerable decline if the country is attacked, leave alone occupied.

That, more or less, is the summary. And let us then listen to the first comments by the reader and the author:

Reader: This may be an interesting programme, but I have had one very important doubt from the very beginning. It is a complex, even a complicated programme. It presupposes a holistic approach, many aspects of the total situation are taken into consideration, certainly not only, as is so common today, missile-counting exercises. But will a total approach not also necessarily lead to a totalitarian approach? Does it not presuppose a very strong government inside a country capable of carrying out all these policies in a relatively synchronised manner, and, in addition, of synchronising it with other countries?

Author: I agree that the approach is holistic, or at least an effort to be so: that was indeed the intention. One might also wish for a political situation to occur whereby many countries would engage in several such policies at the same time. But that is certainly unlikely, and I am not even sure that it is necessary. The point has been made in the first chapter that what matters, at least to start with, is not to carry out all such policies to the letter, but to make clear indications, even only of intentions, in those directions. If there are seven policies I would say that seven small steps in each one of these directions would be much more promising for the future than one big step along one of the dimensions because of the inner logic in all these matters. We have overwhelming evidence that the spirit of any disarmament treaty is effectively counteracted before the ink is dry because nothing is done along the other dimensions. Hence, my general answer would be to try to avoid both the all-out holistic approach and the all-out unidimensional one in favour of many small steps along many dimensions undertaken by many countries. Walking on four legs, in short, if only with the speed of a tortoise.

Reader: But who will then start such a process, where is the beginning?

Author: The beginning is, to my mind, only to be found in the clear realisation of the fallacy of a policy based on a deterrence that has to be provocative; if it is not accompanied by threats it is not credible; if it is not accompanied by uncertainty it could be circumvented, and it is bound to lead to endless arms races. The optimistic assumption, of course, is that there will be some understanding of this at the governmental level before the present policies end with a war. I do not expect an understanding of that type to come in all or many countries at the same time. But it could come in some countries. Thus, it is interesting to note that in 1983 social democrats are in opposition in many countries: Norway, Denmark, the Netherlands, Great Britain, Belgium, West Germany. This may serve to sharpen their senses about alternative security policies when conservative governments try to implement policies that clearly are against the will of the majority of the people, and in addition try to avoid not only plebiscites but also votes in the national assemblies. It is also interesting to note that it is very easy today to find people among the military who have no difficulties with the need for a new military doctrine, although their expertise will bring in all kinds of interesting ideas and nuances in the analysis. Also, it should be remembered that what is asked for here is nothing more radical than the policies already engaged in by countries like Switzerland, Yugoslavia, Albania, Austria, Finland and Sweden, in different ways. It has also been pointed out repeatedly how different these countries are, indicating that these policies should be compatible with very different approaches to political matters in general. No total change is needed.

Reader: But these countries have their security to a large extent because other countries are members of NATO!

Author: I doubt this very much, although it is commonly believed in NATO circles, and perhaps also said by some military and political leaders in some neutral and non-aligned countries. First of all, it should be noted that if anyone of the neutral or non-aligned countries should by force be made militarily much more available to one of the superpowers, I doubt very much that the other superpower would come to the rescue. There may be all kinds of efforts to subvert an invasion, to send arms back with refugees — one case being Afghanistan today. But that is not the same as the type of protection given to an ally according to the principle "an attack on one of us is an attack on us all". Second, as long as one of the superpowers of the blocks has very high offensive capability, it may be in the interest of some neutral or non-aligned countries that there is a countervailing block in the region, for the simple reason that in case of a general war by far the most belligerent activity would be between the two blocks. Any mssile on West German soil not only would focus more belligerent attention on West Germany and less on the United States, but also more on West Germany than on Switzerland, Austria and France. Gradients in the landscape of unavailability will make the unavailable countries stand out and make the available ones more obvious targets. On the other hand, however, the objection to that type of argument would be that a region with two blocks pitted against each other is a very dangerous place anyhow, and it would be far better to have a region with no such blocks and little or no offensive capability at all. In other words, the politics of those five countries throughout.

Reader: Imagine, however, that the type of plan indicated in section 3.4 is carried out. You have said yourself that this might lead to a Europe with France being the only holder of nuclear arms on the European continent, the Soviet Union not counting. Could that not actually be an even more dangerous situation, with bilateral or multilateral co-operation between France and neighbouring countries, even with a European Defence Community with nuclear weapons?

Author: It would, and to be honest I have no answer. As long as France manages to be in the shadows of the superpowers so that all attention is focused on them I can see no dynamism towards nuclear disarmament in that particular country. It is interesting to note that even people highly critical of the peace movement, among other reasons because it is held to be totally unrealistic and ineffective, point to the virtual non-existence of a peace movement, with the exclusion of the classical communist peace movement, in France. As far as I can understand, the only way out is for all true friends of France to encourage a more genuine peace movement and a change in military doctrine in that country, which may now very well risk being the final redoubt, a little bit like Brazil when it was holding out with slavery long after other countries had given it up. The only thing I can say at this point is to elevate France to the same level as the superpowers as a problem country, even suspecting that this is what some of the most nationalist, and for that reason provincial, French elites actually might like because that is the way they see themselves.

Reader: But if this process implies a certain imitation of the five countries you mention, is it not to be expected that there might even be resistance from the neutral and non-aligned countries because their comparative advantage might be reduced?

Author: I would suspect exactly that. My own experience lecturing and discussing these matters in a number of countries is that very many people in countries low on the security scale of 5.1 above would like to get higher up, that establishment people in countries higher up look at this with scepticism, and that anti-establishment people in countries higher up are even more sceptical because they see the shortcomings of their own countries so clearly, and for that reason would never define their own countries as model countries, high up on any index of security.

Reader: I would certainly say that this is particularly true in the case of Switzerland. You have made that country too ideal by far, forgetting about the horrible way in which the country treats its conscientious objectors (not that different from the way it is done in the Soviet Union); the arms exports; and the generally high level of militarisation of the country penetrating everywhere, with arms practice in villages, now possibly women also doing service, with the tendency for high military ranks to go from father to son, the linkage with industry, etc.

Author: I would agree with all that, and if I myself were a Swiss I would certainly spend much of my time fighting along exactly those lines. Being myself a conscientious objector I am happy to be a citizen in a country where that type of objection was permitted, although my own objection to the additional six months on top of the service period in the military — to be spent in a very meaningless "alternative" service — landed me in prison for half a year. However, if I should discuss the case of Switzerland I would use the seven dimensions indicated in that section to get a more complete view. Perhaps it would be useful to start with the last four dimensions and ask the question of to what extent Swiss defence really is defensive. The Swiss may say that the aircraft they have are the only ones available on the market, but the point could still be made that their autonomy is sufficient to look provocative. Perhaps more attention could be given to this point if the intention really is to be non-provocative. And the same certainly applies to the possible acquisition of new tanks, such as the German Leopard II: a weapon system with possible offensive capability. To this it may be objected that Switzerland is surrounded only by other "Western" countries, but that may change in case of a war. Here major criticism should set in. Also the country does not develop non-military defence, probably because the military are so unable to understand conscientious objectors.

Then one might of course also put some question marks in connection with the non-alignment. The experience from the Second World War was that it was a neutrality in favour of Germany, even so much so that the British bombarded the Swiss weapons industry, Oerlikon, on some occasions. And there are many other points such as the trains passing through Switzerland. But to this, in turn, it may be objected that the country did as well as it could, and followed a relatively neutral line, although it helped Nazi Germany unnecessarily by sending back many Jewish refugees, and managed to escape unscathed. What matters today is that it is not under any superpower command, it does not have any nuclear tasks to perform, nor does not have any bases on its territory. These are the big facts, overwhelmingly so relative to smaller points — seen in a European comparative perspective.

Of course it can be objected that Switzerland is far from self-reliant given its present trade structure, which spreads its market connections all over the world, relatively thinly, in terms of exploitation, like 160 cat's paws resting on the shoulders of 160 countries. And yet the country has a planning structure which makes it credible that it cannot easily be blackmailed into submission for lack of what is needed to satisfy the basic needs of the population during a war. But the atomic power plants are totally inconsistent with a policy of invulnerability.

When it comes to "outer usefulness' Switzerland is obviously playing on the second aspect of this dimension, not on direct international co-operation. This has to do with the conflict resolution dimension: Switzerland does not play the useful roles of countries like Finland,

Yugoslavia and to some extent her neighbour Austria, the role as go-between. Switzerland is not only to the right, but to the right of the right, as evidenced by recent behaviour in the Conference on Security and Co-operation in Europe. Switzerland does not enter the international system as a partner but as a facility, charging a hefty price for services rendered. Moreover, not only does Switzerland not contribute to East-West conflict resolution in any significant way but the country also aggravates the North-South conflict by its very low contribution to official development assistance, its non-membership in some UN organisations and a general pattern of non-participation.

Switzerland does not play any useful role in connection with the balance of power either. As a major exporter of arms, arms that are ultimately used in belligerent activity, the country contributes more to imbalance than to balance, and more to war than to peace. After all, most weapons at some point or another are used, including Swiss weapons, and not for parades and for exercises only.

Being a non-member of the United Nations the role of Switzerland seems to be what it was at the Second Special Session for Disarmament in June 1982: to be an observer, sitting by some special desks, marginalised from world society, informing themselves, contributing little or nothing. This is particularly sad since Switzerland has something which could be a major contribution: its military doctrine. With more political will to participate and more ability to present the issue Switzerland might here even make a contribution to the world community of nations, but is probably barred from doing so partly by its self-marginalisation, which puts it out of touch with what is going on, partly by its conservatism which makes the country not even see its own originality clearly, and partly for fear of challenging their great Western friends by putting forward alternative concepts.

In short, I am certainly not suggesting that there is not very much for the Swiss peace movement and other forces for peace in Switzerland to do, every day, every hour. The list could also easily be made longer, including the peculiar practices the Swiss police have in controlling foreigners addressing audiences outside the Universities — again reminiscent of the Soviet Union. But the Swiss peace movement should also be criticised for a certain provincialism in not seeing that judged from the outside, from the standpoint of client countries in the two alliances predestined to be sacrificed at an early stage in a nuclear conflict, the achievements of this little country are still considerable, even so much so that there are things to learn for other countries. It is not against Switzerland that the Soviet Union will direct a paralysing second strike.

Reader: I still do not see how an alternative process could be started. More precisely, what would be the first steps?

Author: To take the seven dimensions again, systematically, here are some typical first steps, very modest. *First,* a country could usefully appoint a commission to study the whole problem of transarmament, and even if the country cannot do so, a major policial part of the opposition could do it. A commission for non-provocative, defensive defence would not only put forward a defence plan based on a change in military doctrine, but would also put forward a conversion plan. That conversion plan would at the same time look for all possible ways of cutting military expenditure, basing itself on the fact that the countries highest on the index of security also are lower in defence expenditure *per capita* than the client countries — thinking now of comparable countries. At the same time it would look for labour-intensive conversion tasks, in other words for ways of creating employment rather than abolishing it as is the case with highly capital and research intensive offensive weapons systems. The plans for conversion would in some countries raise some very sensitive issues, such as how to bring about nuclear withdrawal, and how to bring about the withdrawal of superpower troops. Troops from other countries within the same alliance would be less important, and could stay for collective security.

Then, *second,* there would be a commission to study the possibilities of decoupling from the superpower. This could very well be done jointly with other countries more or less in the same situation, and not necessarily even in the same block — in the latter case it would have to be done somewhat clandestinely. It would be very important to indicate small steps rather than the big ones, and they would be intimately related to a transarmament process. Again, if the government is not in a position to have a commission to study this it could commission an institute half-way related to the government to do so, creating the necessary political distance. What matters most is to have many more possible alternatives than just member/non-member.

Third, the problem of a less vulnerable society. This is by no means unknown: any country today has in its bureaucracy special councils for total defence operating more or less along the lines that have also been discussed here. But one might enrich the perspective by relating it to some of the problems coming out of the current economic crisis, in the minds of many calling for less, not for more dependence than before on a highly competitive world market system. A higher level of self-reliance is on the cards, and what is self-reliance if not precisely defence + autonomy + independence + interdependence?

Fourth, and this could be done right away by the government itself if it has the inclination: stepping up co-operation patterns with the other party, above all having more discussions and more dialogues, and much more in the open, not closed as frequently highly useless expert seminars are. The search for new types of economic co-operation that would be symbiotic, without leading to dependencies, is important. The gas pipeline from the Soviet Union is good, but only if more independent energy conversion with unconventional methods is also developed.

Fifth, related to the preceding point: contribute to conflict resolution by systematically trying to find out what is the most worrisome aspect to the other side, and trying to do something about it. If one's own superpower stands in the way of such efforts then that would be one good reason to have some suspicion about the motives of that superpower. Could it possibly be to keep the conflict alive? Could it also be to keep the conflict away from the superpower, "sharing costs and risks" by maintaining or even creating conflicts between lower rank allies and the superpower on the other side? And would that not exactly be in line with forward deployment, so that the superpowers themselves can withdraw behind solid conflict formations in the lower ranks on both sides?

Sixth, the problem of balance of power. The voices saying today that there is no such thing, that the arms race just goes on and on and that nobody has the faintest idea about how to bring it to a stop are very numerous. The *Stockholm International Peace Research Institute* (SIPRI) has done a tremendous job in making this clear to everybody. Just as for the next point about disarmament, all countries in the world are obligated by UN resolutions to make the dangers of war and arms races clear to the population, and to work for disarmament. Concretely this means peace education, encouraging schools and colleges, mass media and so on at least to discuss all these problems, not necessarily with any particular positions favoured, but certainly not brushing them under the carpet. Discussing, then, means real discussion in the sense of letting all voices be heard, even those critical of governmental positions.

Seventh, in connection with disarmament, put forward some unilateral initiative, however small. Even to do what is mentioned under the preceding six points is already an initiative. But the type I have in mind would be more like this: to invite the other side to put forward a proposal for something that in their mind would reduce tension, on the understanding that there might be a counter-proposal from one's own side. There should then be some willingness to do this unilaterally, with the hope that there might be a follow-up on the other side. Again, it should be pointed out that these initiatives could very well be small ones, such as to change the location of a manoeuvre away from border areas to further inland, or to renounce some particular, provocative type of deployment.

Reader: This presupposes a country where there is some change of political will, for instance because another party has come into power, supported to a large extent by peace movement votes. But will this not run against the danger you yourself warned of, that the superpowers might be terribly frightened by any disintegration in their empires/alliances, and consequently be even more provocative and belligerent?

Author: Yes, this is a major problem. It is also a major reason for the gradualism of everything suggested in this book. I do not at all go along with extremists in the peace movement demanding total disarmament and total dissolution of military alliances here and now, for the many reasons indicated in the text. At the same time there would have to be a certain firmness, communicating to the superpower not only the will to take these small steps, but also that they may be to superpower advantage. It might even relieve the superpowers of the burden of being the "guardians of peace" in such a threatening way, as they think they have to be today. In short, most of the dialogue would have to be within one's own alliance and within one's own country rather than between alliances — in itself an indication that the true nature of the East-West conflict probably is more on the *"intra-*side" than on the "inter-side".

Reader: But would it then not be better simply to leave the matters as they are, if the superpowers are so sensitive?

Author: I do not think that works either, because of the tremendous dangers involved. It is very hard not to let the past be a guide also in the nuclear age, and the correlations between arms races and outbreaks of war as a result of military confrontations is overwhelming. It should be remembered that this correlation also obtains today, in the nuclear age, in an atmosphere of nuclear blackmail even if the bomb was used for military purposes only in August 1945. Hence, what I have tried to do in the book is to steer a middle course between the extremists on either side, both in the superpower and client country governments on the one hand, and some of those in the peace movement on the other.

Reader: I find so far that what has been proposed can best be applied to small countries in Europe perhaps on both sides, not too deeply steeped in clientism, willing to learn from the five model countries, what you referred to as the concrete utopias among us. This will function as a catalyst. But France is a problem in its own right. Also, the thesis for the superpowers seems to be a gradual erosion of their power, trying to do it in such a way that they are not shocked into over-reaction the other way. The general idea is pull-back, and then later on a more conventional approach to superpower over-armament. This may or may not work. But what about the rest of the world, what about East Asia, what about the Third World?

Author: East Asia is the second major cold war theatre. The two Koreas have certain similarities with the two Germanies, but with the major difference that Germany suffers the consequences of the horrible Nazi regime and the Hitler war that Germany imposed on almost all of Europe; Korea was a victim, not an aggressor. A policy of transarmament and decoupling, combined with inner strength and peaceful co-existence would be what Korea would need, possibly even on the way to unification. Most writers on this topic have emphasised such themes, but perhaps not seen it in the context of a general security theory. Some type of confederation is actually the most likely outcome.

Then there are the two major actors in East Asia: China and Japan. China has offensive weapons but is reasonably decoupled in spite of what the United States might believe — if Washington thinks China is an ally she may be very disappointed. Japan is very much linked to the Western superpower, being militarily available in many ways, but is, so far, relatively defensive in military posture. Both may change: a very far from unlikely development would be decoupling combined with an increase in offensive capability. The present Japanese policy, which can only be described as stepwise militarisation, is compatible with that perspective. Far more useful for the whole area would be a policy that would combine decoupling with an entirely defensive military posture, putting Japanese ingenuity to the difficult task of developing new classes of defensive weapons, possibly miniaturised, highly efficient and compatible with the general pattern of defensive defence based on small, autonomous, mobile, locally supported units. It would also be entirely in line with Japanese scientific/technological patterns to be the first to develop an efficient anti-ballistic missile defence, in which case one might hope that the invulnerability obtained would be put to constructive political use.

Then there are the other East and South-east Asian countries. Personally I have always been of the opinion that what used to be referred to as "North Vietnam" had, and still has, as a basic ambition to fill the void created by the Japanese and French and later American withdrawal from "French" Indo-China. This means that Hanoi expansionism will include Laos and Kampuchea, but will stop at that point. Thailand is not in danger. In general, the only way in which the ASEAN countries would be endangered would be by policies so much against the people in general that they see no alternative to a communist type revolution and take-over, in which case all three of the socialist actors in the area, the Soviet Union, China and Vietnam, might do something, singly, in co-operation or in conflict. But the key to that problem would be in the internal situation of the country, and it would be entirely compatible with the programme put forward here for alternative security under "inner strength".

Much more problematic is the Third World in general, for the simple reason that there is so little consciousness about these matters. Political theory and political practice have focused so single-mindedly on "development", not on "peace and security" — and it is only recently that these issues have surfaced in the East and South-east Asian countries. It is only in that part of the world that people seem to be conscious of the possibility that a decrease in tension and withdrawal of weapons in Europe might well lead to an increase in tension and even more forward basing in other parts of the world. In short, I would be inclined to give the highly unsatisfactory answer that just as the First World still has not managed to understand problems of development, the Third World has yet to come to grips with problems of peace and security. In other words, we are in the first phase of conflict resolution, the consciousness formation phase. There is such a gap in thinking about these matters when one compares much of South America and Africa with, for instance, Hong Kong. That little city state may serve as a rather good example of how one can create security out of an outer usefulness, a factor that certainly will be able to survive the possible transfer of sovereignty from Great Britain to China at the end of the century.

Reader: Let us now go back for a moment to the model itself, and particularly to the transarmament aspect of it. If we just make use of the distincton between offensive and defensive arms there are three possibilities: both parties are offensive, one is offensive and the other defensive, both parties are defensive. The first possibility is the present one, and the general thesis is that this inevitably leads to arms races, in the longer run probably also inevitably to wars even if most of the wars so far have been dislocated, outside the European "theatre". The third case is the most hopeful one: both parties are defensive only, and when that is combined with decoupling, inner strength and mutual outer usefulness, I understand your thesis to be that one would arrive at a rather beautiful Europe. It would still be l'Europe des patries and the only danger might be that it would be l'Europe de Paris because of the French force de frappe.

But leaving all of that aside, most interesting is the offensive/defensive combination which would come about if one of the parties, or only one country in one of the parties, unilaterally underwent transarmament. A sudden transition from the offensive/offensive combination to the defensive/defensive combination is highly unlikely; a gradual, well-synchronised but slow transition is also unlikely. What is most likely is an imbalance of the type mentioned. Of course, to have a defensive posture is very far from the same as being in a military vacuum, but would this still not invite an attack?

Author: Let us first note that the countries in Europe that have been attacked by the Soviet Union, and we are usually thinking of the Soviet Union as the aggressor in that region, are the members of the Warsaw Treaty Organisation, not the neutral/non-aligned. The Soviet Union has invaded Hungary in 1956 and Czechoslovakia in 1968; not countries outside the WTO. One interesting point about Afghanistan was that it probably had a higher level of security when it was a feudal monarchy, that in no way could be suspected of being aligned with the Soviet Union than after the communist take-over that took place in various phases and raised the question of whether it was loyal or not.

Nonetheless, the question remains whether the defensive defence argued for is sufficient to survive reasonably intact in case the war should come to one's own country, not only in reducing the chances of a war by counteracting the arms race. Perhaps it should also be added to this that war by accident would be less likely, not necessarily because defensive arms are less complicated and for that reason less likely to go wrong, but essentially because if they go wrong it would only hurt the country itself. Moreover, a war by escalation would also be less likely since the ties of alignment, the aligned system itself, would be so loose that a war-like action in one corner of the system is less easily transmitted all over the place.

Having said that, it is clear that even the strongest defensive defence has nothing to set up against a nuclear attack. A one megaton bomb is already sufficient to eliminate most of the population when exploded over the bigger cities in the world. Clearly the threat of this can be used for blackmail. But my point would be that this is already the case today, that nothing would become much different if the changes argued for in this book were implemented. It is even today entirely possible for a terrorist organisation, governmental or non-governmental, to smuggle an "atomic device" into another country, deposit it somewhere, attach it to an ignition mechanism that can be triggered electronically at a distance and then write a letter to the government of the country informing it about the situation and demanding something. They do not even have to sign the letter, only notify the "host" government that any effort to find and even dismantle the "nuclear device" might lead to its detonation. As I have said before, this is the nature of the nuclear age. We are infinitely vulnerable in any case. One may answer that when both sides possess offensive weapons they can retaliate and that the threat of retaliation would stave the hand of the aggressor. But what if one does not even know who the aggressor is? And what if that policy of nuclear deterrence decreases rather than increases the security? Moreover, when is it more likely that nuclear weapons will be used: against a totally non-offensive country or against one with a highly provocative type of international behaviour, including offensive arms? In short, I do not think at all that the transition from offensive to defensive weapons implies any increase in susceptibility to nuclear blackmail. And non-alignment would decrease the susceptibility to blackmail from "one's own" superpower.

The question is then whether the defence is efficient against a conventional attack. But that seems to me to be a question of military technology combined with the question of morale: both vertical morale in terms of loyalty/discipline to the authorities, and horizontal morale in terms of solidarity with the rest of the population. A surprising amount of military have come out recently testifying to the technical possibility of conventional defence, along the lines of the discussion in earlier sections and chapters. And as to the question of morale: this is a problem of social construction and reconstruction, of building strong societies. Just as the general thesis that "the more vulnerable the society the more likely that it will rely on offensive arms" constitutes a rather major argument against dominant military doctrine, the opposite thesis "the less vulnerable a society the more likely that it can adopt a defensive military posture" is the key to understanding the whole transarmament process. The reader os asked once more to have a look at the dimensions indicated in 5.4 above and simply put them together, the dimensions of economic, ecological, political and social invulnerability and so on, and ask himself whether this does not constitute a rather decent society. But nonetheless, even if I feel that the arguments are in favour of the model proposed one should not entertain any illusion of perfect security. That commodity is simply no longer available in the nuclear age, even much less so than it ever was.

Reader: But does the model not presuppose a relatively high level of mobilisation of the people with Feindbilder and even militarisation in the country? Put differently, might this not mean that peace and security would be obtained at the expense of freedom?

Author: This would be to me a major danger. However, I do not think that the examples of Finland and Austria suggest that such dangers are imminent, although both countries can be criticised for not realising the model as far as they could and should. Switzerland is a case in point with its high level of militarisation and its extreme cold war stance. That is the reason why I have made use of it pedagogically in a dialectical manner, exploring both the strong and the weak sides of Swiss policy. But in general terms I would tend to see a defensive military posture as something institutionalised and routinised through governmental decision and supported by bureaucratic action. It is not that different from militias found in most countries, only built much more explicitly into the military doctrine of the country, and made much less dependent on superpower support and command. Non-alignment would also make it possible to develop a more symmetric image of the world, to see that the threat comes not only from one side. In Europe, West and East, the Soviet Union is the threat; in Latin America, North and South, the United States is the threat. Europeans East and West will have a tendency to forget the aggressive

nature of the United States just as Latin Americans North and South
would be ignorant of the Soviet Union. And yet the United States might
one day behave aggressively for instance in Southern Europe and the
Soviet Union might one day intervene, for instance, in the Carribean area.
Preparedness is not the same as mobilisation. Mobilisation including
Feindbilder would be the necessary and inevitable outcome of belligerent
activity against the country in question. And the preparedness, if carried
out according to the model, would be so decentralised as to counteract the
type of militarisation that goes with strong, centrally located, hierarchical
organisation. Admittedly, however, it could also go together with a more
dispersed type of militarisation that could run contrary to freedom.
However, if Yugoslavia has a freedom deficit it is hardly because of the
military factor but much more because of the political factor. I would tend
to conclude that this problem can be solved, and also insist that important
in the model are the dimensions, and that one should not be too mesmerised
by the concrete cases, neither by their weak nor by their strong sides for
that matter.

*Reader: Well, I guess I am not fully convinced, but the gist of your argument
is actually to compare the likely consequences of the model not with an ideal
world of peace, security and freedom — but with the real world in which we
live where freedom is trampled upon, security has become insecurity and
peace is overshadowed by the threat of a catastrophic war.*

Author: That is exactly the point. Let me go one step further. Concluding,
let us permit outselves just to dream a little. The superpowers have pulled
back, there is still an ultimate nuclear deterrent between the two of them
but even that deterrent is in the process of being reduced. The alliances
continue as consultation organisations. Transarmament and decoupling
have come very far in many countries. Partly as a consequence of changed
security policy, mainly as a consequence of the economic crisis, countries
have become more self-reliant. And in the centre of Europe co-operation
between the two parts of Europe starts taking on more natural forms. The
regime in the GDR manages what the regime in Hungary has done: great
portions of the population travel abroad as tourists and return. To cross the
border between the two Germanies, form Bayern to Thüringen or *vice
versa* is about as easy as between Bayern and Tirol. The Eastern European
countries have been "Finlandised" and the Soviet Union has discovered
that this increases her security rather than decreasing it. Some type of
socialism is even blossoming in Eastern Europe; there is a more
experimental attitude. Some of it receives the attenton of groups in
Western Europe that used to disregard Eastern, secondary Europe
completely for a generation or two. In the West the crisis is mastered; all
kinds of US forward basing are withdrawn.

And then, a number of all-European institutions start taking shape:
economic, political, social, cultural and security institutions, for instance, a
Security Commission for Europe, under the United Nations. And where
should they be located? No place would be better than Berlin, including
making Berlin a *Freistadt Berlin*. To me it is not quite obvious whether it
should contain both parts of Berlin or only the Western part, whether it

should be with a wall (around all of Berlin, or only as present) or without a wall. These are questions to be discussed. But I can hardly imagine a more beautiful way of ending the Second World War and of starting a real period of European peace and security than by converting that major symbol of Nazi horror into an autonomous peace capital for Europe as a whole. And with that I simply conclude. The book is written in Berlin; I can find no more appropriate concluding vision for that magnificent city, that troubled nation, for Europe and for the world.

Suggested Reading

In order to save space (and not to make the book too expensive) footnotes have not been included. The following are some books the reader might find useful, roughly organised according to the chapters in the present book.

Chapter 1

Ulrich Albrecht, *Kündigt den Nachrüstungsbeschluss!*, Fischer Frankfurt, 1982.
Johan Galtung, *Environment, Development and Military Activity*, University Press, Oslo, 1982.
Erhard Eppler, *Die tödliche Utopie der Sicherheit*, Rowohlt, Hamburg, 1983.
Sir John Hackett, *The Third World War; a Future History*, London, 1978.
Daisaku Ikeda, *A Lasting Peace*, New York, Tokyo, Weatherhill, 1981.
Mary Kaldor, *The Disintegrating West*, Pelican Books, London, 1978.
Dieter S. Lutz, *Weltkriegwider Willen*, Rowohlt, Hamburg, 1981.
Alfred Mechtersheimer, *Nachrüsten?*, Rowohlt, Hamburg, 1981.
Arfred Mechtersheimer, *Rüstung und Frieden*, Langen-Müller/Herbig, 1982.
Johan Niezing, *Sociology, War and Disarmament*, Rotterdam University Press, 1973.

Chapter 2

Johan Galtung, *The True Worlds*, The Free Press, New York, 1980.
István Kende, *Kriege nach 1945, Militärpolitik, Dokumentation*, 1982.
Dieter S. Lutz, *Sicherheitspolitik am Scheideweg?*, Bundeszentrale für politische Bildung, Bonn, 1982.
Peter Wallensteen, *Structure and War*, Uppsala, 1973.

Chapter 3

Gert Bastian, *Frieden schaffen!*, Kindler, München, 1983.
Nigel Calder, *Nuclear Nightmares*, The Viking Press, New York, 1979.
C.G. Jacobsen, *The Nuclear Era*, Spokesman, Nottingham, 1982.
Gert Petersen, *Om Fredens Nødvendighed*, Vindrose, Copenhagen, 1981.
Alva Myrdal et al, *Dynamics of European Nuclear Disarmament*, Spokesman, Nottingham, 1981.
SIPRI, *The Arms Race and Arms Control*, Taylor & Francis Ltd., London, 1982, 1983.
E.P. Thompson and Dan Smith, *Protest and Survive*, Monthly Review Press, New York and London, 1981.
H.W. Tromp and G.R. La Rocque, (eds.), *Nuclear War in Europe*, Groningen University Press, Groningen 1982.
Arthur Westing, *Warfare in a Fragile World*, Taylor & Francis Ltd., London, 1980.

Chapter 4

Magne Barth (red.) *Frys*, Pax, Oslo, 1983.
Michael Clarke and Marjorie Mowlam, *Disarmament*, Routledge & Kegan Paul, London, 1982.
Johan Galtung, *Peace, War and Defense, Essays in Peace Research*, Vol.II, Ejlers, Copenhagen, 1976.
Jozef Goldblat, *Arms Control Agreements*, Praeger, New York, 1982.
Ekkehart Krippendorff and Reimar Stuckenbrock, *Zur Kritik des Palme Berichts*, Verlag Europäischer Perspektiven, Berlin, 1983.
Alva Myrdal, *The Game of Disarmament*, Spokesman, Nottingham, 1976.
Alva Myrdal et al, *Dynamics of European Nuclear Disarmament*, Spokesman, Nottingham, 1981.
Palme Commission, *Common Security*, Pan books, London, 1982.
Marek Thee, *Armaments, Arms control and Disarmament*, UNESCO, Paris, 1981.
Paul Walker, *Seizing the Initiative: First Steps to Disarmament*, American Friends Service Committee, Philadelphia, 1983.

Chapter 5

Horst Afheldt, *Defensive Verteidigung*, rororo aktuell, Hamburg, 1983.
Alternative Defence Commission, *Defence without the Bomb*, Taylor & Francis, London, 1983.
Arbeitskreis atomwaffenfreies Europa, *Alternativen Europäischer Friedenspolitik*, Berlin, 1981.
Dietrich Fischer, *Preventing War: A Rational Strategy for Peace in the Nuclear Age*, Littlefield, New Jersey, 1984.
Berge Furre and Ingolf Hakon Teigene, *Forsvar for Fred*, Pax, Oslo, 1983.
Johan Galtung and Sverre Lodgaard, *Co-operation in Europe*, University Press, Oslo, 1970.
Johan Galtung and Per Hansen, *Totalforsvar*, Universitetsforlaget, Oslo, 1981.
Johan Galtung, *Anders verteidigen*, Rowohlt, Reinbek bei Hamburg, 1981.
Robert C. Johansen, *Toward an Alternative Security System*, World Policy Institute, New York, 1983.
Komitee für Grundrechte und Demokratie, *Frieden mit anderen Waffen*, Rowohlt, Hamburg, 1981.
Dieter S. Lutz/Annemarie Große-Jütte, *Neutralität eine Alternative?*, Nomos, Baden-Baden, 1982.
Johann Löser, *Weder rot noch tot*, Günther Olzog Verlag, München, 1981.
Gert Petersen, *Om Nødvendigheden af Dansk Fredspolitik*, Vindrose, Copenhagen, 1982.
Roy Preiswerk et al, *Formen Schweizerischer Friedenspolitik*, Iustitia et Pax, Freiburg, 1982.
Emil Spannocchi, *Verteidigung ohne Selbstzerstörung*, Hanser, Wien, 1976.
Carolyn M. Stephenson, *Alternative Methods for International Security*, University Press of America, Washington, 1982.
Svenska Freds-Och Skiljedomsföreningen, *Program for Fred*, Stockholm, 1982.
Jan Øberg, *At udvikle sikkerhed og sikre udvikling*, Vindrose, Copenhagen, 1983.

Heresies
Resist Much, Obey Little
by Ken Coates

At the beginning of the first nuclear disarmament movement, Russell and Einstein published a famous declaration which became known as the Pugwash Manifesto. At that time, the world was divided into two powerful blocs, each of which gave the impression of internal unity and external intransigence. But the unity of the blocs has been breaking down, year by year. Today, both East and West are deeply divided. Ken Coates analyses the divisions in communism, in a series of essays which cover the thoughts of major Eastern heretics. With the rebirth of the European peace movement, many of the issues which are discussed in this little book begin to present themselves in a new light, with new urgency.

"'Tell that to the Russians', people say to supporters of nuclear disarmament. The point about Ken Coates, a founder and leader of European Nuclear Disarmament, is that he does — as these humane and intelligent essays show."

Ben Pimlott, *New Socialist*

"A heretical vision of this sharpness must necessarily be a two-eyed one. Meanwhile, this handsomely produced volume — some of the accompanying photographs are semi-archival items — is good news enough."

Perry Anderson, *Tribune*

"This is a book to dip into, focusing contemporary issues through a range of historical and literary arguments. One of the sources of its author's wisdom is that he was one of the few who continued to see, through the seventies, the nuclear frame in which our policies are contained."

Martin Shaw, *New Statesman*

Paper £3.50
Cloth £13.95
158 pages with 14 illustrations

ISBN 0 85124 356 8
ISBN 0 85124 355 X

**Spokesman, Bertrand Russell House, Gamble Street, Nottingham
Tel. 0602 708318**

Distributed in U.S.A. by Dufour Editions Inc.

Dynamics of European Nuclear Disarmament
by Alva Myrdal and others,
edited by Ken Coates

Europe is now in very great peril. The arms race between the two great super powers rushes forward without restraint. Detente flounders in obvious crisis. The threat of war becomes more and more evident. Nuclear war, which used to be styled "unthinkable", is nonetheless being thought by modern strategists; and their modern doctrine of "limited" nuclear war has particularly fearsome consequences for Europe.

Our continent is stiff with arms emplacements and heavy with stockpiled warheads. It is the most militarised zone in the world. Yet it has nothing to fight about, when left to its own devices. Its nations confront one another in the increasingly reluctant blocs which have formed around the super-states. Apprehension grows among the peoples of the smaller nations, as they realise that their protectors might well prefer to restrict their future wars to territories outside their own boundaries.

The threat of a "theatre" nuclear war in Europe is stimulating a continent-wide Resistance. This book enlists to that Resistance the aid of some of the most distinguished peace researchers in Europe's universities, whose careful analyses will be discussed from Poland to Portugal, from Scandinavia to Sicily, wherever the menace of nuclear war preparations is opposed.

Contributors include Rudolf Bahro, Ken Coates, Johan Galtung, Robert Havemann, Carl J. Jacobsen, Fernando Moran, Alva Myrdal, Marek Thee, Raimo Väyrynen plus key documents from the US Library of Congress Research Service, the Socialist International, the Communist Party of Italy **and from various European disarmament movements.**

"The great merit of this book is that it moves beyond the inspiring general intention to many of the hard details, informing and preparing in notably mature and rational ways".

Raymond Williams, *The Guardian*

Paper £5.50   Cloth £17.50

Available from bookshops and from Bertrand Russell House, Gamble Street, Nottingham NG7 4ET, Tel. 0602 708318

Distributed in U.S.A. b, Colour Editions Inc.

DATE DUE

N